The Image of God in Man

David Cairns is emeritus Professor of Practical Theology at Christ's College, Aberdeen, a position he held from 1948 to 1972. He was also Reader in Systematic Theology at Aberdeen University.

He studied at the universities of Oxford, Tübingen, Zürich (under Emil Brunner), and Aberdeen. For some years he was a parish minister at Bridge of Allan, Stirlingshire and, from 1940 to 1945, a chaplain to the forces.

He has held various lectureships in this country and two in the United States of America, and he sat on the Faith and Order Commission for a number of years. Among his published works are several books and also some theological translations from the German, the most important of these being Volume III of Brunner's *Dogmatics*.

DAVID CAIRNS

The Image of God in Man

with an *Introduction by*
DAVID E. JENKINS

COLLINS
FONTANA LIBRARY
THEOLOGY AND PHILOSOPHY

The Image of God in Man was first published by SCM Press, London in 1953
Revised edition with additional material first issued
in the Fontana Library of Theology and Philosophy in 1973

Revised edition with additional material
© David Cairns 1973
© in the Introduction David E. Jenkins 1973

Printed in Great Britain
Collins Clear-Type Press
London and Glasgow

To my wife

Acknowledgments

The author and publisher wish to acknowledge their indebtedness for permission to reproduce copyright material as follows: from *The Dignity of Man* by Herschel Baker, published by Harvard University Press, Massachusetts, 1947; from *Creative Evolution* by Henri Bergson, published by Macmillan, Basingstoke, 1911; from *The Young Marx* by Bernard Delfgaauw, published by Sheed & Ward Ltd, London, 1967; from 'Inhibitions, Symptoms and Anxiety' in Volume XX of *The Standard Edition of the Complete Works of Sigmund Freud*, revised and edited by James Strachey. Reprinted by permission of Sigmund Freud Copyrights Ltd, The Institute of Psycho-Analysis and The Hogarth Press Ltd; from *Marx's Concept of Man* by Erich Fromm, published by Frederick Ungar Publishing Co., New York, 1961; from *The Christian Faith and the Marxist Criticism of Religion* by Helmut Gollwitzer, published by The Saint Andrew Press, Edinburgh, 1970; from *Personality Structure and Human Interaction* by Harry Guntrip, published by The Hogarth Press Ltd, London, 1961, and Indiana University Press, Indiana; from *Teilhard Reassessed* edited by Anthony Hanson, published by Darton, Longman & Todd Ltd, London, 1970; from *Sigmund Freud: Life and Work*, Volume I by Ernest Jones, published by The Hogarth Press Ltd, London, 1953. Reprinted by kind permission of Mrs Katherine Jones and The Hogarth Press Ltd; from *Man in the New Testament* by W. G. Kümmel, published by The Epworth Press, London, 1963; from *The Biblical Theology of Saint Irenaeus* by John Lawson, published by The Epworth Press, London, 1948; from *Early Writings* of Karl Marx, translated by T. B. Bottomore, published by C. A. Watts, London, 1963; from 'Critiques Re-considered' by Charles M. Savage in *Study Encounter*, IV, 1, 1968, published by World Council of Churches, Geneva; from *The Book of Isaiah* by G. Adam Smith, published by Hodder & Stoughton Ltd, London, 1910; from *Human Nature: The Marxian View* by Vernon Venable, published by Dobson Books, Ltd, London, 1946.

The author wishes to thank T. & T. Clark, Edinburgh and Lutterworth Press London, for their kind permission to allow him to use his own translations from Emil Brunner's *Man in Revolt* and Karl Barth's *Church Dogmatics*.

The Scripture quotations are from the Revised Standard Version Bible, copyright 1946, 1952 and © 1971, by the Division of Christian Education, National Council of the Churches of Christ in the USA and are used by permission.

Contents

Preface to Revised Edition

The main aim of this book is to give some account of the Christian doctrine of the image of God in man, starting with the biblical sources, and tracing some of the historic Christian interpretations from early times to the present day. Two chapters which were inserted in order briefly to set forth and compare two influential non-Christian understandings of man, the Marxian and the Freudian, have been rewritten, and a new chapter on Teilhard de Chardin's view has been added. It is my opinion that he has something important to say on this theme. Teilhard was practically unknown to the wider theological public when this book first appeared. The chapter is submitted in the hope that it may encourage English-speaking readers to take his thought rather more seriously than a number of them have recently done.

When this book first appeared, the world was still shaken by the impact of National Socialist racialism and by the revelation of the deliberate cruelties which it had been prepared to inflict upon vast numbers of the human race. At that time a German theologian wrote the following words: 'A superficial glance at the publications of the contemporary anti-Christian movements will convince any man of clear perception that the point where the Christian faith is most hotly opposed is in the doctrine of man. . . . The debate about the new "national" or "racial" conception of man has thrust the debate about God quite into the background.'[1]

Although the inflated German racialism to which special reference is here made is now a thing of the past, another type of racialism and oppression has become more marked in the intervening years, and more and more obviously intolerable, the racialism which declares that a man's dignity depends on the colour of his skin, and the oppression which results from the division of nations into 'haves' and 'have-nots'. Thus the nature

1. Bachmann, *Gottes Ebenbild* (Furche Verlag, Berlin, 1938) p. 1.

of man has become more and more the subject of intense interest, not only for Christian thinkers, but also for those who believe with Marx that 'the criticism of religion has, in essence, been largely completed'[2] and that the question of God is no longer a living issue.

Here, therefore, Christian thinkers, whose faith forbids them to allow the abstraction of man's nature from his relation to God, will have vigorous rejoinders to make. 'You are not interested in God,' they will say, 'but you are intensely and increasingly interested in man. Yet your whole doctrine of man is faulty because you do not understand his essential relationship to God.'

There is, however, a very considerable and hopeful change in the international atmosphere which could hardly have been foreseen in 1953 when this book first appeared. This is the opening of a genuine philosophical and even theological dialogue between east and west, which has indeed received severe setbacks, but which can hardly fail to continue, and, indeed, to deepen, especially now that Communist China has been admitted to the United Nations. Dr Johnson once said that the immediate prospect of hanging had a remarkably clarifying effect on a man's thinking, and it may be that the possibilities of atomic destruction have had something of the same effect on the minds of Marxists and non-Marxists alike. 'Today, perspectives change. What was then (over a hundred years ago) insurmountable may today be approached. Real differences do remain between Christianity and Marxism. No one will deny this. However, the immediate problems of our world—hunger, population, illiteracy, pollution, urban development, technology and the spiritual confusion of our day—demand an end to the luxury of just hurling condemnations and anathemas from one walled camp towards another. The Cold War has cancelled out potentially creative forces which could be used to deal with these problems. The "economic" gap between the richer northern nations and the poorer southern nations is a greater menace to the world than the "ideological" gap between Capitalism and Communism.'[3]

2. The opening words of 'Criticism of the Hegelian Philosophy of Right'. See *Early Writings* of Karl Marx, translated by T. B. Bottomore (C. A. Watts & Co. Ltd., London, 1963) pp. 43-4.

3. Charles M. Savage, *Study Encounter*, iv, 1, 1968, p.3.

Christians and Marxists have not been the only groups involved in such conversations. The World Council of Churches' Conference at Geneva in 1967 recommended a dialogue between Christians and 'advocates of non-Christian social ideologies', believing that 'this would increase the "possibilities of co-operation between Christians and non-Christians, irrespective of their ideologies, for the furtherance of peace and progress for all mankind".'[4]

It appears therefore that the vital discussion between Christian and non-Christian minds in the next decades, is likely to take place in this area, the doctrine of man, a discussion which, we may hope, will not be a mere idle wrangle, but a genuine meeting between mind and mind, between man and man, thrust forward into dialogue by the urgent pressures of our world situation, where, without being sentimental or untrue to our deepest insights, we may learn from one another. May it not be that, as Teilhard de Chardin suggested, there is something providential in these pressures to which our world-environment is subjecting us, so that we must learn to love one another or perish?

Hence a study of the Christian doctrine of man in the various forms which it has taken, may be offered again to the public in the hope that it can help Christians better to understand their faith and some of its implications in the modern world, and aid them in reasoned opposition to views and attitudes that deprive man of his rightful heritage, and give a firmer foothold to them in their dialogue with other men of goodwill who share their concern for the future of humanity, but who cannot as yet share their Christian faith.

The subject of the image of God in man covers really the wide field of the whole Christian doctrine of man, for there is no part of man's nature which was not created to serve that image, and no part which is without relation to the image even in man's blindness and sin. But naturally the treatment of this vast theme is not possible here, and many points relative to the Christian doctrine of man will be omitted.

But to embark even on the more limited enterprise to which this study is committed was a sufficiently stimulating and even daunting prospect. Human history is so splendid and so tragic

4. Ibid.

that only the providence of God can carry it to its consummation, and the doctrine of the image touches on the providence of God in creation, history and consummation. The writer has done his best, but as the work proceeded, he has frequently asked himself, 'Who is sufficient for these things?'

Introduction

When the future is so problematic why bother with what some men used to believe in the past?

Can man survive? According to René Dubos (member of the American National Academy of Sciences, prominent writer on topics relating medical and biological sciences to human affairs and joint author of *Only One Earth*, the popular account of the resources of, and threats to, our planet prepared for the Stockholm Conference of the United Nations on the Human Environment), the answer is almost certainly yes, because the human race is quite remarkably adaptable. But the real question is 'Will it be worth surviving?' Men and women can and do survive in the most appalling conditions of urban noise and squalor. Probably some ways will be found for some to survive on the edge of a nuclear desert or spread thinly across any dust-bowl which might remain after over-population, over-exploitation and pollution had eroded most cultivable land and killed off most of the teeming populations. But what would this survival be worth 'humanly speaking'? It might well show, what many have suspected, that the universe is nothing but a sequence of meaningless accidents and that the peculiar nature of the human accident is that it has achieved the potentiality of accidentally terminating itself.

Or would this be so? Does the prospect of the miserable near-extinction of the whole human race call in question the meaning and value of you, me and those we love in any different way from the undoubted fact of our respective and individual deaths? It depends, perhaps, on the pictures we have become accustomed to cherish, however unconsciously, about the world as a whole. It may be that the prospect of my death is easier to ignore or even to face if I can imagine that everything goes on more or less as before but simply 'without me'. But if there is to be nothing to 'go on as before' then the radical nothingness of my future becomes as bleakly inescapable in imagination as in fact.

However that may be and whatever are the subtle and complicated pressures upon us now, it certainly seems that the trends, possibilities and struggles of the present face us with such urgent decisions about the future, or, failing those decisions, with such imminent and monstrous threats, that we can have no time for reflective study of the past. Men who lived, so it seems to us, under human conditions and prospects so different from ours, can scarcely have anything useful or powerful to say to us through what they believed, hoped and argued about, concerning the human condition, its dimensions, its distortions and its hopes. Their narrow and local worlds are gone and we have to face for ourselves a situation so changed that they can be of no help. It is we who have seen the pictures from the moon of one limited globe, lonely in space and inhabited by a growing spawn of those who are rapidly making it uninhabitable. We are really those upon whom a prospect of the end of the world has come, if not for ourselves, at least for our children or grandchildren.

Since our predicament is so unique and so sharply and presently pressing, why trouble to make available again a book originally prepared twenty years ago which goes carefully over certain features of the biblical and Christian traditions of understanding man, his nature and his destiny, grouped around the central picture of man as in the image of God? It is true that the last section of the book (chapters XV-XVIII), which has been in part rewritten, and in part written especially, for this new edition takes up Marx and Freud as the 'revolutionaries' in our western understanding of man and so moves through them into our current debates and confusions. But even Marx and Freud (particularly the latter) are suspected in many parts of the world of being old-fashioned, far too much the product of a particular phase of European culture, or even dangerously irrelevant. (This applies to Freud as a whole and to Marx at least in the way in which certain forms of Marxism have developed.) Further, some of the most challenging questions and hopes about man, his nature and his future are clearly arising at present from developments in Mao's China and in the increasing contributions from the traditions of the cultures and religions of Asia. (Not to mention what is developing in both Latin America and in Africa as men and women in these continents struggle in various ways to be their distinctive selves and play their own parts in human history.)

This book, however, is largely arranged historically and follows up certain ideas from the Bible, through their handling in Mediterranean Christianity as it grew to their development and discussion in mediaeval Christianity and then in modern European Protestantism. All books are necessarily selective. But why be concerned to make this particular selection available again when we are having to face a global anxiety about our human future?

The book is to be welcomed as a very useful tool for, and contribution to, the task of facing the future with all the resources that are available to us. In particular, and from the point of view of committed Christians, I believe it could make an important contribution to removing one of the reasons for the frequently continuing poverty of the Christian response to our present human struggles. One of the reasons for this poverty of response lies in the poverty of current Christian knowledge of accumulated Christian resources and our consequent unreadiness to contribute from these resources to the current human predicament.

Perhaps it is now more widely felt and more appropriately felt than ever before that a gigantic question mark embraces both our particular futures and our common future as human beings. Perhaps also, and again as never before, every particular portion of the human race is affected, both in its present and in its prospects, by the present experiences, the past histories and the struggles for particular futures, of all other human beings in their common needs and diverse traditions. A common reaction to the felt uniqueness of this present and to the comprehensiveness of the future threat is to turn away from our particular and narrower pasts as necessarily irrelevant and dangerously hampering. How can 'they' who neither knew nor imagined either our science or our scene have anything to say to us who have to face for ourselves our own new world, whether it be brave, beastly or boring? But such an abandonment of the past, however narrow it may seem to us, is, surely, no human way of facing the expanding present or the exploding future.

To imagine that every human experience which took place before the splitting of the atom can have neither any significance to us nor help for us is a combination of conceit and cowardice which can commit us only to despair. The conceit is shown in the unquestioning assumption that our powers and experiences render totally obsolescent what other men and women have learnt, suffered and enjoyed. Our reality is real while theirs was superstitious, trivial and false. The cowardice lies in the panic in face of our problems combined with our insecurity in face of ourselves which prevents us from daring to take time to look back at, and down into, what it has been to be human. The conceit is not strong enough to be questioned even though it more than suspects that the future already casts a shadow which negates it. The combination commits us to despair because it leaves us poised between a past which is held to be devoid of meaning and a future which is held to be full of threats. The human present in which we live is, therefore, merely a turbulent flux, deprived of roots and highly uncertain of fruits. The death of the past reduces the present to either a neurosis or a psychosis.

But this is false. The past is not wholly irrelevant to us. Just as it is part of human experience, so it provides a part of human resources. The suffering, learning, living and dying of our ancestors were no less human than our own. They too had to live with the problem of whether man was lost in the universe, alone, at home, or on his way to possibilities more abiding and more fulfilling. Their considered and reflective experience offers us, therefore, at least a potential reservoir of provocation, hope, comfort, insight and stimulus to experiment. We have no absolute need to be a generation entirely on our own facing hitherto totally unimagined problems with tools and resources which have to be invented and fashioned from a beginning which can only now be discovered. The rediscovery of past reflections may pay high dividends by way of stabilizing, directing and encouraging us.

For those who, among the struggle to be human, intend and attempt to profess themselves Christians the death of the past is, all the more, an impossibility. Or, conversely, if the past is totally dead to us and without meaning for us then so is Christianity and naming the name of Jesus is a game we should not play, save perhaps as our own neurotic contribution to the fantasies of our present state. If, however, there is something sane, healthy and saving in those things which surround and are pointed to by Jesus then one of our concerns and of our hopes will always be to draw on the Christian past under the pressures of the human present for the sake of a universal future. For it is of the essence of our belief that God has from the beginning been involved in the processes of creation and in the affairs of history. Through this involvement men and women have been given the opportunity of discovering together both the presence of God and the shaping of their own identity and future and to do this in their encounters with living and in their attempts both to make sense of, and receive sense from, what happens to them and how they respond to these happenings. Thus a certain tradition of knowledge of God and expectation from God has been built up in human affairs and in relation to human affairs. To neglect this tradition is to neglect an important human and Christian resource.

In returning to this resource we have, of course, to take full account of those factors which make it a symptom of health rather than of neurosis to wish the past dead. For it is not only the pressures of the prospective future which urge us (as I would believe, wrongly) to kill off the past by neglect, and obsessive and short-sighted concern with our problems. The past projects into the present its own burdens which keep men back and bind them down by both concepts and institutions which dominate, distort and detract.

Episodes in the Christian doctrine of sin, for example, can be taken as a case in point if by 'the Christian doctrine of sin' we mean a composite tradition which includes a whole series of understanding about sin which have, from time to time, been fashionable, and also the use which has been made of these understandings in relation to the running of institutions and the treatment of, and relationships with, men and women. Clearly, in the name of 'the Christian doctrine of sin' much tyranny of authoritarianism has been justified and much barbarity of punishment and allocation of guilt has been allowed or even encouraged. The notions of sin and the sanctions

19

against sin have sometimes been sinfully developed and sinfully abused. Thus there is a past within the tradition, with
effects in the present, which needs to be decisively repudiated
and left behind for the sake of any more human future.⌋

But here again, what should be meant by 'leaving the past
behind'? The most healthy and hopeful thing would seem to
be to attempt to come to terms with these abuses in the past
with the help of our present perspectives and future pressures in
such a way that both positive and negative things can be discovered to help and guide us in our present efforts. That is
to say, an understanding, from a fresh perspective, of past
abuses with present effects should help us to discern obstacles
of which we must be wary in our present practices. (What is
the evidence that we are any the less prone to ignore pitfalls
than our predecessors?) While, on the positive side, a fresh
understanding of the abuses of a doctrinal tradition may
uncover for us positive insights of that tradition in a way
which makes these insights relevant and illuminating for us
with our present perspectives and questions.

Christians at any rate must, it would seem to me, approach
their traditions with these expectations. The biblical pictures
and presentations about the history of the people of God do not
suggest that these people, in their self-understanding and in
their responses to God, are ever right in any persistent or
lasting way. That is to say they do not produce an established
pattern either of understanding or of behaviour which is left
alone to be practised as the one guaranteed to be conducive to
human fulfilment and the divine purpose of salvation. Rather
they are constantly being proved wrong in being brought to
understand that they were or are in the wrong in some vital
matter connected with their future development and with
the expanding purpose of God for the world as a whole.⌋

But while every attempt to settle down as being in the right
is shown up as a betrayal of the very calling to be the people of
God, the repeated disturbances to which they are subjected are
the occasions of building up a continuing knowledge and experience of the righteousness of God. That is to say that there
is a repeated and cumulative discovery of a power who is
consistently and faithfully at work to advance and enlarge
purposes of love and of justice in which men and women will

find fulfilment. Hence creative discoveries of new possibilities and resources which relate the troubled present to a more hopeful future are to be found most especially in concentrations of circumstances and convergencies of pressures which serve to throw into relief the abuses and errors of the past tradition and understanding and so set the past free to make its proper (and essential) contribution to the learning of the present and the building of the future.

Thus neither the undoubted ambiguity of the past nor its seeming irrelevance cuts us off from it as a source of hope, strength and insight, least of all for those of us who are Christians. But it is no use conducting merely theoretical discussions about either the usefulness or the uselessness of what has gone before and been recorded by our predecessors. The object of the rather theoretical arguing which has been set out in this introductory essay has been simply to clear away likely objections to the relevance, desirability and usefulness of republishing a considered treatment of a particular strand in biblical and Christian thought about man at this particular juncture of human affairs and in the climate of thought which tends, at present, to prevail. I am, myself, clear that it is desirable, indeed necessary, to regain a hearing for the type of careful reflection on past reflection and controversy of which this book is largely constituted. Seeing that we are in a crisis, and sometimes even in a panic, about man and about his future we need more than ever to reconsider and make available for renewal our accumulated resources.

But it has not been very much the fashion to do this, even in Christian circles. Christian writers, thinkers and speakers have found it appropriate to rush to the manifest and public points of controversy and there manage as best they could in a style as near to the current and contemporary as could be produced. This has certainly 'brought theology into the market-place' and I, for one, hope that it will never again withdraw and never forget that one of its absolutely essential tasks is to sustain a presence in that human market-place, while one of its most essential needs is to learn from, and respond to, all the other needs and experiences in that same place. However, if I may be allowed perhaps to over-expand the metaphor, once one has firmly set up one's stall in the place where the ordinary, daily and pressing affairs of ordinary men and women are conducted, then it is necessary to have for sale something more than a few hastily gathered rotten tomatoes or else some second-hand fruits which have been either purchased or filched from other farmers or producers. The offering of one's own produce is all the more necessary if it is even remotely possible that among that produce could be found some food-stuffs which would not otherwise be available.

Yet once again, of course, it is necessary to be very aware of the proper and necessary grounds for turning away from the traditions of the Christian faith as actually handled in so much of current Christianity and especially in traditional methods and traditional formulae. Instead of living out of the tradition into the world and so becoming part of the current human struggle with consequent effects of judgment on what we have made of the tradition so far and of renewal for a fresh sharing in and contribution to the life of men, we have lived inwardly and formalistically. 'The Christian Tradition' has, in practice, too often been characterized by cowardice and by defensive looking back rather than by courage and expectant looking forward. Thus it has seemed necessary to get away from all traditional aspects and considerations in order to find a renewed life and faith. But now that this struggle for renewal has been well and truly launched it should be possible to return to a healthy and proper use of the tradition. Further, as I have argued, it is now necessary to return to such a use if Christians are to discover and make a truly Christian contribution to our present human worries and hopes.

Professor Cairns' book provides us with the sort of material from the tradition about which we need to reflect if we are to be equipped to discover Christian contributions in depth and distinctiveness to contemporary debates, decisions and disturbances. Moreover he presents the material in such a way as to make it available for our use without over-insisting about what that use should be. Apart from the last few chapters he does not write primarily with current controversies in mind but primarily with the intention of enabling an understanding of the material in its various contemporary contexts. He evaluates this material enough to set our own minds going in the contemporary direction but he does direct us to the material itself. This is important for we have left behind the time when systematic dogmatic edifices could be of use in the facing and handling of our problems. What we need to know about are the insights which our Christian predecessors drew from the tradition as it came to them and from their own wrestlings with faithful living and hoping in their own times. We need to know also of the pitfalls into which they fell or the limitations which subsequent events and reflections show to have been theirs. From opportunities to learn about and reflect on their experiences and conclusions we can ourselves be put on the way to discovering the insights, hopes and tentative conclusions which we can contribute to the experiment of faithful Christian living and, through this, to the whole struggle of human living.

If I may put it so, we are in an age of 'do-it-yourself' theology. No one can work out Christian contributions in the psychological or industrial or technological or political struggles to be human apart from Christians who are involved in psychology or industry or technology or political activity – and so on for the many interlocking forms which life now takes. What theologians can and must do is to make available the material from the tradition for those 'do-it-yourself' kits which so-called 'lay' Christians more and more need. (And doubtless, also, the theologians must discover how to be available to share in this doing of 'lay' theology but this cannot be discussed further here.)

I have personally taken some initiative in trying to get this work of Professor Cairns easily available again because it seemed to me to contain so much material (which is not easily and readily available) for a 'do-it-yourself' kit in the Christian understanding of man. And it is in this area above all at the present time that talk about God, faith in Jesus Christ and belief in the power and presence of the Holy Spirit has to be brought to bear. Consequently it is in this area of the understanding of man that Christians need to be most informed about the resources and reflections of the Christian tradition so far. Only so will they be in a position to make their own contribution both from the riches of the tradition and to the enrichment of the tradition, which is ultimately concerned not with the Christian doctrine of man but with the fulfilment of all men in the love of God and of one another.

The focusing of this material around the notion of man as in the image of God seems to me to be of the utmost importance and of particular relevance. Our present human predicament arises as much as anything out of the unique human powers over our environment and ourselves and of unique human demands for justice and for freedom. Man has, as never before, power to do most things, including to destroy himself, and men and women, as never before, are all over the world refusing to be left in conditions and positions which are less human than those enjoyed and occupied by that minority who are their privileged fellows.

The understanding of man as in the image of God speaks, or should speak, directly to these features of our life. A creature in the image of God is a creature destined for immense and creative powers. A creature destined to be fulfilled in the image of God is a creature destined to enjoy absolute justice, freedom and love. But a creature in the image of God is a creature and not an accident. Hence somewhere in his relationship to God and in the potentialities of this image should lie the sources and resources which will make the future not a question either of survival or of extinction but a certainty of human fulfilment.

Since, however, these questions are so urgent, it is vital that we do not neglect any relevant resources. It is my belief that this book directs our attention to some of the most important of such resources and offers us the material from which we have to go on for ourselves to enable these resources to be lively and relevant.

Geneva, November 1972   DAVID JENKINS

CHAPTER I

The Old Testament Teaching

1 Explicit References: Their Fewness and Importance

In the Old Testament, the image of God is directly mentioned in only three passages: in Genesis 1:26-7; in Genesis 5:1-3, and in Genesis 9:5-6. It will be worth our while to reproduce these short passages here.

In Genesis 1:26, after the creation of living things, God says, 'Let us make man in our image, after our likeness; and let them have dominion over the fish of the sea, and over the birds of the air, and over the cattle, and over all the earth, and over every creeping thing that creeps upon the earth. So God created man in his own image, in the image of God he created him; male and female he created them. And God blessed them, and God said to them, "Be fruitful and multiply, and fill the earth and subdue it; and have dominion over the fish of the sea and over the birds of the air and over every living thing that moves upon the earth." '[1]

In Genesis 5:1-3, the writer says, 'This is the book of the generations of Adam. When God created man, he made him in the likeness of God. Male and female he created them, and he blessed them and named them Man when they were created. When Adam had lived a hundred and thirty years, he became the father of a son in his own likeness, after his image, and named him Seth.'

And the third passage, Genesis 9:5-6 runs as follows (God is speaking to Noah): 'For your lifeblood I will surely require a reckoning; of every beast I will require it, and of man; of every man's brother I will require the life of man. Whoever sheds the blood of man, by man shall his blood be shed; for God made man in his own image.'

Arguing from the fewness of these explicit references, and from the fact that they all belong to 'P', a writer of the fifth century BC, and are therefore comparatively late, Anders Nygren[2] does not scruple to reject as non-biblical the conception of the image of God in the sense which it bears in these passages. He claims that it is alien to the thought of the Bible, and is an invasion from the Hellenistic world of thought. It is not possible to accept this cavalier rejection of the concept; it will be our contention that, though only thrice actually mentioned, it is implied in the whole thought-world of the Old Testament.

In contrast with Nygren, Gerhard von Rad,[3] the author of the article 'Image of God in the Old Testament' in Gerhard Kittel's *Theological Dictionary*, does not think that the fewness of the references means that the concept is of no importance for Old Testament thought. He points out that the Old Testament does indeed emphasize the distance of man from God. Man is dust, and must be consumed before the divine holiness. Therefore the biblical witness to the image in man appears only, as it were, on the margin of the Old Testament message. But, he adds, it is very significant that it does so appear, and that it appears at that point where the Old Testament has to deal with the mystery of the origin of man.

Eichrodt's[4] conclusion on this point is practically the same. He points to the overmastering conviction of the Hebrews that God was supreme over nature, as over history. It was this religious conviction that saved them from any attempt at mystical union with a supposedly divine power of nature by means of sexual orgy or worship of idols. At the same time, the Hebrew perceived that he was himself a spiritual personality; he realized his own distance from nature, and in his relationship to God he became glad and certain of his own dignity as a responsible spiritual being.

Our conclusion is that the exaltation of God over nature, as perceived by the Hebrews, did not lead them to class men as wholly one with nature as over against the divine otherness. On the contrary, what one finds is the same kind of effect as is seen when one looks at a double picture through a stereoscope. The entities nature, man, and God, which to the one-eyed vision of the heathen religions seemed to lie all more or less in one plane, are now revealed in the light of a new dimension of depth. God is far above nature and man, but man, in his own lesser degree, has been lifted out of the plane of nature by virtue of his special relationship to God.

And further, this effect of what we might call stereoscopic depth can be seen increasing as time goes on. Let us take the account of creation given in Genesis 1, and compare it with the account of Genesis 2. The earlier account in time is that of Genesis 2, which belongs to 'J', the Jahvist document. The account of Genesis 1 belongs, as we said, to 'P', the Priestly document, which is roughly some four hundred years later. 'J' is anthropomorphic in its description of God, but 'P' belongs to a time when the centralization of worship and the development of a legal and priestly system had accentuated man's sense of the exaltation and unapproachable holiness of God. This tendency is clearly to be seen in the general account given of the Creation by 'P', whose emphasis all the time is on the distance of God from the world which he is creating.

Instead of the world being created by the direct act of God, as in the 'J' account of Chapter 2, each plant and creature is recorded as having been created through the medium of God's word. But this does not mean that 'P' regards man and nature as all one over against the distant creator. For, before man's making, there is another pause, counsel is taken in the heavenly places, and then man is created in God's image.[5] Thus here in 'P', and here alone, does the Old Testament rise to the formation of a special concept to mark man's otherness from the rest of the world, and his kinship with God.

It is worth-while to pause and reflect here that the Bible, which exalts the otherness and the glory of God, which emphasizes as no other ancient book the twofold barrier of creation and sin that separates man from him, yet speaks of man as created in the divine image. It never so exalts God as to turn man into a mere thing, or to annihilate him. The Bible does not talk of irresistible grace; something of man's freedom is left to him, even in his sin; he is a responsible being, and therefore a guilty being; God always deals with man as a person.

2 *Some Early Interpretations Criticized in the Light of the Text*

It will be our task at a later stage to inquire in more detail into the teaching of some of the Fathers. At this point it will be of value to reject some of the interpretations which do not tally with the text itself.

In the first place, we must reject the view of Irenaeus who, in his exegesis of Genesis 1:26 made a distinction between *tzelem* and *demuth*, image and likeness. The latter, he thought, referred to man's original righteousness, lost at the Fall, while the former referred to the divine image, which still continues to exist, even in fallen man. The text gives no basis for this view. 'Image' and 'likeness' cannot refer to two quite different things. What we have here is a Hebrew parallelism, or, as Eichrodt thinks, the second term defines more closely than the first what is meant. 'In God's image, that is to say, in his likeness.'

Further, the text hardly permits us to look on the image as *constituted*[6] by man's dominion over nature. Eichrodt points out that a blessing is given to man when he is created in the divine image, but that a second blessing is necessary before the dominion over nature is given. The dominion is certainly connected with the image, and one might say that, without the image, the dominion would never have been given. In Psalm 8, the dignity of man and his dominion over the earth are brought into very close relationship, though the words 'image' and 'likeness 'are not actually mentioned. Our conclusion is that, though related in this manner, image and dominion are not identical.

Again, Genesis 9 shows that the image, as the Old Testament conceives it, cannot have been lost at the Fall, as was asserted at the Reformation. In this chapter, God tells Noah and his sons that the dominion over nature is theirs. If the dominion is still there, after the Fall, the inference is that the image also is still there, and this is at once stated to be the fact. The life of animals belongs to God, therefore the blood of animals shall not be eaten. But when the life of a man has been taken, that is a different affair. The animal or man that has killed him shall be put to death. And the ground of this precept is man's creation in the divine image. Therefore the image is still there today in sinful man.[7]

A further point may be inferred from the ninth chapter, though it is not stated in so many words. The image is universal; it belongs to the human race as such. Not only Hebrews, but Gentiles also are created in it, and not only man is in

God's image, but woman also.

And, lastly, because of the image, man's life is sacred. In the case of the animals, there is a limit to man's dominion. Their blood, that is to say their life, belongs to God. But with regard to man's own person, the limitation on the dominion of man is much more rigorous. For the image of God marks man as God's possession, as holy.

3 Some Modern Interpretations

These reflections bring us rather nearer to an understanding of the meaning of the author of 'P' when he says the words, 'image of God'. We can agree with von Rad, when he says that 'P' is trying to express the mystery that man is like God, and that he is to be described as a creature whose being comes, not from below, but in its origin points to the upper region.[8] Can we go further than this?

Eichrodt, in his *Theology of the Old Testament*,[9] dares to go a good deal further. He says: 'If we remember the whole manner and fashion in which the Godhead is pictured in Genesis 1, how he appears from the first lines as conscious and powerful will, and continually bears witness to himself through insistent purposive creation, we shall be forced to find man's likeness to God as indicated by the author, in his spiritual superiority, which expresses itself not only in his higher rational endowment, but above all in his capacity for self-consciousness and self-determination; in short, in those capacities which we are accustomed to regard as typical of personality . . . The gift to man of the *imago dei* in the formal sense indicated by us implies nothing less than a connection with God through which man, even as a sinner, remains a rational being capable of spiritual fellowship with God. His pre-eminence over all other creatures consists in the fact that as a conscious self he can be reached by God's word, and thereby called to responsibility.'

What are we to make of this definition? One might be prepared to go a good deal of the way with Eichrodt. And yet one feels that it is hard to say at what point he is still giving the thoughts of 'P', and at what point he begins to comment on their implications in the light of Emil Brunner's *Man in Revolt*. With what Eichrodt says here I am in agreement, believing it to be a Christian development of the implications of 'P' 's account, but were these thoughts in the mind of 'P' as he wrote?

In his book, *The Bible Doctrine of Man,* Dr Ryder Smith claims that Genesis 1:26 refers to a physical resemblance between God and man. He thus explains the retention of the image after the Fall, and asserts that the terms used in relation to the image, both in Hebrew and in Septuagint Greek, all refer to a visible form. He believes that the Hebrews thought of God as having visible form, though not a material body. Man is indeed made to be like God morally and spiritually, but this is not the truth which Genesis I:26 teaches; it is a doctrine of the prophets.[10]

It may be remembered that the Genesis story has certain affinities with the *Gilgamesh Epos,* which tells how the man Enkidu was created in the image of the god Anu, while other forms of the story relate that a sketch of the man to be created was made by the god on a tablet. Here indeed a definite physical likeness is indicated. Eichrodt says that no physical resemblance can have been in the mind of the author of 'P', in whose eyes there was no parallel in heaven or on earth to Jahveh. The reverence of 'P' is, he says, everywhere apparent, and the notion of a physical likeness simply does not fit into his world of discourse.[11]

On the other hand, von Rad says that the argument as to whether the image of God refers to man's physical or spiritual being is not very profitable. But if we do use the alternative spiritual-physical, we must decide to take the image of God in man in a predominantly physical sense.[12] Where specialists disagree, a certain liberty is left us.

In my view, the essential thing about the image in 'P' is man's personal nature, his link with God, his dignity above other creatures, darkly felt rather than clearly thought out. The Hebrew did not so sharply distinguish between body and spirit as does western thought, and the body for him was, so to speak, a sacrament of the spirit. It would not therefore upset our view if there were also what we may call physical overtones in the conception of Genesis 1:26, and there would be a line of development through to the notion of the image in the New Testament, where transformation into the

mage involves also a new physical life, and where it is promised that the believer will be clothed also with a new
spiritual body when the spiritual likeness is revealed in its
glory.

In his *Church Dogmatics*[13] Karl Barth gives a number of
definitions of the image of God supplied by various theo-
ogians, concluding with a couple of quotations from Bieder-
mann and Troeltsch. Troeltsch's view Barth summarizes as
follows:

'The image of God does not signify a lost original condition, but rather, presupposing the kinship of man's soul with
God, a longing which "reaches out in struggle and growth towards perfection, and which is consequently the principle of
historical development".'

This definition starts innocently enough with the assertion
that the image was not lost at the Fall, but it finishes with
words which seem to belong to the thought-world of evolutionary optimism rather than to that of the Bible. It is clear
that, whatever is being described here, we are very far away
from the thoughts of the author of 'P'.

There is surely therefore in this case some justification for
the criticism made by Barth himself when he says: 'We may
indeed discuss which of all these and the many other similar
explanations of the concept is the finest or the profoundest or
the most serious. But one cannot discuss which of them is the
right interpretation of Genesis 1:26 seq. For it is crystal clear
that after their originators found the concept in our passage,
their interpretations were one and all fabricated out of thin
air according to the different anthropologies of their authors.'[14]

What are we to say of Barth's own interpretation of the
concept 'image of God' in the Old Testament? We shall have
to deal with it at greater length later on, but it will be sufficient at this stage to say that Barth seizes upon the fact that
twice the author of 'P', after saying that God created man in
his own image, adds the words, 'Male and female he created
them'. There is, Barth claims, a simple and clear correspondence between the being of God and the being of man in
this point, that in both there is included an 'I' and a 'Thou'.
In the case of man, you have the man and the woman; in the
case of God, the confrontation is, later in the Bible, more

fully described in the doctrine of the Holy Trinity.[15] If the critic objects that 'P' was surely too early a writer to contain even traces of Trinitarian doctrine, Barth has an answer ready. He claims that when God says in Genesis 1:26, 'Let us make man in our image',[16] it is not to a mere divan of supernatural beings that the words are addressed, but that the person or persons to whom they are spoken is, or are, associated with God in the act of creation. Therefore there is at least a hint here in the direction of the Trinity.

The reader may well ask whether Barth is not guilty here of just the fault of which he accuses Troeltsch. But one thing must be noted, even if there be here too a reading of ideas into the text, rather than out of it, Barth is not on a level with Troeltsch, whom he has condemned, for it is the New Testament which he is using to interpret the Old, and not, like Troeltsch, a series of ideas which have little kinship with biblical thought. My own conclusion is that 'P' means by existence in God's image a personal responsible existence before God, and that this implies what Barth and Brunner read into it, though I very much wonder how deeply 'P' saw into the societary nature of personal being, both divine and human.

4 *The Image of God and the Glory of God*
If there were no New Testament, then there would hardly be justification for introducing a paragraph in this chapter on the relationship of the image of God in man to the divine glory. For the two concepts are like lines which indeed converge in the Old Testament, but can hardly be said to meet until the New Testament. There is not space here to distinguish at length between the various strands of thought on God's glory in the Old Testament.

The word is used to describe a property of God himself. His glory is revealed in the thunderstorm, the lightning, and the thick cloud; it is also revealed in the temple. For Ezekiel it is associated with a visible splendour and the vision of a form like the human one. There is also a more general use of the term where 'glory' means almost the same as 'honour'. The glory of God is God in his revelation. Here we find a curious tension. For on the one hand God revealed is God

32

directly present. On the other hand, even in the Old Testament, the revelation of God is not conceived of as a crude theophany. If God's glory is revealed, it is also wrapped in thick cloud and mystery. There is a strong forward-looking tendency in many of the passages which refer to the divine glory. God is besought to reveal his glory to all peoples, and the implication is that it has never yet been fully revealed. There is urgent expectation of the day when the earth shall be full of the glory of the Lord as the waters cover the sea.

But man too is described in the Old Testament as possessing his own proper glory, and this word can be used to describe a number of things – a man's riches, or the dignity or honour in which he is held – and the word can sometimes be used to describe a man's soul or personality in its essential worth.

There is hardly, however, in the Old Testament any notion of man's sharing in the glory of God; though von Rad says that the act of salvation at the last is pictured as being so universal that there is little distinction between God being Israel's glory and Israel created for God's.[17]

The only passage where man is spoken of as actually reflecting or shining with the divine glory is in the passage later quoted by St Paul in an 'image' context in 2 Corinthians 3.[18] But in general the Old Testament speaks of the faithful as merely beholding God's glory at the day of his coming.[19] The Rabbinic writings, coming at a time when the hope of life beyond the grave had grown clearer, speak with less reserve. They say that the righteous will be renewed in the next world with the splendour of God. The apocalyptic writings assert that the blessed shall see God's glory, which shall be visible at the Day of Judgment, and the righteous shall shine reflecting it.[20]

This is exactly the view expressed in Matthew 13:43: 'Then the righteous will shine like the sun in the kingdom of their Father.' But this carries us beyond the Old Testament. We shall have to consider in the next chapter the way in which the notions of the divine glory and the human image of God are developed in the New Testament and brought into relation with each other.

Does the Old Testament regard the glory of God as a visible or a moral and spiritual glory? The answer certainly is that it does not make a rigid separation between the spirit and the body, as western thought is apt to do. The Hebrews regarded the outward form as an expression of the inward reality; and, for example the vision of Isaiah was both a vision of light and of spiritual holiness. It is fortunately not our task to decide whether the Hebrews thought of God as possessing physical form, though not a material body.[21] But at least we can say that God is a God who can naturally reveal himself, and even become incarnate in the physical world, and the physical world is one which is sacramentally fitted to reveal his spiritual nature.

5 *Help from Biblical Psychology?*

Is any guidance given to us in our inquiry by a study of Old Testament psychology? Is it possible, for example, to locate the image of God in any of the different parts of man's personality of which the Old Testament writers speak?

The Old Testament itself nowhere undertakes to do this. Indeed, such a quest as I have suggested would be illegitimate, since Hebrew psychology does not divide up man's nature into mutually exclusive parts. When soul or spirit or reins or heart are spoken of, it is the whole man that is described in each case, but one term is chosen in preference to another, according as one aspect or another of man's life is emphasized. Where it is the life, or the individuality, or strong desire, then it is the word 'soul' (*Nephesh*) that is used. Where eternal influences, or a power above the individual, then 'spirit' (*Ruach*) is the word. Where intellect, will and conscience are to the fore, then it is the word 'heart' (*Lebh*), and where motive, or that which is known to God but hidden to men, then the Old Testament writers use the word 'reins' (*Kelaoth*).

Thus, though the same word (*Ruach*) is used for the Divine Spirit and the spirit of man, it would not be fair to lodge the image of God in man's *Ruach* alone, for the Old Testament does not only make a sharp distinction between God's Spirit and man's, but those aspects of human life indicated by the words heart and soul and reins are also relevant to man's existence in God's image.

We may say, however, in general, that the impression left

upon us by Hebrew thought is, that man's nature is twofold. One cannot speak of a dualism, but of a twofold nature, in which the links between spirit and body are extremely intimate. The body is neither the tomb of the soul, as idealism is apt to regard it, nor is it the man himself, as the materialists claim. In Eichrodt's words: 'It is rather the living form of our being, the necessary expression of our individual existence, in which the meaning of our life must find its realization.'[22]

But, as we have already indicated, the image is to be found rather in man as a spiritual being than in his physical nature, though the intimate connection of the spiritual with the physical will make it natural that the image should leave its trace on the physical nature of man. There is no direct mention in the Old Testament of such a physical reflection,[23] though possibly the 'glory' mentioned in Psalm 8 is an indication of it. (Verse 5: 'Yet thou hast made him little less than God, and dost crown him with glory and honour.')

Here a word must be said about this magnificent psalm, although the words 'image of God' do not occur in it. There can, however, be no doubt of the affinity between Psalm 8 and the priestly account of creation which we have been considering. In spite of the melancholy results of sin, the Bible, which is so realistic in its view of fallen man, does not hesitate to let ring out this voice of praise to God for his glory in nature and in man. While the psalm cannot be taken as giving in itself the whole biblical teaching about man, yet it must not be silenced from the choir of witness. Here there is an echo of Eden, even in the midst of sin and mortality; here there is a promise of what will yet be. And this hope the author of Hebrews finds fulfilled in Jesus, through whom a restored humanity will one day give unbroken praise to God.

6 Importance of the Concept in Old Testament Thought

At the beginning of this chapter the claim was made that, though the term 'image of God' was only thrice mentioned in the Old Testament, the reality for which it stands has a not unimportant place in Old Testament theology. It is now necessary to give some grounds for this belief. There is surely an indication of it in the Jahvist document which deals in Genesis 10 with the common descent of man, and the fact of a common language, although this was said to have been annulled by the confusion of Babel.

While the common language of mankind was reported to have been lost at Babel, 'P' says that Adam was created in the likeness of God and begat a son in his image, after his likeness (Genesis 5:1-3). Thus it is indicated that all mankind is in the image and likeness of God, being the descendants of Adam.

But it is through the prophetic writings that this universal sacredness of man first becomes clear. There was one very important fact in the history of Israel that tended to obscure it. That was the fact of the covenant. The first thing that God had to teach Israel was the reality of the covenant, which was the basis of their special relation to him. It was exceedingly difficult for a primitive people to keep a fast grip of this primary truth, and yet to realize that God had also a care for the other peoples, and for every man on earth. It was, one might venture to say, almost impossible for Israel securely to hold both these truths together, the reality of the covenant and the universality of the image, until it had dawned on them that there was but one God and that the gods of the other nations were idols. For were not these other peoples enemies of Israel, serving other gods? But when the revelation of God as universal Lord became clear, and the gods of the other nations dwindled away into idols, then the notion of an image of God as wide as humanity could take fast hold. Up till then the notion of the covenant would always be accompanied by a temptation to the thought of favouritism. The true harmony of the two notions, that of the special covenant and the universal image, lay in the conviction that it was God's purpose that in Abraham's seed all the peoples of the earth would be blest.[24] The covenant of the Old Testament was thus clearly realized as being the prelude to a universal covenant, and the promise of this was part of the prophetic message. It is then, in the prophetic teaching, that we must look for the clearest witness to the universal image, and it is here that we shall find it. Once it is even expressed in terms that seem to endanger the covenant, in Amos 9:7, ' "Are you not like the Ethiopians to me, O

36

people of Israel?" says the Lord. "Did I not bring up Israel
from the land of Egypt, and the Philistines from Caphtor, and
the Syrians from Kir?"'

The deliverance from Egypt should give Israel no grounds
for self-congratulation. Had not God done the same for other
peoples? When we reflect how continually this fact of the
deliverance from Egypt is interpreted in the Old Testament
as a proof to Israel of her covenant-relationship with God,
we can see how desperately the prophet must have been convinced of the danger she was in, from a selfish interpretation
of the same deliverance. For he strikes at the selfishness even
at the risk of destroying faith in the special revelation and
covenant altogether.

If God has a care for the other peoples as well as for
Israel, it expresses itself also in his anger at these Gentiles
when they do not respect the divine image in each other.
Let it be granted that the main denunciation is to fall upon
Israel and Judah for their sins, and that this is the climax of a
famous passage Amos 1 and 2). But the fact remains that the
people of Damascus will be punished 'because they have
threshed Gilead with threshing sledges of iron', and Gaza will
suffer because 'they carried into exile a whole people to
deliver them up to Edom', and Tyre will be punished for the
same reason. The lesson of Jonah, whom the Lord rebuked
for his lack of pity for the people of Nineveh, points in the
same direction.

One must then conclude that while the doctrine of the
universal image of God as the source of the sacredness of
human beings is not a predominant doctrine in the Old Testament, it has a secure lodgment there. This is the only doctrine
of the image which is found *by name* in the Old Testament.

7 *The Old Testament Concept of the Image in the New Testament*

We shall see in the next chapter that a different doctrine of
the image is to be found in the New Testament. The New
Testament doctrine pictures the image as a likeness to Christ,
a likeness for which God has planned our being, a likeness
into which we must be restored by the grace of God in Christ.
This is a likeness which has been lost by sin. In this book I

37

shall henceforward refer to these two doctrines as the Old
Testament and New Testament doctrines of the image respectively.

But while the one doctrine is to be found chiefly in the
Old Testament and the other in the New, it is not possible
to say that the Old Testament doctrine of the image is not
to be found in the New Testament. It is found quite explicitly
in one passage, and that is, as one might expect, in the letter
of St James, who of all the New Testament writers remains,
both in his language and thought, the most clearly a man of
the Old Testament. In his Epistle 3:9, he is talking of the
dangers of the tongue and says, 'With it we bless the Lord
and Father, and with it we curse men, who are made in the
likeness (*homoiosis*) of God. From the same mouth come blessing and cursing.'[25]

The other passage is one which does not actually mention
the image; but appears to make a clear reference to it. When
Jesus asked for a *denarius* (Mark 12:16) and said, 'Whose
likeness and inscription is this?' and as a result of the Pharisees'
answer rejoined, 'Render to Caesar the things that are Caesar's,
and to God the things that are God's', the unspoken argument
surely is: 'Give to Caesar the taxes that are his due. But the
image that is printed on you is not Caesar's, but God's;
therefore you yourselves belong to God.' And this is quite
clearly the Old Testament use of the term in the mouth of
Christ himself. (I have seen no modern writer who has noticed
this important point, save Dorothy Sayers[26] in her play, *The
Man Born to be King*.)

While the Old Testament conception of the image is thus to
be found in the New Testament, it is also fair to say that
though the New Testament sense is not to be found in so
many words in the Old Testament, yet the achievement of the
image and likeness of God in his people is also the goal of the
Old Testament revelation. It will perhaps be asked: Are
there two senses, after all, the one clearly distinct from the
other?

There are a number of theologians who have denied that
two senses can be so distinguished. The view that I have
followed is close to that of Emil Brunner, and I have followed
it because it appears to me to have better scriptural foundation

than the opposing view.[27] Those who maintain that there is
in the Bible only one sense of the term 'image of God' are
driven to exclude the typical Old Testament sense altogether.
As a result they are driven to define the image in terms of an
integrity lost at the Fall, or as existing merely in God's
purpose and election. And this is in clear opposition to the
teaching of the Old Testament.

CHAPTER II

The New Testament Teaching

In the New Testament, the image of God is mentioned less than a dozen times. But the teaching on the image is more important than this might lead us to think, for some of the passages are among the greatest in the Bible, and the image of God is often the subject when the term 'image' is not itself used. Most of the 'image' passages occur in the writings of St Paul.

1 *The word 'image' is used in three main senses in the New Testament: firstly, to describe Christ's singular dignity and divine Sonship; secondly, to describe the likeness of God into which believers enter through faith in Christ; and thirdly, to describe man's humanity. The third sense is marginal in the New Testament, and the second is the central one*

Let us first consider Colossians 1:13-18. The context here is a polemic against those heretics in Colossae who believed that faith in Christ needed to be supplemented by worship of angels and principalities and powers. Paul is concerned to assert the supremacy of Christ over all other powers in the universe. The nearer context is a hymn of praise to the Father who 'has delivered us from the dominion of darkness and transferred us to the kingdom of his beloved Son . . . He is the image of the invisible God, the first-born of all creation; for in him all things were created, in heaven and on earth, visible and invisible, whether thrones or dominions or principalities or authorities – all things were created through him and for him. He is before all things, and in him all things hold together. He is the head of the body, the church; he is the beginning, the first-born from the dead, that in everything he might be pre-eminent.'

Here the whole emphasis is laid on the supremacy of Christ, over all thrones and powers. He is distinguished from all subordinate beings. Therefore the word *Prototokos*, 'first-born', as we come upon it the first time in the passage, in verse 15, 'first-born of all creation' does not mean that Christ is a creature. Indeed, it is specifically said that all things were created through him. We must, of course, remember that the issue of Arianism, which asserted Christ to be a created being, had not yet arisen, and that Paul was not talking dogmatically precise language. But the whole force of the passage strains in the contrary direction. It asserts that Christ is supreme over all created beings, and thus different from them. He is the image of the invisible God.

The commentators are not agreed as to the exact meaning of *Prototokos*. Some say that here it means only pre-eminence in authority, and the possession of dominion, others claim that it means also temporal priority.[1] In any case it cannot here afford a basis of kinship with other, created, beings.

In this sentence, then, when Christ is called the image (*Eikon*), the meaning is precisely the same as when in Hebrews 1:3, he is called the 'express image' (*Charakter*) of God's glory. In both passages a glory absolutely singular is ascribed to Christ, and a relation which none other can share. This is the divine Sonship.

If this be so, then it may well be asked why the word *Eikon* is here used of him, since in the Old Testament that word is used to describe man generically in his humanity. Our answer might be along the following lines. It is probable that Paul and Philo were too nearly contemporaries for Paul to be acquainted with Philo's writings, but it is very likely that teaching of a Philonian type was current in the Hellenistic world at the time that the Letter to the Colossians was written, and that St Paul was familiar with it. Philo gives a strange interpretation of the two accounts of creation in Genesis 1 and 2. He holds that they refer to different men. The man spoken of in Genesis 1:26 seq. is a heavenly man, and he is in the image of God. The second man, to whom reference is made in Genesis 2:7, is a creature of the creator, and not his offspring, like the first man. Philo's heavenly man might be described in Platonic terms as the idea of man, whose home is in Paradise, as the Platonic ideas are said to be 'laid up in the heavenly places'. Most writers identify Philo's heavenly man with the logos, who in spite of his title, is probably not conceived of as personal.

If we assume that such ideas as these were current in Colossae, we may assume that Paul was not asserting merely Christ's superiority to angels and principalities, but to have been attacking such speculations of a Philonian type.[2] Confronted with the view that there is an impersonal logos which is the image of the invisible God, a logos which receives the title 'Heavenly man' and is therefore termed the image of God, Paul answers: 'No. The dignity which you Hellenistic Jews ascribe to your logos, I ascribe to Jesus Christ. All wreaths of empire meet upon his brow, and he is the true logos, who was with the Father from the beginning. He and not your phantom logos is the image of God, through whom all things were created.' Whether or not this be the way in which Paul comes to use the term 'image of God' to describe Christ in his divinity, there can be no doubt that here in Colossians 1:15 he does so, and also in 2 Corinthians 4:4 where he speaks of the 'gospel of the glory of Christ who is the likeness of God.'

Let us return to the exposition of Colossians 1:15-20. Though we claim that the first reference of the word 'image' in verse 15 is to our Lord's divinity, yet we must grant that Paul later hints at another sense of the word, though the term *Eikon* does not actually occur again. For the word *Prototokos* is mentioned again, when in verse 18 Christ is described as 'the first-born from the dead'. The thought that links the two parts of the argument is surely that, just as Christ, though not created (verse 16), is first-born in the order of creation, so also he is first-born in the order of the new creation, the order of the resurrection. Here then, the word 'first-born' has a different sense from that which it had in verse 15. Here Christ is the first to rise from the dead, but others will follow him, and will share in the glory of his resurrection. It is impossible to read these words about Christ being the first-born from the dead without thinking of 1 Corinthians 15:20: 'But in fact Christ has been raised from the dead, the first fruits of those who have fallen asleep. For as by a man came death, by a man has come also the resurrection of the dead. For as in Adam all die, so also in Christ shall all be made alive. But each in his own order: Christ the first fruits, then at his coming those who belong to Christ.'

Here we have the doctrine of the first and the last Adam, which is very important for the New Testament teaching on the image of God in man. The parallelism runs thus: As Adam was the first-born of mankind, so Christ is the first-born of the resurrection. Adam's sin led to death for himself and all humanity. Christ's death and resurrection reversed the verdict of death. He became the first of a new humanity, and in his glory all who believe in him are destined to share.

So that Paul, without actually mentioning the image a second time in this passage, Colossians 1, seems to have passed over from the first sense of the word 'image' to a second one. Hitherto the word 'first-born' has been used in this passage to describe a dignity which cannot be passed on to any other person. Now, in verse 18, it is used to describe an experience in which Christ is the first of a long series of men. And this second sense of the word 'image', which is only hinted at here, is in fact the central use in the New Testament, and with it we shall be mainly occupied in the rest of this chapter. This second sense of the word 'image' describes Christ's perfect humanity, in which by faith men can share, and in which they hope to be perfected.

It is worth-while recalling that there is a third sense in which the term 'image of God' is used in the New Testament. Reference was made to it in the last chapter. Owing to its prominence in the Old Testament, we shall call this the Old Testament image. This sense is found in James 3:9 where the term used is *Homoiosis*, or 'likeness'. It is clear that a character is here indicated in which all men share. In the story of Jesus and the *denarius*,[3] there is also an indirect but unmistakable reference to man being, as man, in the image of God.

While both the New Testament image and the Old Testament image are found in the New Testament, there is no attempt made to show the relation between the one and the other. It is in the field of soteriology that certain principles are laid down in the New Testament which have important results for our doctrine of the Old Testament image. Such statements as 'there is no other name under heaven given among men, by which we must be saved',[4] forbid us to think of the Old Testament image as implying man's essential and continuing moral goodness. We shall later trace the development of theories of the image, some of which do not avoid dangerous error on this point.

2 *The image of God or of Christ, to which believers are conformed through faith, is an existence in love to God, responsive to God's love to man. This existence is not a discarnate life*

Let us turn to Romans 8, a chapter whose theme is the unshakable purpose of God, which is leading to a glorious consummation, to which the whole creation looks forward with an indescribable mixture of agony and hope. Meanwhile, God's Spirit is within us, who believe, teaching us to love him and call him 'Abba, Father' (verse 15). We need have no doubt of the triumph to which all things are moving, for all things work together for good to them that love God. Paul says (verse 28): 'We know that in everything God works for good with those who love him, who are called according to his purpose. For those whom he foreknew he also predestined to be conformed to the image of his Son, in order that he might be the first-born among many brethren . . . What then shall we say to this? If God is for us, who is against us? He who did not spare his own Son, but gave him up for us all, will he not also give us all things with him?' And the chapter closes thus: 'For I am sure that neither death, nor life, nor angels, nor principalities, nor things present, nor things to come, nor powers, nor height, nor depth, nor anything else in all creation, will be able to separate us from the love of God in Christ Jesus our Lord.'

What is the meaning of the words, 'the image of his Son'? The main theme of the chapter is certainly God's eternal love to us in Christ, and therefore the main content of the image is surely the answering and grateful love of the believer towards God. It is what we have called the characteristic New Testament image. This love is given by the Holy Spirit. But there is something else to be noted. The image is the image of God's Son, and there is in the passage more than a hint of future physical likeness to Christ. Verse 23 says: '. . . We ourselves, who have the first fruits of the Spirit, groan in-

wardly as we wait for adoption as sons, the redemption of our
bodies.' Here we have the same kind of double character
which we found in our handling of the Old Testament image.
There is present a spiritual element, and there is present also a
physical element. There is no need to assume as an inference from
this fact, that God has a visible form. But he is such that his only
Son can take upon human nature. There is thus, for all God's
difference from created being, a certain kinship between him
and his world, so that Christ was able to become man; and we
who have in this world a physical nature and expect to have a
glorified physical nature in the next, may yet be in the divine
image. Of this physical element we shall have more to say
in the next paragraph.

3 *The image of God is pictured as glory reflecting God's
glory revealed in Christ. It is not purely moral, but will
shine forth not only in our spirits, but in our redeemed
bodies. This glory is conceived of as something already
given, as being given in the present, and as something lying
still in the eschatological future*

We said before that the glory of God is God in his revelation.
The New Testament sees in Christ the crown of God's revelation, and consequently it sees in Christ the perfect revelation
of the glory of God. This appears as early as Luke 2:9,
where the glory of the Lord shines round the Bethlehem
shepherds, and the angels praise God, saying: 'Glory to God
in the highest, and on earth peace among men with whom
he is pleased!' Such ascriptions of glory do not imply that
God is given something which he did not possess before.
They are rather the due acknowledgment by men or angels of a
glory which is already God's. In the praise of the angels he is
glorified because of the revelation of his love and greatness
in the coming incarnation, and shepherds and angels acknowledge his glory. And so it is reported in the Gospels that
when the people saw Christ's mighty works of healing, they
glorified God (Mark 2:12, healing of paralytic; Luke 7:16,
raising of young man at Nain).

But the glory of God is revealed especially in Christ's
resurrection and ascension ('God raised him from the dead

45

and gave him glory' 1 Peter 1:21; 'Was it not necessary that the Christ should suffer these things and enter into his glory?' Luke 24:26). But the death of Christ is for the author of John the central focus of his glory, while the transfiguration is for the synoptic writers a foretaste of that glory. It must be noted that in the New Testament even more clearly than in the Old the divine glory is not the glory of a theophany which all can behold – it is a hidden glory, which can be seen only by the eye of faith. The transfiguration followed on Peter's confession, and was seen only by the three disciples nearest to our Lord. After his resurrection he appeared not to all and sundry, but to those who loved him. 'We have beheld his glory, glory as of the only Son from the Father,' says John (1:14). This is probably a reference to the whole of Christ's life and death, and where glory is associated with his death, there even more emphatically it is such only to the eye of men whom the Holy Spirit has taught to see glory where it might least be expected. Together with this incognito of glory there goes the eager hope for that day when the disguise will be laid aside and the glory openly revealed.

In the Old Testament, as we saw, the term 'glory' is used both to describe God and, in a different sense, to describe man. In the New Testament the gap is bridged in the person of Christ, who is both God and man. And yet he never seeks his own glory, but the glory of the Father who sent him (John 7:18, 8:50). The Father glorifies him as he glorifies the Father by finishing the work allotted to him in his cross and passion (John 17:1-4). Through his revelation in the Son, the Father glorifies both himself and the Son. Christ rejects as a temptation of the devil the glory of the world (Luke 4:6) and gives himself wholly to the task of serving the Father. Other men too must not boast themselves by reason of their own achievements, or seek glory there. Where they can glory, and must glory, is in the cross of Christ, and in the destiny to which it has opened up the way for them. They are encouraged, and even bidden, to look for a glory which comes from union with Christ. So strong is this emphasis that sin itself is once defined as 'falling short of the glory of God' (Romans 3:23). By this is clearly meant the glory of the image of God; the glory of man being to reflect God's glory, and sin being

Thus if in sin (OT) then image is lost

46

the condition wherein this image is not reflected. And the
eschatological 'hope of glory' which is so frequently referred
to in the writings of Paul and Peter, is not merely the hope of
a day when God's glory will break forth in unimpeded
splendour in the world. It is the hope that we may share in
the glory of the image. Thus St Paul can speak of rejoicing
in the hope of sharing the glory of God (Romans 5:2) and
of the glory which is to be revealed in us, and Peter of 'the
unfading crown of glory' (1 Peter 5:4). It is unnecessary to
give fuller references to the passages where this coming
glory is mentioned. It is enough to say that once our attention
has been drawn to it, we shall find it constantly recurring
throughout the New Testament.

It must further be noted that, as we saw in the last paragraph, while the image of glory is a spiritual and moral likeness, the physical element cannot be eliminated from it. The
resurrection body shares in glory. 'It is sown in dishonour, it is
raised in glory. It is sown in weakness, it is raised in power.
It is sown a physical body, it is raised a spiritual body.' (I
Corinthians 15:43-4) 'The first man was from the earth, a
man of dust; [Adam] the second man is from heaven.' (verse
47) 'Just as we have borne the image of the man of dust,
we shall also bear the image of the man of heaven.' (verse 49)
It is true that we are speaking here of a *spiritual* body, and
therefore by analogy, for the only bodies we know directly
are our human bodies. But the analogy holds, and is close
enough for the experience of Christ's transfiguration and of
his resurrection to have been available through the power of
the Spirit to men who were still in the natural body. In this
light we must read the words of 1 John 3:2: 'Beloved, we
are God's children now; it does not yet appear what we shall
be, but we know that when he appears we shall be like him,
for we shall see him as he is.' In this sentence we must see
both a spiritual and moral likeness of the glorified believer
to Christ, and a quasi-physical likeness of our spiritual bodies
to his.

The theme of the glory of the image receives perhaps its
fullest treatment in the great passage in 2 Corinthians, the
third and fourth chapters, where St Paul is speaking of the
glory of the Christian gospel. Here he contrasts it with the

lesser glory of the old covenant. Moses, who came down from Mount Sinai, bearing the tables of the law, had to put a veil on his face. He did this, either because the people of Israel could not look steadfastly on the brightness of his face, or, as the modern scholars are more inclined to suggest, because his glory was a fading glory, and he did not wish them to see its transience.

We, however, says Paul, proclaim our gospel without any veil. 'We are very bold', and 'we all, with unveiled face, beholding the glory of the Lord, are being changed into his likeness from one degree of glory to another; for this comes from the Lord who is the Spirit.' (2 Corinthians 3:18)

Moses looked on God, and his face shone with a reflected glory. We, looking at Christ, shine also with a reflected glory, but ours is not fading and transient, as was that of Moses. It is rather changed from radiance to radiance. This brightness is nothing of our own, but a constant gift, since we reflect the light of the love of God shown to us in Christ. The very light and essence of our being becomes gratitude.

The next chapter goes on to deal with the difficulty: 'How is it, if this gospel is so glorious, that men can reject it?' Paul sets it down to a blinding of their hearts. We read, in 4:3-6: 'And even if our gospel is veiled, it is veiled only to those who are perishing. In their case the god of this world has blinded the minds of the unbelievers to keep them from seeing the light of the gospel of the glory of Christ, who is the likeness of God. For what we preach is not ourselves, but Jesus Christ as Lord, with ourselves as your servants for Jesus' sake. For it is the God who said, "Let light shine out of darkness", who has shone in our hearts to give the light of the knowledge of the glory of God in the face of Christ.' Here all our themes are touched, the moral and physical splendour revealed in Christ, and God's glory incarnate, which glory we reflect.

The New Testament considers this image both as a gift in the purpose of God from the beginning, as actually now given to believers with the gift of faith, and as an inheritance into which they are exhorted to enter now, and also as a future promise, which will be revealed at the end of our era. Since the thoughts related to the image and glory are so closely interwoven, we have not been able to avoid mention of the eschatological nature of the image doctrine. But it is worth our while now specifically to draw attention to its threefold character, as past, present and future. It is true that salvation and man's sonship of God have also the same threefold pattern, as has also the doctrine of the Kingdom and the Lordship of Christ, for all these doctrines are but facets of the one Christian truth.

The image is there in God's predestination of his own. 'For those whom he foreknew he also predestined to be conformed to the image of his son,' says Romans 8:29 – and here all the verbs are in the past tense, as if to emphasize the sureness of God's purpose, which is already as good as complete, when looked at in one way. 'And those whom he predestined, he also called; and those whom he called he also justified; and those whom he justified he also glorified.' (verse 30)

past tense

In 2 Corinthians 3:18, the tense is the present. 'We all . . . are being changed into his likeness', and the imperative, the perfect, and the indicative alternate in Colossians 3:8-10, 'But now put them all away; anger, wrath, malice, slander, and foul talk from your mouth . . . seeing that you have put off the old nature with its practices; and have put on the new nature, which is being renewed in knowledge after the image of its creator.' We are reminded also of the passage in Philippians, 'work out your own salvation with fear and trembling; for God is at work in you.' (2:12-13) Here we seem to have got beyond the sphere where we can pose an alternative, God or the Christian, for the action is in the highest degree that of both. And here also we have got beyond the ordinary notion that part has been done while part remains still to be achieved. We may and must use figures of speech from other parts of life, such as that of the possession of the title-deeds of a mine, while the working out of the seams remains still to be completed. But we must be ready to acknowledge that salvation is something to which there is no exact parallel in the rest of life, and that all illustrations are not more than analogies which are imperfect. Thus we have salvation, and glory and the image, we have these things truly, but we have them under the guise of faith. And that does not mean that we do not really have them yet. But our possession

present

of them remains yet to be revealed to all. And this will not
be shown until the end of the age.

4 *This sharing in the divine glory does not amount to the divinization of believers*

One last question must be briefly discussed under this heading. Does the description of the image as a reflection of God's
glory, and in a sense a sharing of it, justify the use by the early
Greek theologians, especially Irenaeus, Athanasius and Clement
of Alexandria, of the language of divinization? Is there any
scriptural reference to divinization?

There is only one New Testament passage which is in clear
support of their views. This is 2 Peter 1:4, where the writer
speaks of the gospel, 'by which he has granted to us his
precious and very great promises, that through these you may
escape from the corruption that is in the world because of
passion, and become partakers of the divine nature.' The
Greek words are *theiou koinōnoi phuseōs*. It is generally
agreed that this phrase means what it appears to say, that the
believers actually share in the nature of God.[5] It is probable
that the writer is speaking, as it were, off the record, and the
words are connected with a reference to immortality, as
often in the Greek theologians we have mentioned. The question may be raised as to how much more than this is implied,
and it will be hard to give an answer.

But it is clear that no other New Testament passage goes
so far in the direction of divinization as this. The word
koinōnia and its derivatives when employed by St Paul are
commonly used of a personal relation to Christ, as in 1
Corinthians 1:9: '. . . you were called into the fellowship
koinōnia of his Son, Jesus Christ.' This describes a mystical
fellowship with the exalted Christ, but not a mystical absorption in him or an absorption of the divine nature into oneself;
it is a personal relation. The Pauline conceptions of life in
Christ and of membership of his body again do not appear to
justify the concept of divinization, wonderful and mysterious
as is the truth to which they point. Life in Christ is always
mediated by faith, as is the membership of his body, and
faith is always a relation of persons. The passage in St Paul
which seems to come nearest to the language of divinization is

50

the famous verse, Galatians 2:20: 'I have been crucified with Christ; it is no longer I who live, but Christ who lives in me; and the life I now live in the flesh I live by faith in the Son of God, who loved me, and gave himself for me.' Yet here, where it would appear that the relation passes, as it were, beyond the personal, with the death of the individual and the assumption of his place by the living Christ; the apostle explains his meaning in terms which show that his own personality has not been replaced by that of his Lord: 'The life I now live in the flesh, I live by faith in the Son of God, who loved me and gave himself for me.'

There are other passages which refer to Christ's presence in the Christian in Paul's writings. In these it appears that what Paul is saying is nothing essentially different from what he expresses elsewhere in terms of the possession by the Christian of the Spirit of God. This is clear in Romans 8:10, where he says: 'But if Christ is in you, although your bodies are dead because of sin; your spirits are alive because of righteousness.'[6] Now the gift of the Spirit does not imply the divinization of the believer, or of the Church. In this relation the Spirit remains the Lord, and is not fused with the believer.

Thus our conclusion is that 2 Peter 1:4 goes beyond anything in the Pauline writings in the direction of divinization. And while it may not mean to teach a doctrine which is unbiblical, yet it is open to misinterpretation, and has in fact been misinterpreted. We would state the New Testament position as follows, by faith in Christ men share in the gifts which he brought, and share even in his glory in the sense that we shall be together with him, in that union whereby the Church is united to the Lord. But if to become partakers of the divine nature means more than this, then the notion, in spite of the reference in 2 Peter, is unbiblical.

5 *In all the New Testament passages the image renewed in believers is spoken of as existing, not in the solitary individual, but in the person as a member of the redeemed community*

It will be remembered that St Paul teaches the solidarity of all men in Adam, and finds a parallel to it in the solidarity of believers in Christ, the last Adam. The unity of all men in Adam was a Rabbinic doctrine, and various stories were told of the creation of his body from dust taken from various parts of the earth, and tales were also told about the creation of men from various parts of his body. These crude stories were doubtless meant to suggest that there was a profounder unity between mankind and the first man than could be accounted for by merely physical descent. Paul finds a similar profound and mysterious unity of believers with the last Adam and each other. As W. D. Davies says: '. . . (life in Christ) is a social concept, to be (in Christ) is to have discovered the true community . . . Paul knows nothing of solitary salvation; to be "in Christ" is not for him the mystic flight of the alone to the alone.'[7] It is therefore natural that St Paul always speaks of 'you' and 'us' in the image passages, for the individual is not in the image alone, but as a member of the redeemed community.

It must however be admitted[8] that for Paul the individual is never swamped in the Church; his salvation must be personally appropriated from Christ, just as a man's desperate condition without Christ is his own, whether he realizes it or not. 'Wretched man that I am!' says St Paul; 'Who will deliver me from this body of death? Thanks be to God through Jesus Christ our Lord.'[9] And just as it is the individual-in-the-community – rather than the community itself – that is in the image of God, so also the individual element is emphasized in the physical aspect of the image. The Church is indeed Christ's body, but the spiritual body of the individual believer will also be revealed in the day of Christ's appearing. Though *we* bear the image of the man of heaven, it is as a redeemed member of Christ that *each one* of us will bear it.

6 Comparison of the Threefold Image with the Threefold Fatherhood of God

Such then is the gist of the New Testament teaching on the image of God in man. But our task will not be completed until we have seen how this teaching fits in with the rest of New Testament thought about God and man. I can only very briefly indicate what profound agreement I believe there to be between this doctrine and the rest of the teaching of the

ew Testament. A sketch will be given of two other concepts
the New Testament, the first being that of the divine
therhood, and the second that of sonship of God. The
ntention will be made that, just as there is to be found in
e New Testament a threefold use of the words 'image of
od', so there is also a threefold use of the words fatherhood
nd sonship.

(a) There is, first, a Fatherhood and Sonship in which God
he Father and Christ the Son alone are related to each other.
here is a second sense in which God is the Father, and all
elievers are his sons. And there is a third sense in which
e is the Father of all men, and even a sense in which they
re all his sons.

We shall mention first the divine Fatherhood and the divine
onship, but we shall mention them only to leave them, for our
heme here is not Christology, and, further, the days are past in
which it was possible to deny that Jesus claimed to be the
on of God in a singular sense. It is beyond doubt that the
New Testament claims for him such a dignity.

(b) Therefore we may at once pass to that sonship of the
divine Father into which Jesus claimed to lead his disciples.
If Jesus said almost nothing in his teaching about the image of
God, it was because he had said all that he needed on that
subject in the terms of Fatherhood and sonship. And a few
moments' reflection on his teaching and example, so closely
intertwined will help to make clearer our picture of that
Fatherhood and that sonship.

It must be here pointed out that all through his Ministry
he was not merely teaching men about their sonship of God,
but opening up for them an entry into that sonship. His role
was never that of one who encouraged others to enter into the
possession of a treasure that had been always there. His
claim was to have brought that kingdom with him in a mysterious way, and now, with his coming, it was possible for men to
enter it as it had not been possible before. Entry into the
kingdom is also entry into the sonship of faith. Christ was
able to say, 'and no one knows the Father except the Son
and any one to whom the Son chooses to reveal him.'
(Matthew 11:27) The Fatherhood of God could only be
known in this intimate way by those who belonged to the

53

kingdom which Jesus brought with him.

But in this bringing of the kingdom to men the teaching and example of Jesus had a large place. 'Our Father' was the name which they were taught to use to him, and his coming near to them was a revelation of his character and mind and relationship to all his creation. Because he was like this, they could trust him absolutely, and have confidence to enter into the new relation of intimacy which he was making possible.

It was only gradually that these things were taught to them, nor is a full understanding of the sonship of believers necessary even today, in order that a man should enter into this experience. Different people use the same words, and one man may mean much by them, another little. It is the sincerity of the man which indicates how much he means, the tone of his voice, and also, even more, the degree to which he is willing to commit himself to the cause or person he believes in. Some of the words of Jesus have been preserved for us in the original Aramaic, for those who knew him could still hear them spoken in the tones and timbre of his voice. In the garden of Gethsemane the disciples heard him pray 'Abba, Father, all things are possible to thee; remove this cup from me; yet not what I will, but what thou wilt.' (Mark 14:36) Twice, in different letters, St Paul quotes this phrase: 'And because you are sons, God has sent the Spirit of his Son into our hearts, crying "Abba, Father!"' (Galatians 4:6); and again in Romans 8:15: 'For you did not receive the spirit of slavery to fall back into fear but you have received the spirit of sonship.' From the prayers of their master, and perhaps most of all from that last prayer in Gethsemane, where he expressed finally and fully the love and obedience unto death which every man owes the Father, the disciples learnt what is the divine Fatherhood, and what the sonship of believers.

In this sonship which is open to all believers, the human bond is faith. In the Gospels faith always seems to be a relationship to Jesus and God at the same time. No doubt it was sometimes very rudimentary, and in its earliest stages was hardly more than reliance. But when Jesus encouraged men to rely, on whom was it he asked them to rely? On himself, the visible healer and teacher, and also on the God who has

the power and the will to help. To a man whom he healed Christ said: 'Go home and tell what great things the Lord hath done for thee.' God is the ultimate object of the faith for which Jesus asks.

We have already, almost insensibly, begun to make the transition from our Lord's teaching to his example. Let us look at one of his wonderful actions, an action eloquent of his faith in the Father. It might well pass unnoticed. It comes in the story of the healing of Jairus' daughter (Mark 5:22-43). While Jesus was speaking to the woman he healed of the issue of blood, 'There came from the ruler's house some who said, "Your daughter is dead, why trouble the teacher any further?" But ignoring what they said, Jesus said to the ruler of the synagogue, "Do not fear, only believe." '

Here is a confidence expressed by Jesus in his Father which is quite staggering. Who would have blamed him if he had turned back there and said: 'Sickness and ills I can cure, but death is beyond me. It must have been the will of God that she should die.' But he went on, and that simple action said more than many words. And, further, he encouraged Jairus also to share that faith, and therefore also to share the relation of sonship.

It was not merely to an inner circle of his own disciples that he opened wide the doors of the sonship of God. They had the deepest understanding of God's kingdom and Fatherhood and they were indeed the inmost circle, but all who had faith, in the measure that they had it, found the doors of the kingdom opening to them. And this faith was not confined to members of the Jewish race, even during Jesus' lifetime. So we may say that all who have faith in God through Christ have the sonship, just as they also have the image of God in the second sense, though these words are not used in the Gospels.

The example of Jesus was the example of an absolute unquestioning obedience, and his love was like a clear flame without the slightest wavering before the winds of fear or self-seeking. Such a love from all his children is what the Father desires. Had it merely been told us that this was what the Father required we would probably have thought it was a hard or impossible exaction. But now that we have seen

the Son's will, not hard or legal in its obedience, but shining in the perfect freedom of love and devotion, a whole new world of man's possibilities has been revealed to us. We are shown that so many of our anxieties about ourselves, our desires to secure our own interests, our self-insurances, are not natural, but sinful, because tinged with doubt of the Father's love and power. This we could never have known had not the one life of perfect sonship been lived before our eyes. This image of God is what we were made for. For this every man was made. All the broken and disordered fragments of fear, self-will, sensuality and pride can be healed of their disorder and reunited into that living whole from which they have been broken. All man's instincts can be brought into harmony under the rule of love and obedience to God. They can be reunited in a self from which all selfishness shall at last have been purged away. That is the sonship of the heavenly Father which is offered to faith, and that is the life in the image of God which Christ has opened to all believers.

This teaching is common to the whole New Testament, and the gift of the Holy Spirit, adoption, and the earnest expectation of the whole creation – all these envisage one thing, the perfected sonship of believers, which is also their perfection in the divine image. On this theme all Christians will be found in agreement.

(c) We must now consider a belief which Christians have unfortunately made the subject of bitter controversy, the question of a universal Fatherhood of God and universal sonship of man. We must first examine three texts which by some are taken to exclude a universal Fatherhood.

The first is Matthew 11:27 which runs as follows: 'All things have been delivered to me by my Father; and no one knows the Son except the Father, and no one knows the Father except the Son and any one to whom the Son chooses to reveal him.'

The second is John 14:6, which runs as follows: 'Jesus said to him, [Thomas] "I am the way, and the truth, and the life; no man comes to the Father, but by me."'

And the third is Acts 4:12, where St Peter says: 'And there is salvation in no one else [but Christ], for there is no

other name under heaven given among men by which we must be saved.'

From these three verses it has been inferred that there can be no universal Fatherhood of God. Only if approached through Christ is God the Father of men, only the Christian believer can be called a son. But do the passages really mean, as Luther taught, that God is only fatherly to those who believe in Christ and that to all others he is a God of intolerable wrath, and pure righteous indignation? If they do, the question we are considering is settled at this early stage. There is no need to inquire further, for there can be no universal Fatherhood of God.

But do these verses demand such an interpretation? If we take it that they exclude the universal Fatherhood, we shall have no alternative but to go on and assert as Luther did, that all who, even through invincible ignorance, have not saving faith in Christ, will be damned, since they are dealing with a God of pure wrath. But the words 'there is no other name under heaven' do not, as Leonard Hodgson[10] has shown, demand this cruel condemnation of the heathen, nor yet the damnation of those who have never had the gospel brought effectively to their attention. Unless one accepts the very grim result which Luther accepted, one has no right to deny a universal Fatherhood on the strength of these three texts.

There may, however, be a universal and divine Fatherhood which has no counterpart in a universal human sonship. It may be claimed that, far from men in general being considered in the New Testament as sons of God, sonship is there claimed to be given only by adoption. Another figure used is that of the second birth. If this be necessary to make men God's sons, it is clear that physical birth has nothing to do with sonship of God.

Let us at once admit that any claim that the New Testament teaches a universal Fatherhood and sonship would at once founder if it were implied that men living in a state of sin were not in need of reconciliation with God, and that no second birth was necessary. Similarly, any teaching which claimed that the wrath of God was an illusion of man could not base itself on scriptural authority. But the universal

Fatherhood and sonship we are asserting is not bound up with these mistaken views. All that we are claiming is that there is a universal Fatherhood of God which makes his relation to sinners one of both love and wrath; of love because they are his creatures and children, of wrath because they are sinners. But the wrath is a fatherly one, and God longs to be able to express himself to them in pure love. It is this longing in the Father which is the ground of revelation.

The well-known reference of St Paul to adoption as necessary to sonship is not hostile to the notion of a universal sonship and Fatherhood, for the metaphor is actually mingled with another, that of tutelage (Galatians 4:1-7). In the figure of adoption men are considered as having been slaves of the law, and now rescued from such slavery by adoption as sons. But in the preceding verses there is given the other picture of men as sons and heirs by nature; and subject for a while, during their minority, to the tutelage of the law. It is clear that neither of these illustrations was chosen with the purpose of serving as a basis of a general doctrine such as that of a universal or restricted Fatherhood of God.

There is another passage which may be cited by the opponents of the belief in a universal Fatherhood. In John 8:42-4, Jesus is depicted in open conflict with some of the Jews. They even want to kill him. He has told them that he can make them free. They answer that they are not slaves, but Abraham's children. He retorts that if they were, they would believe, as Abraham did. But now they do the acts of their father. They then claim that God is their Father, and Jesus says: 'God forbid – you belong to the devil, he is your father and you are his children.'

But Jesus does not mean literally that Satan had created the Jews, and that they were in the devil's image, and God no longer loved them. He does not mean this any more than he meant literally that Peter was Satan when he rebuked him for choosing the cross (Matthew 16:22-3). Had he meant literally that they were the children of the devil, how could he have said a few verses earlier that they were in bondage to sin, and that he would make them free? (John 8:32)

What are the biblical passages which, on the other hand, go to prove a universal Fatherhood of God? I can only treat

of this matter in the shortest possible way, and would refer anyone who wishes to read a full discussion on it to Dr Scott Lidgett's fine book, *The Fatherhood of God*.[11]

The belief that God, outside his revelation in the Old and New Testaments, is purely a God of retributive justice and anger, is at once refuted by St Matthew's Gospel, which of all the Gospels contains by far the greatest number of references to the divine Fatherhood. Of course, not all these references are to a universal Fatherhood, but a number of them are.

In Matthew 5:44-5 the disciples are told to love their enemies, that they may be the children of their heavenly Father, 'for he makes his sun rise on the evil and on the good, and sends rain on the just and on the unjust.' True, he is 'your' heavenly Father – that is, the Father of believers, but his mercy and tenderness are shown to all, the unjust as well as the just. Here, quite unmistakably, is the universal Fatherhood, shown even to the fowls of the air and to the lilies, in so far as they are able to receive it.

Luke 6:35 expresses the same truth: 'for he is kind to the ungrateful and the selfish.'

There is, however, one parable which quickly settles the whole matter, the parable of the prodigal son (Luke 15:11-32). Here the reference is quite indubitably universal. Although the introduction to the parable refers to a contrast between the Pharisees and the publicans and sinners (Luke 15:1), not even a purist would argue that the publicans and sinners are forgetful children of the covenant, and therefore in a sense believers. The prodigal is the personification of lost sinful man in general, and he is thought of, not only as a prodigal, but also as a son. And if the prodigal is every sinner, then God is the loving Father of all, who seeks all.

Thus our second investigation has borne out the conclusions arrived at by our first. The New Testament speaks of the divine Fatherhood in three senses, and of sonship in three senses also. And this confirms our assertion that the New Testament also has three uses of the term 'image of God'. First, it is applied to Christ alone; secondly, to all believers; and, thirdly, to all men, even in their sin.

The Image of God in Man

NOTE ON THE BIBLICAL USE OF THE TERM 'IMAGE OF GOD'

In all the passages in the Old Testament where the image of God is mentioned, it is said that man is created *in the image* of God.

In the New Testament, Christ is twice said to *be* the likeness or the image of God (2 Corinthians 4:4 and Colossians 1:15), and once only, in a colloquial passage, is man said – in contradistinction to woman – to *be* the image (1 Corinthians 11:7). The common usage in the New Testament is that man is said to be 'predestined to be conformed' to the image (Romans 8:29) or 'changed into his likeness' (2 Corinthians 3:18) or 'renewed . . . after the image' (Colossians 3:10) or 'made in the likeness of God' (James 3:9). Here the divine purpose for man's existence is life in the image, or the image itself. The image of God in man is nowhere mentioned in the Bible. Are then all attempts to describe it as a quality of human existence due to a misunderstanding?

It should already be clear to our readers that this is not our opinion. In the characteristic Old Testament sense of the term 'image of God', man still after the Fall is 'in God's image', and this term refers not only to a divine purpose for him, but also to a character of his existence today. The typical New Testament usage of the term refers to a character for which God destines man, which he has lost by sin.

The English language suffers from the lack of a word like the German *Ebenbildlichkeit,* which may be translated either as 'man's character as God's image' or 'man's existence in the divine image'. To use such periphrases always to describe the main theme of our study would be intolerably clumsy, and therefore the phrase 'the image of God in man' is frequently used. It must be understood that this usage does not imply any belief in a divine spark, or an area in human nature untouched by sin. It indicates, first, a purpose of God for man, and, secondly, a quality of man's existence.

CHAPTER III

The Image of God in the
Mystery Religions

We must now consider very briefly the relation of the Pauline teaching on the image of God to the teaching of the mystery religions of the Hellenistic world, since it has been claimed by Reitzenstein and other scholars that their influence on Paul was very great. Indeed, if Reitzenstein's claims be conceded, the thought of St Paul on man and God would hardly be a true branch springing out of the parent oak of Hebrew religion. It would rather be a mistletoe branch sprung from a seed which had blown in from the world of oriental religious rites and Hellenistic speculation. This world is extremely hard to describe, because there grew up in the centuries before and after Christ a perfect jungle of syncretistic ritual and speculation. There were a number of cults, originating in different countries, most of them connected with the notion of fertility or the dying and resurrection of vegetation every year. There were the rites of Isis, of Cybele the great mother, the Eleusinian and Orphic mysteries, there were the rites of Mithra and others. There was a strong syncretistic tendency which led the worshippers to assimilate one rite to another. This assimilation was largely due to the influence of Stoics and other philosophers who claimed that the various rituals of worship were all ways of approach to the one true deity, and that the various gods were but names for the one great principle that stands behind the universe.

Reitzenstein draws our attention to the distinction between the public mysteries which in dramatic form celebrated the experiences of the gods and goddesses worshipped and the purely personal mysteries which we can find in the Egyptian, Phrygian and Persian cults in their later developments.[1] It is these private cults of Isis, of Attis and Cybele, and of Mithra, which have especial relevance for our subject. In the private cults the syncretistic influences appear to have worked most

strongly, and a very considerable resemblance appears to have existed among them. But our evidence is scanty, and the date of our documents is often uncertain or late, so that there is need for a good deal of conjecture as to the meaning and exact character of the rites. In general, we may say that their goal was salvation (*Soteria*), and that this was conceived of as union with the god or the goddess. Sometimes this union was of a crudely sexual form, sometimes it was pictured as a spiritual union.

In Apuleius' description of the Isis mysteries at Cenchreae, near Corinth, Lucius, the hero of the story, desires to become an initiate. He has volunteered for the service of Isis, and lives as her captive in the temple precinct until by favourable dreams she grants permission to his request. Dedication rites, including baptism, are then administered. Dedication is a freely chosen death, and a new life is granted to the initiate by the grace of the goddess.[2] He enters thus into her kingdom: he is holy. His being is changed, and he is reborn. In the *Metamorphoses* of Apuleius, Lucius descends at last to the shrine where the great change takes place. He tells us that he came to the threshold of the world of the dead, and through all elements. 'I visited the bounds of death: I trod Proserpina's threshold: I passed through all the elements and returned. It was midnight, but I saw the sun radiant with bright light. I came into the very presence of the gods below and the gods above and I adored them face to face.'[3] As morning appeared, he put on the heavenly garment and took a flaming torch in his right hand. A garland was put on his head, and he stood on a pedestal before the goddess as a statue of the sungod, and was honoured as a god by the assembled congregation.[4] There followed a festal meal, and for some days Lucius was the image of God (*Eikon*). Then he left the heavenly garment in the temple, where it was laid up for him, and returned to the workaday world. We hear, says Reitzenstein, of another community that dressed an initiate after his death in the shining garment of Osiris which he had worn at his initiation, and also of another simpler garment of black and white which marked the wearer as the logos of God.[5]

We can see here a certain striking, superficial resemblance

to the doctrine of the image taught in 2 Corinthians 3, where it is said that by reflecting the glory of God seen in the face of Jesus Christ we are transformed into his image. And there is also a distinct resemblance between the bright garment worn by the initiate and the spiritual body spoken of in the Pauline writings. There are more striking resemblances of the mystery religions to Pauline doctrine which are not relevant to the teaching on the image. But there is something so crude in the story of Lucius, for all its charm, that we can understand the complaint of the early Christians that the mysteries were devilish imitations of Christian doctrines.[6] This explanation is not possible for us today, and we would have to give another account of the resemblances.

It would be useless here to go into a full discussion of the question raised by Reitzenstein about the ancestry of Pauline Christian teaching. It has been fully answered by H. A. A. Kennedy in his *St Paul and the Mystery-Religions*. We must concede that there are striking parallels to Pauline thought in the language and ideas of these religions. But the claim that Christian and Pauline thought is a changeling in the cradle of Judaism is demonstrably untrue. The fundamental conceptions of the New Testament are the legitimate descendants of those in the Old Testament. The meanings of words in the New Testament are invariably nearer to the meanings of the same words in the Septuagint and their Hebrew equivalents in the Old Testament than to the meanings of the same words in classical Greek. It is therefore unnecessary to go hunting for parents of New Testament concepts or experiences in the mystery religions. It is true that Christ's birth and life, his death and resurrection have entered as a tremendous new factor into the life and thought of the New Testament writers. But the personal devotion of St Paul to the Lord 'who loved me and gave himself for me' belongs to a wholly different world than that of the mysteries, where salvation 'was invariably assured "by the exact performance of sacred ceremonies".'[7] Here too the image was conceived of in a thoroughly individualistic manner and the eschatological emphasis is missing. There are various ways in which we may account for the remarkable though superficial resemblances between Pauline conceptions and those of the mysteries. The

kinship may be due to the fact that such figures as those of
rebirth and likeness to the divine, the concept of the divine as
visible radiance, and of man's true being as a reflection of it,
are natural to the human soul in its search for God.

Again, many of the documents quoted by Reitzenstein and
his school are of uncertain date, and some are certainly post-
Christian. For example, the *Metamorphoses* of Apuleius, from
which comes the story of the initiation of Lucius into the Isis
mysteries, were written about AD 150. There may therefore
well be, in this book, and elsewhere in the mysteries, the
influence of Christian ideas. And in much earlier documents,
Jewish conceptions akin to the Christian may be at work also.[8]

A third reason for similarity will undoubtedly be this, that
St Paul was acquainted with the world of the mystery religions,
and as one who became a Greek to the Greeks, and was all
things to all men, if by any means he might save some, he
would be ready to use the current terminology both in an
apologetic and in a polemical way.

Just so a missionary to India today may describe Christ as
his *Guru,* or teacher, and just so did the author of the fourth
Gospel speak of Christ as the Logos. The danger of making
such points of contact with contemporary thought is that one's
readers or hearers may not realize that the apologist is
straining and changing the concepts he adopts, to make them
fitted to bear their Christian content. There is clearly a
polemical use of the word 'knowledge' (*Gnosis*) in 1 Corinthians 8. Here the word has a special sense common to the
mystery religions and Gnosticism. It refers to a specially revealed knowledge of God which confers on man the blessings
of immortality and, indeed, is said to make him divine.

There is, however, one aspect of the doctrine of the
mystery religions of which the New Testament writers make
almost no use. And that is this notion of the divinization of
the believer. The Jewish writers were equally chary of using
it. Kennedy says that 'We are not confronted in Judaistic
thought with the notion of absorption in the Deity. Nor does
there ever, apparently, occur the conception of the deification
of mortals through mystic communion with God.'[9]

This idea does, however, occur frequently and unmistakably in the mystery religions. In Poimandres[10] it is said: 'This

is the blessed issue for those who have attained *Gnosis*, to be
deified.' Plutarch says, as we have seen, that in a certain
cultus a black-and-white garment was put on the initiates after
their death, which marked them out as the logos of God.
And Reitzenstein quotes[11] an Egyptian magic formula whereby
a mystic to whom his god has appeared prays, 'Come unto me,
Hermes, as children to their mother's womb', and describes
the effect: 'Thou art I and I am thou, thine is mine and
I am thine, for I am thine image' (*Eidolon*). The first phrase
of this second quotation is subtly and yet profoundly different
from Paul's 'it is no longer I who live, but Christ who lives
in me', which Paul so carefully qualifies by the words that
follow: 'and the life which I now live in the flesh I live by
the faith in the Son of God, who loved me and gave himself
for me.'[12]

This change of the substance of the believer into divinity
in the mystery religions is accomplished by a supernaturally
and often magically acquired knowledge. It is bound to lead
to a fusion of the initiate with God which from a Christian
point of view is blasphemous. Eckhart expressed a similar view
when he said: 'If I am to know God directly, I must become
completely he, and he I: so that this he and this I become
and are one I.'[13]

We shall see that the Eastern theologians, Irenaeus, Athanasius and Clement, developed a doctrine of divinization[14]
of the Christian. But it must be admitted that while their
teaching is objectionable and dangerous, it does not ever go
so far as the teaching of Eckhart and the mystery religions.
It is carefully qualified in a manner which we shall later
have to examine. But it is very probable that where the
eastern theologians go beyond the reserve of the Bible, as
they undoubtedly do, they are acting unconsciously under the
influence of the mystery religions.

CHAPTER IV

Human Reason as a Spark
of the Divine Fire

1 *Introduction*

In this chapter we shall consider a thought which has played a large part in the doctrine of man: the concept of the essential divinity of man's reason or soul.[1] It is true that the phrase 'image of God' is only found clearly expressed in Hebrew and Christian thought, but before Philo we find a very similar concept in Stoicism, and since Stoicism is itself dependent on the teaching of Heraclitus, it will be advisable to refer shortly to his thought on the reason of man. For this line of thought which runs from Heraclitus through the Stoics to Philo has had a twofold influence on later thinkers.

Firstly, Christian thinkers up to and including St Thomas are in part dependent on this pre-Christian thought, regarding the image predominantly as rationality, though Augustine and Aquinas do not define it in the Stoic manner, and are free from any tendency to regard the image as a spark of the divine in man. And, secondly, there is a tendency in thought influenced by idealism, even today, to regard the image of God in man as a spark of the divine. In this respect at least such modern thought follows Stoicism. It is therefore good to go back to the first roots of such thinking. For while we have not the space to describe its later ramifications, our objections to it from the Christian point of view may hold good against this type of thought in its later developments also.

In this short review we shall not try to give more of the background of the thinkers and their thought than is necessary for an understanding of their teaching on our subject. In all the thinkers mentioned in this chapter, there is a tendency to think of man's reason as the essential thing in him. Our task will be to ask how they conceive of this rationality, and how they relate it to God, or the divine Reason.[2]

2 *Heraclitus*

Heraclitus is best known for his principle of the universal flux. All things, he teaches, are in continual change, and passing into their opposites. But such change is not without rationale. There is order in it. The primitive substance is fire, from which all things are derived. Change is either upwards or downwards, by rarefaction or by condensation. In the downward direction, fire changes into water, and water into earth, under which heading all solids are comprised. The rivalry between things, which are constantly passing into their opposite, is the ultimate logos, or cause, of phenomena. It is also described as destiny, or justice, and, oddly enough, is also identified with fire. Heraclitus thus recognized an immanent reason in the universe, but probably did not think of it as conscious, though he used language which was susceptible of such an interpretation. The soul of man also consists of fire – not the pure primitive element, but the fire which on the way upward develops itself out of the moist exhalations of the world. A drunk man has a wet soul, and cannot guide his steps. The dry soul, said Heraclitus, is the best. (It is curious how primitive thought has affected our language today, so that, without thinking of him, when we speak of 'the dry light of reason', we are influenced by this Greek philosopher who lived at Ephesus five hundred years before Christ!)

The soul of man is thus a part of the universal fire, the logos. The soul is not permanently separated from that fire, for, like the rest of things, it is in a state of flux. All round us is the atmosphere, which is a part of fire, since air and fire are akin, and Heraclitus suggests that we maintain our rational life by breathing it. At other times he suggests that our connection with the universal logos is through our perceptions. When our eyes are closed in sleep, we are not more than potentially rational. Heraclitus seems to have had no exalted view of man's nature, and probably thought that the source of errors lay in his tendency to follow individual thought instead of universal reason.

In this system there is really no God; the logos is the rational, self-evolving principle of the world. Like man's mind, it is material, and the relation of man's mind to it is that of a part to the whole.

3 *Anaxagoras*

Anaxagoras of Clazomenae had a less naïve view of Mind. For him it was the first mover, and was either immaterial, or the subtlest form of matter, omnipotent and omniscient, though terms are also used of it which can hardly be reconciled with the notion of conscious existence. The human soul, as in Heraclitus, was a part of Mind, and of the same substance. This meant that for Anaxagoras it was essentially eternal and divine.

4 *Socrates*

Socrates probably believed in one supreme God and a number of local and inferior deities. Since he left no writings, there is a well-known difficulty in determining what his teaching was, and we are dependent on the very different pictures of Xenophon and Plato for what we know of him. It is certain that he taught that God seeks man's good, and is omnipresent and omniscient, interpenetrating nature, and ruling it as the mind rules its body. His theism depends on the conviction that there is a certain community of nature between man and God. 'The soul, if anything else that is human does so, partakes of the divine',[3] and this partaking seems to be the possession by the soul of a part of the divine substance.[4] On this basis, and on the existence of design in nature, which is planned for man's good, an elementary system of natural theology is built up. In spite of his teaching about participation in divine substance, the very moving picture of Socrates in Plato's *Apology* shows that his belief was far more of a theistic nature than pantheistic, and his influence and that of his great successor and disciple had an important humanizing effect on the thought of the Stoics who followed.

5 *Stoic Philosophy*

Stoic philosophy developed at a time when the speculative interest of men was declining, and it expresses a strongly practical, ethical tendency. This moral and religious earnestness could find no metaphysical support in Aristotle's transcendent and unheeding God and, curiously enough, the Stoics chose the Heraclitean philosophy, with some modifications, the most important of which was the adoption of the Socratic and

Platonic teleology. Thus, as we saw, the Socratic and Platonic God, who is transcendent, and purposes good to his world, has some influence in humanizing the world view of Stoicism, though Stoicism officially is based on a philosophy which has no right to such a concept of a good purpose for the world, since its system is essentially pantheist.

Stoicism is thus a philosophy in which there is at times a real conflict with the implications of the materialistic monism which it has adopted as its metaphysical basis, and it continually tends to regard the deity in a manner inconsistent with its own philosophic first principles. The above mentioned adoption of Socratic teleology is only one instance of this. Thus in many ways Stoicism has ethical affinities with the Hebrew-Christian way of thought, a characteristic perhaps due to the Semitic origin of some of the early Stoics.[5] The concept of God as impersonal is doubtless predominant, and is expressed in such words of definition as: 'A rational fiery spirit having no shape, but changing to what it will, and made like to all things.'[6] On the other hand, Antipater of Tarsus defines God as 'A living being, blessed, imperishable, the benefactor of mankind.'[7] And Aratus of Soli writes the words which St Paul has made famous: 'For we are indeed his offspring.'[8]

Since it is here our purpose to examine chiefly the manner in which the relation of man and his reason to the divine is conceived, the Stoic conception of God, with its inconsistencies, must be further examined. Belief in God is an article of the Stoic creed, but he is identified with the universe, which is itself spoken of as wise, good and perfect. It is a Stoic tenet that all causes are corporeal, and therefore that God, the First Cause, is also corporeal. He is identified with 'ether' or fire – not exactly ordinary terrestrial fire, which is destructive, but with a more subtle fire, like that in the human body, which is creative. He is called the 'fiery mind of the universe',[9] and also a spirit, but this word is to be taken in the literal physical sense, as meaning breath, though, again, a breath more subtle than ours. Like air, he is omnipresent and all-pervading. In one sense, he is the essential element in the universe, since he is fire. In another sense, since fire is the fundamental constituent of all the elements, he may be equated with the whole universe. Thus the universe is God

in the full sense; the divine and the natural wholly coalesce, and there is no logical place for any divine transcendence over the world.

The same curious identification of fire and logos is to be seen here as in Heraclitus, for this divine fiery spirit is also intelligent, identical with universal Mind. Stoic thought made much use of the notion of 'seeds'. In the seeds of living things was obviously latent the fully developed life of the adult being. This life was supposed to be of an airy or fiery nature. If seeds were kept long enough, they lost their power of growth. This notion of the seminal logos was in the first place applicable to plants and living beings, but it was afterwards extended to apply to other entities of a non-organic kind. Fire is regarded as the seed of the whole universe, having in it the whole possibilities of the universe latent at the beginning. The seminal logoi of various realities within the universe have their unity in the universal logos, God.

We must now consider shortly the Stoic conception of man, in so far as it is relevant to our purpose. Man is privileged above all other things. There is an ascending scale of dignity from inanimate objects, through plants and animals, and finally culminating in man. To him alone the gods have sent down the logos out of heaven to make him rational.[10] 'Reason is nothing less than a part of the Divine Spirit immersed in the human body.'[11] It is variously described as 'a piece drawn off from Zeus' (*Apospasma*), or 'an emanation of him who administers the universe' or 'a god dwelling as guest in the human frame'. There is thus only one intelligent soul,[12] and men and gods have communion with each other through participation in the logos. Man's interest in physics and astronomy proves his divinity.[13] Epictetus uses the notion of the inborn divinity as an urge to ethical uprightness, much as St Paul uses the notion of the union of the believer with Christ. 'When you are in social intercourse, when you are exercising yourself, know you not that you are nourishing a god, that you are exercising a god? Wretch, you are carrying about a god with you, and you know it not!'[14] The sovereign principle of the soul is thus the rational faculty, though the word 'logos', oddly enough, is not used for it. Instead it is called the sovereign principle (*Hegemonikon*), which is one of

eight faculties of the soul. The other seven are the five senses, and the powers of speech and generation. All of these are subtle breaths, lodging in the body, of a material nature, and extended from the sovereign principle in the heart to their special organs.[15]

It is clear from this that in Stoicism, as in the earlier systems, man's reason is considered as essentially a spark of the divine. And we shall find that the nearly universal perception of the dignity of man will almost inevitably produce some such conclusion, except where the biblical teaching on creation is taken with full seriousness. For the gist of the doctrine of creation is surely this, that man's being, though linked with the divine, is itself essentially not divine, but created, and thus dependent on God, and of a different order from his own being, though akin to it. We must admit that Genesis 2:7, 'then the Lord God formed man of dust from the ground, and breathed into his nostrils the breath of life; and man became a living being', is, if taken in isolation, susceptible of an interpretation other than this. It might be taken to teach that man's soul is, as Stoicism holds, an emanation of the divine Being, while his body is of a lower order. But the general doctrine of the Bible is decisively against this doctrine of emanation. We must further admit that the relation of God to man is sometimes seen by Stoicism as an I-Thou relationship. But this I-thou relationship is never secure so long as God can be identified with the whole of nature, or with Fate and Destiny. Further, it appears that in Stoicism the personal relation between God and the soul, where it appears, is ontologically not prior to the participation by man in the logos, but secondary to it. In our opinion, which will be later expounded fully, the personal relation of the creator to his creature is fundamental, and any power of reason given to the created person is secondary to this. It appears that only the Christian doctrine of creation, with the gulf which it makes between the being of the creator and that of his creature, can secure this priority beyond all doubt.

We must also note that Stoicism regards man's likeness to God as fundamentally his rationality, a view whose dangers we shall later see. In Stoicism we actually do find the concept 'image of God' to describe man's being, though there is here,

of course, no dependence on the Genesis account of creation.
This concept occurs in the hymn of Cleanthes to Zeus, of
which the second four lines are:

> *Hail! For 'tis meet that men should call on Thee,*
> *Whose seed we are, and ours the destiny*
> *Alone of all that lives and moves on earth*
> *A mirror of Thy deity to be!*

The words translated, 'mirror of Thy deity' are in the Greek
Theou Mimēma – a representation of God.

It is interesting that the Bible itself notices this approxi-
mation of Stoic thought to its own doctrine of the image of
God in man. Our consideration of the Stoic teaching has been
specially important for our study because, second to Christianity, Stoicism has been in all ages a main route of thought
about the dignity of man, a conception that has had, and
will have, such importance for human law and society. Indeed,
some time ago, Kingsley Martin went so far as to say in
The New Statesman and Nation that Stoicism was a better
and sounder basis than the biblical teaching for the notion of
human dignity. We shall have to return to this question at a
much later stage.

6 *Philo of Alexandria*

Philo was a Jew who lived from about 20 BC to about AD
45. He considered himself devoutly orthodox, and was accepted as such by the Jewish community of Alexandria, who
chose him to represent them on one important mission to
Rome to present their case to the Emperor Caligula. He
believed that the law of Moses was unchangeable and eternal,
and that Moses' authority as a religious teacher was supreme.

And yet, living as he did in the city where the learning of
the Greeks was like an atmosphere which a man could not
help breathing, Philo was bound to be much influenced by it,
especially by Stoicism. His task was somehow to make a
synthesis between the Jewish and the Greek elements in his
thought without in any way compromising that Old Testament
revelation. This he attempted to do by a method of allegorical
interpretation of the scriptures perhaps more thoroughgoing,
fanciful and florid than any other man has ever developed.

In respect of the doctrine of God, his great problem was

how to modify Greek thought so as to make room for a
God who is so strictly supreme in his universe, and so transcendent, as is the God of the Old Testament. And the concept which be used to solve this problem was that of the
logos. It is interesting that Christianity, which also teaches
that God is transcendent, and yet graciously related to the
created world, has the doctrine of the Trinity as one of its
central tenets, and its own form of the logos teaching. There
can be no doubt that the thought of Philo has here left its
impress on Christian doctrine, though Christian teaching about
the logos is by no means identical with Philo's.

In order to understand Philo's teaching about the image of
God in man, we must first learn a little more about his
doctrine of God. It is, fortunately, not necessary to go into
the details of his very complicated and possibly incoherent
exposition of this doctrine.

Philo believes, first and foremost, in God's self-revelation
through the Old Testament. But he also believes in the
cosmological argument to Mind as the first mover of the
universe. There is, moreover, a more direct way to God for
our minds than that of natural theology; by means of intuition. But none of our knowledge of God is knowledge of his
essence. The direct intuition just mentioned does not give us
an insight into the divine essence. And indeed this limitation is
not surprising, since we cannot know the essence even of our
own souls.[16] A further element of scepticism is introduced
by the following fact. In our thought about God we are
dependent on the argument from analogy. What we do know
directly of mind is what is revealed in our self-consciousness,
but we cannot apply this univocally to God, for the good
reason that he is not related to the universe as we are to
our bodies, but is its creator, and transcendent. This does not,
however, lead to pure scepticism about God, but only to
rejection of crude anthropomorphisms. Passages in the Old
Testament are allegorized away, but God is left the attributes
of personality, freedom, perfection and goodness, among
others. There can be no doubt that the source of Philo's
knowledge about these attributes is really the Old Testament
revelation. It might be thought that the attributes we have
named are surely descriptions of God's essence, but it appears

that Philo, in saying that we do not know God in his essence, means only that we have to use terms to describe him which we know to be inadequate. God is free, but not free precisely as we know ourselves to be; he is good, but good with a goodness transcending what we can understand. In fact, Philo's scepticism is not more radical than that of St Thomas, who states that when we predicate qualities of God we do not do so univocally, as if they meant exactly the same thing as when they were applied to men. Philo is here merely asserting that all predication which we make of attributes to the divine nature is analogical in character, a view that is held by all sound theologians.

Since God is thus not known in his essence, how is he known? He is known through his powers, the highest of which, comprising all the others, is the logos. These powers are very similar to the seminal logoi of Stoicism; they are the intelligible ideas which hold together the parts of the universe, and make them rational. Passages in the Old Testament referring to angels are taken by Philo to refer to the powers. They are the thoughts of God, which are expressed visibly in the universe, and form a hierarchy, of which the culmination is the logos, which includes them all. The logos is God's thought displayed in the whole system of the universe. It can be conceived of in two aspects — first, in its relation to the mind of the creator. The logos was present in his mind before the created world came into being. And, second, the logos can be seen in the created universe, for it is the principle of rationality and cohesion in the world. The logos there expresses visibly the mind of the creator, just as a cathedral is the visible expression of the architect's mind.

The kinship and the difference between this teaching and that of the Stoics is at once evident. This logos is certainly different from the Stoic logos since it is not material. It differs also from the Stoic logos in its function of mediation between the creator and the created world. It is not sheerly identical with God as is the Stoic logos, though it can be called God.

But the kinship with Stoic thought is also evident. For example, there is surely here the danger of a pantheistic influ-

ence being carried over from Stoicism. Hebrew thought could never admit, as this doctrine seems to do, that the created world as it stands is in an unqualified fashion the expression of the logos of the creator.

There has been much discussion as to whether Philo regarded the logos as personal or not. Drummond admits[17] that he frequently describes it in personal terms, but points out that his whole literary style is one that makes much use of personal figures, many of which cannot possibly be taken literally. If the logos is sometimes described as God's Son, the world is also often described in the same terms.[18]

Philo has a singular exegesis of the two image passages at the beginning of Genesis, which he claims refer to two different creations. The account in Genesis 1:26 seq. tells of the Creation according to God's image of an ideal man, incorporeal and incorruptible, before the material man was moulded out of clay on earth (Genesis 2:7). This 'idea of man' had to be in existence in the heavenly places as a model for the other. Most modern commentators take it that Philo meant by the heavenly man of Genesis 1:26 the logos. If this be the case, then our existence in the image of God is existence in the image of the logos.

Philo's teaching on man is that he is a link between the physical world and the invisible. In this way, he is akin to the logos itself. Again, Philo says that we share physical constitution with inanimate objects, growth with plants, life or soul with animals, but the power of intelligence is peculiar to Mind.[19]

Here we may note in criticism, that if this possession of intelligence be the criterion of man's existence in the divine image, then it is hard to see how man's intellect is the divine image in any sense that the rest of the world is not.[20] The stamp of the logos is on the universe, and on its constituent objects – that is, they are rational in the sense of being intelligible. But man is rational in the sense of being a reasoning subject, and this only a person can be, and this the logos is not.

Philo teaches that man is a two-natured animal, consisting of body and soul; the soul has two sides, the irrational and the rational. The lower, irrational, part of the soul is mortal,

75

the higher was breathed into man at creation, and this part is, probably, immaterial. Moses recognized the substance of our rational faculty as 'spirit', meaning thereby 'not air in motion, but a certain stamp and character of divine power, which Moses calls by a proper name, "image", intimating that God is the archetype of rational nature, and man an image and copy.'[21] It is clear that the divine archetype here mentioned is the logos. Man's reason is sometimes called a ray or fragment of the divine nature, or 'a copy and imitation of the eternal and blessed idea, the most closely related of all things on the earth to the Father of the cosmos'[22] – a further reference to the logos. But, according to Drummond, the governing conception of man's relation to God and the logos is that the human mind is divine, and emanates from God. He says: '. . . Philo did not recognize the distinction between a being who is made in the likeness of God and one who emanates from God.'[23]

Be this as it may, the notion of emanation is one which is not true to the Hebrew Christian thought-world, while that of a copy or imitation is actually biblical.

Our study of Philo has shown us, then, the modifications which have to be made in a pantheistic logos doctrine if it has to be fitted into a theistic system, where the notion of divine transcendence is well developed. The logos is not identical with God, but mediates between him and the world. But the notion of transcendence has not been able to permeate the whole of Philo's system, and in particular the doctrine of man's rational spirit is still conceived in a pantheistic manner. If Drummond be wrong, and if Philo's descriptions of the relation of man to the divine are not all synonyms for emanation, then we see in his anthropology the traces of a view more consonant with the genius of Hebrew and Christian thought. From our point of view, the notion of the image as a divine spark in man is a cul-de-sac. The barrier falls, in fact, not between the divine-rational and the sensuous, as it tends to do in Philo, but between the divine and the human, which is not only created, but also, in point of fact, sinful.

In making these criticisms of Heraclitus and the Stoics, we must, however, remember the vital concern which was in

their minds as they developed the doctrine of the divine spark. Without the clearer light which has been given to us, they were trying to account for, and to safeguard, the almost universal instinct about the dignity and sacredness of humanity. The truth that lies behind the error of the divine spark is, that a doctrine of man which tries to deal with man in separation from God has committed an error which will distort every truth which it discovers. We shall attempt to do justice to this link between God and man in two aspects. Firstly, man is always with God; confronted by him: 'He is not far from each one of us; for in him we live and move and have our being.' And, secondly, man's being cannot be understood apart from the divine election; God's purpose of salvation for him.

In the next part of our study there is a certain difficulty which must be met. It is this; there is no massive general growth in the doctrine of the image from one theologian to another, no clear line of development which can be traced from century to century. Thus a study of the teaching of each theologian separately would be in danger of confusing the reader, who would find the account disjointed, and have great difficulty in seeing whither it was leading him. A different method of organizing the material in this part of the book has therefore been attempted.

There are certain problems and dangers which each one of the early theologians has faced, problems immanent in the reality which they were studying, or dangers which threatened them. I have taken as the themes of my next four chapters these problems and dangers, hoping that thus a greater unity and direction will have been given to the argument of the book than if each man's contribution on the whole doctrine had been considered in turn. Thus our study will be preparing us for our own conclusions and the evaluation of the answers submitted to the same problems by later thinkers. It is hoped that at the same time adequate information will be given as to the teaching of the early theologians on important points. The thinkers dealt with in this second section of the book are St Irenaeus, St Clement of Alexandria, St Athanasius, and St Augustine.

*

The Teaching of Two Thinkers on 'Image' and 'Likeness'

1 St Irenaeus

(a) Introduction

In Irenaeus we have the first of the Church Fathers who has much to say on our doctrine. In himself he is a most interesting and attractive figure, and his early place in church history gives a special importance and fascination to his writings. Born probably about AD 130, he writes his memories of his old teacher, Polycarp of Smyrna, who 'was instructed by apostles and conversed with many who had seen Christ . . . whom I saw also in my early youth, for he tarried on earth a very long time, and when a very old man gloriously and most nobly suffering martyrdom, departed this life'. The death of Christ preceded the writing of Irenaeus' great work, *Against Heresies,* by about as long an interval as has passed between the accession of Queen Victoria (1838) and the present day.

In the hundred years that had passed since the death of St Paul the teachings of the Gnostics had made great inroads on the Christian Church. Were it not that Gnosticism had then been so dangerous a rival to Christianity, and had it not been a kind of fifth column also within the Church, the pretentious nonsense of its teaching would have been long ago forgotten. The details of the heresy in its various forms can be found in the first two books of Irenaeus' work, *Against Heresies.* All that needs to be said here is that both Valentinus and Marcion asserted that the creator of the world was not the true God, and that salvation was a redemption into the realm of a transcendent, hidden God who was first revealed through Christ. The teaching of Marcion was very much less nonsensical and objectionable than that of Valentinus. The point relevant to our purpose is that the doctrine of the image of God which is to be found in both Testaments was naturally

a powerful weapon against Gnosticism in the hand of Irenaeus, and he did not fail to use it. For the doctrine of the image, found in both Testaments, proves that the Bible teaches that it was the same God who created us in his image at the first who will also perfect us at the last.

When this has been said, we must, however, admit that Irenaeus seems more directly interested in the unity of history and the agency of the one logos throughout it, and in his doctrine of Recapitulation, than in making unmistakably clear his views on the image and the likeness. Often his argument is driving in some other direction, when he makes some parenthetical mention of the image or the likeness, and it is these parenthetical statements that form much of the material we have to put together. Klebba is probably right in saying that the confusion of the debate about Irenaeus' views on image and likeness is due, not only to his careless use of terms, but also to the fact that critics have not noticed that the references are sometimes to the fallen Adam, sometimes to his state of integrity, sometimes to mankind in the various stages of its history from sin to redemption.[1] We must also remember, as Struker points out,[2] that a great part of the works of Irenaeus are only preserved to us in Latin, a language much poorer than the original Greek, and that it is not always clear what Greek word stood in the original in the place of the Latin word *similitudo* in the translation.

(b) Uses of the Terms 'Image' and 'Likeness'

It is generally accepted that in the main Irenaeus based himself on a certain interpretation of Genesis 1:26, which says that God created man in his image, after his likeness. According to this interpretation, the likeness was lost at the Fall, while the image remains even today in all men. The most important passages on the image in Iranaeus support this view.

In *Adv. Haer.*, V, 6, 1, the writer is arguing that not only man's soul, but also his body is destined for salvation, and he is led into a disquisition on psychology. Here he says: 'But if the Spirit be wanting to the soul, he who is such is indeed of an animal nature, and being left carnal, shall be an imperfect being, possessing indeed the image in his formation, but not receiving the similitude through the Spirit, and thus

80

is this being imperfect.'

To one not familiar with Irenaeus' thought this passage may seem only to add to the darkness, but to those acquainted with him the meaning is clear. The man 'of an animal nature' is here the natural man after the Fall, who has still the image, while a special gift of the Spirit is needed to perfect him, and give him the likeness or similitude which was lost at the Fall. There are a great many more passages which support this interpretation.

But there are a number of passages in which at first sight it would appear that Irenaeus is using the term 'image' and 'likeness' as synonyms. But it is doubtful whether this is the case, since of the six passages where the use of the two terms seems to be synonymous, five refer either to unfallen man, or to man regenerate, and therefore do not contradict the generally held view since, even if the likeness was lost at the Fall, the humanity here described would be in possession of it.[3] One of the passages, however, states that both image and likeness were lost at the Fall. It is most probable that in this passage at least Irenaeus is talking carelessly, and reckoning 'image and likeness' as one term. A similar carelessness is to be found in the image doctrine of St Clement of Alexandria, the other thinker whose work we shall be examining in this chapter.

(c) Meanings of the Word 'Image'

Brunner is right in saying that for Irenaeus, the image of God in man is summed up in his nature as a rational and free being, a nature which was not lost at the Fall.[4] In support, let us quote from *Adv. Haer.*, IV, 4, 3, where Irenaeus is answering critics who argue that if Jerusalem, God's own city, were destroyed, then God could not be good. He argues that both Jerusalem and wicked men in general are destroyed without God becoming unjust by his act of punishment: '. . . the wheat and the chaff, being inanimate and irrational, have been made such by nature. But man, being endowed with reason, and in this respect like to God, having been made free in his will, and with power over himself, is himself the cause to himself, that sometimes he becomes wheat, and sometimes chaff. Wherever also he shall be justly condemned

because, having been created a rational being, he lost the true rationality, and, living irrationally, opposed the righteousness of God, giving himself over to every . . . earthly spirit, and serving all lusts. . . .'

It seems clear, then, that man's freedom and rationality here mentioned are for Irenaeus at least a dominant part of the image of God which cannot be lost by sin, although the rationality here mentioned is compatible with a failure to be truly reasonable, when 'man opposes the righteousness of God, gives himself over to every earthly spirit, and serves all lusts.'

There is, however, another element in human nature on which Irenaeus lays emphasis in speaking of the image in man. This is the body. There are two important passages where this is clearly stated. One is the long passage in V, 6, 1, already quoted in another context, where the argument is that God wishes to give salvation to the whole man, body, soul and spirit. Here Irenaeus says: 'But if the Spirit be wanting to the soul, he who is such is indeed of an animal nature, and being left carnal shall be an imperfect being, possessing indeed the image in his formation (*Plasmate* – body) but not receiving the similitude through the Spirit.'

Even more explicit is another passage: 'And then again, this Word was manifested when the Word of God was made man, assimilating himself to man and man to himself, that by means of his resemblance to the Son, man might become precious to the Father. For in times long past, it was *said* that man was created after the image of God. Wherefore also he did easily lose the similitude. When, however, the Word of God became flesh, he confirmed both these, for he both showed forth the image truly, since he became himself what was his image, and he re-established the similitude after a sure manner, by assimilating man to the invisible Father through means of the visible Word.'[5] Here is a clear reference to Christ's incarnation, defined as 'becoming what was his image'. Certainly we must not exclude the other aspects of humanity, but the emphasis is surely on the visible tangible side of the human nature which Christ took upon himself. The image has a strongly physical emphasis. This line of thought is in harmony with Irenaeus' whole anti-Gnostic polemic. The whole

of nature is, he claims, of value to God, and destined for redemption. This is one of his most valuable contributions to theological thought.

But how are we to get over the difficulty that the image seems to be associated with two very different elements in human nature? Struker[6] has attempted to do so by means of a distinction which he claims Irenaeus makes between the image of the logos in man (*Logosebenbildlichkeit*) and the image of God in man (*Gottebenbildlichkeit*). The bodily nature of man, including his whole humanity, is the image of the logos, and is not destroyed by sin. The free and rational nature of man is the image of God. This also is not destroyed by the Fall.

This bold solution solves also another difficulty. If Irenaeus, in saying that man is in God's image, lays such emphasis on the physical side of our nature, is he not committed to the most gross anthropomorphism in his doctrine of God? God will literally have a face and eyes, and will blow with his breath, and so on. But Irenaeus teaches quite explicitly a doctrine of the spirituality of God.[7]

The answer to our problem is thus, that God the Father is not pictured in physical terms, but that the reference in these passages where the bodily emphasis is clear, is to the Son incarnate, in the image of whom man was made. As Irenaeus himself says: '‘And it is for this that he appeared in the fullness of time, to show that his image is like him.’[8] Gross comments thus: 'Irenaeus was thus able to locate the image in man's body, since according to him it was formed in the likeness of the logos incarnate ideally present from all eternity to the Creator.’[9]

There is a profound truth here in the linking up of the whole of man's nature to that of Christ the incarnate Son of God. Had man not been created in God's image, the incarnation would not have been possible. Or, rather, we should say, it was in order that Christ should become incarnate that man was made in God's image.[10] In Christ we see the true nature of man, and man is destined to attain this nature by union with Christ in faith.

(d) Meaning of the Word 'Likeness'

We have now to consider what meaning Irenaeus attached to the term 'likeness'. It is probable that he believed Adam to have been created in the likeness as well as in the image of God, for he frequently confirms the statement of Genesis 1:26 that this was so. It remains, however, certain that Irenaeus thought that regenerate man has a far firmer possession of the likeness than Adam, whom he does not picture as the paragon of maturity and virtue that Augustine and Luther thought him. In III, 22, 4, Irenaeus indicates that before the Fall Adam and Eve were children, who would have taken time to grow up, had not the Fall intervened. Therefore Brunner is right in saying that the likeness was in them 'only present in germ', and 'rather a promise for the future than a present reality'.[11]

For Irenaeus the image in man is, as we have seen, linked in its two aspects to the psycho-physical nature, body and soul. 'Soul' here includes man's power of freedom and his reason. 'In the Christian believer there is a third element, the indwelling Spirit of God. This divine principle is not part of man's nature, but is a supernatural gift of God.'[12] Thus believers have three components in their being, the body, or handiwork of God, the soul, and the spirit. Sinners, on the other hand, have only souls and bodies. The spirit in man, though supernatural, is distinguished from the divine Spirit, which creates it as an organ whereby the believer receives divine influence, and knows divine truth. This view is very strongly suggested by (II, 35, 5,) where it is said that at the Day of Judgment, those who are written in the Book of Life will rise with their own souls, bodies and spirits, while those who have merited chastisement will go to suffer it with their bodies and souls. Thus the wicked appear to have no spirits. The evidence is uncertain, but the view should probably be accepted that, according to Irenaeus, God's Spirit creates, or makes active in man a spirit which is the bearer of the likeness. Thus for Irenaeus the human spirit would not be a gift universal and common to all mankind, as in the thought of Philo. It would not be spirit – the bearer of reason – *Geist* as the word is used by the German idealists. It would be rather the correlative of the special revelation in Christ, a revelation

84

known prophetically under the Old Testament dispensation, and consummated when we behold God face to face at the end of this dispensation.'

The agents of sanctification, who perfect the likeness, are, as at man's creation, the Son and the Spirit. 'We do now receive,' says Irenaeus, 'a certain portion of his Spirit, tending towards perfection, and preparing for incorruption, being little by little accustomed to receive and bear God, which also the apostle terms "an earnest" – that is, a part of the honour which has been promised us by God. . . . This earnest, therefore, thus dwelling in us, renders us spiritual even now, and the mortal is swallowed up by immortality. . . . If therefore, at the present time, having the earnest, we do cry "Abba Father", what shall it be, when, on rising again, we behold him face to face; when all the members shall burst out into a continuous hymn of triumph, glorifying him who raised them from the dead, and gave the gift of eternal life?'[13]

It is true that such passages as this might be interpreted as implying a gradual divinization of the believer through an impartation of the Holy Spirit conceived almost as a physical replenishment. It is, however, our view that this conclusion is hardly fair to Irenaeus, and that this passage and others like it should be interpreted in a genuinely eschatological sense. The revelation in Christ, appropriated by faith in the agency of the Holy Spirit, gives us the true likeness of God, but in a concealed manner. The mode in which we possess that likeness is the mode of faith, which at the resurrection will be transformed into sight.[14]

John Lawson is thoroughly justified in his general contention that the view of salvation given in Irenaeus' image doctrine is not erroneous so much as partial.[15] Irenaeus is apt at times to cast his theology in terms of the vision and 'enjoyment of the paternal light', and it is natural that this type of figure should predominate in teaching about the image and likeness of God in man, where the metaphors and figures to hand are all visual ones. We must, however, remember that he has developed also a powerful theology of salvation, wherein Christ is the recapitulator of history, who with saving power enters into conflict with sin and the devil, turning human defeat into victory.

(e) Conclusions

Such in brief is the doctrine of St Irenaeus on the image and
likeness of God in man. What are we to make of it, what
signposts and danger signals are we to see in it, whereby we
may be guided in the finding of our way towards a true
doctrine? Firstly, whether we accept or not Struker's view
that there is a distinction made in Irenaeus' teaching between
man as the image of God and man as the image of the
incarnate logos, the prominence of the bodily element in his
teaching on the image makes it inevitable that we should
think of man as created in the image of Christ incarnate.
There is in the New Testament a line of teaching which
develops this thought, that Christ is the revelation, not only
of God to man, but also of true humanity. Its importance is
only second to that about Christ as the image and revelation
of God. It is exceedingly important both for New Testament
ethics, and for New Testament beliefs about the resurrection
and the resurrection bodies of the faithful. Since God became
man, and this kind of man, then this kind of man is man
created in God's image. And there is a kinship between true
human nature and the divine nature, otherwise the incarnation would not have been possible. But the doctrine of man
in the image of the incarnate logos is a different one from
that of man in the image of God, and therefore, while admitting the truth of Irenaeus' teaching, and concluding that man
is in God's image in the way that it is possible for a physical
being to be so, we will not locate the image of God as clearly
in man's physical formation as Irenaeus locates the image of
the incarnate logos in man.[16] We shall admit, with Calvin
and Aquinas, that there are traces of the image, in all man's
being, including the physical side of it. But we shall centre
the image, so to speak, rather differently from Irenaeus.

In the second place, Irenaeus has acted with true insight in
seeing that within the concept of the image, a distinction must
be drawn between that which remains to man even in his sin
and that which God purposes for him in Christ – between
what we have already called the Old Testament image and
the New Testament image. Granted that he attaches his
two concepts of image and likeness by a wrong exegesis to
Genesis 1:26, introducing the double sense to a passage where

no double sense was intended by the writer. Yet there *is* a line of cleavage in the concept 'image of God', and, as we shall see, doctrines which try to get on without noticing it always come into difficulties. So by drawing our attention to the cleavage, Irenaeus has done a service to theology.

Thirdly, the question remains: Has he rightly defined what lies on each side of that cleavage? Brunner's criticism is well known.[17] He maintains that here we have the origin of the scholastic distinction between natural and supernatural (though these terms were not actually used till much later). This is a distinction which permits later Catholic writers to grant full freedom of will to unredeemed man, and an intact power of reason which may serve as the organ of a trustworthy natural theology. If this be true, it was an unfortunate step, to draw the line of cleavage where he did, since it was by following his example that scholastic thought was enabled to accept much too uncritically as its foundation the system of Aristotelian metaphysics, building thereon as a second storey the system of revealed truth.

Further, this criticism continues, this way of thinking tempts us to conceive of man's relation to God as something added to his nature, whereas in truth man's relationship to God (*Gottesbestimmtheit*) is the ground of his original true nature, and what we now know in man is a 'denatured' nature. Man has not lost a supernature through sin, but his divinely given nature has become unnatural and inhuman. We shall have to consider this criticism more fully in our discussion of the thought of St Thomas Aquinas, the great scholastic. For the present we must confine ourselves to the study of Irenaeus. Does he consider human freedom and human nature and human reason in man's fallen state as entities intelligible in themselves, without reference to God and his will for man's salvation?

We remember that for Irenaeus fallen man possesses a body and soul, but apparently no spirit, while the believer has in addition a spirit. If this be a true interpretation, then it does appear that Irenaeus thought of the Fall in this respect, not as changing for the worse the whole of man's nature, but as cutting off its supernatural element. And human freedom is regarded by him in what we might today call a rather Pela-

gian fashion, as more or less intact after the Fall. But, as Lawson points out,[18] we must remember the Pelagian controversy was far in the future, and the Faith was being attacked by the Gnostics, whose whole onslaught demanded the rejoinder that man is in a real sense free and responsible for his actions.

With regard to the Irenaean conception of reason, Brunner remarks that 'It is indeed true that for Irenaeus God is himself the true reason, and man's rationality is therefore a *participatio Dei*. But that does not go beyond the Stoic concept of man's rational nature. Human reason is conceived wholly in the sense of Greek rationalism, as something which is intelligible in itself, not existentially related to God.'[19] (*auf Gott aktual Bezogenes*)

There are certainly passages in Irenaeus which give grounds for this criticism, but there are others where man's reason is conceived in much more dynamic terms. V, 1, 3, for example, speaking of man's rational endowment, Irenaeus says: 'For never at any time did Adam escape the hands of God.' The hands of God are for Irenaeus always the Son and the Holy Spirit, and it is clear that in this passage man's reason is brought into a relation of confrontation with the logos and the Spirit much as in Brunner's own thought. IV, 4, 3 also points in the same direction when it is said that man, having been created a rational being, lost the true rationality when he opposed the righteousness of God.

To sum up our conclusions on Irenaeus' work on the image and likeness, we may say that he is right in seeing a line of cleavage in the general concept, but that he wrongly attaches the terms 'image' and 'likeness' in Genesis 1:26 to the two realities indicated, and that to some extent he was the unconscious originator of the dichotomy between the natural and the supernatural which led later to the acceptance of a natural theology as valid, and the undue dominance of the Aristotelian system in the mediaeval synthesis.

2 *St Clement of Alexandria*

(a) Introduction
There is another writer, almost contemporary with St Irenaeus,

whose teaching falls naturally to be considered at the same time, since he was confronting the same Gnostic heresies as Irenaeus, and therefore naturally made a similar use of the doctrine of the image of God to confute them. This is St Clement, whose theology was developed in Alexandria about the end of the second century of our era. He was thus rather younger than Irenaeus. There is no evidence that the two men ever met, and their works give no indication that either had read or influenced the writings of the other.

At the time when Clement's reputation was at its height, the great city was full of thought and speculation. The Platonic and Neo-Platonic philosophies and the various types of Gnostic heresy were current there. Clement's mind was unusually hospitable, and he absorbed much more easily than Irenaeus the ideas of others. Though this was doubtless a tendency of his whole temperament, he certainly had far more opportunity for eclecticism than Irenaeus, who wrote in the beginning of his treatise against heresies. 'Thou wilt not expect from me, who am resident among the Keltae, and am accustomed for the most part to use a barbarous dialect, any display of rhetoric. . . .'[20]

But it is certain that the thought of Clement is less seriously influenced by idealistic and Gnostic ideas than we might imagine from his language.

One of his leading ideas is that of the unity of all history in the logos, who was incarnate in Jesus Christ. The life of the Saviour, with his death and resurrection, is for Clement the central point of history. Clement's tendency to stress the unity of history is polemical. So is his view that both heathen philosophy and Old Testament revelation were in their own special ways preparations for the gospel. It is thus that he counters the heresy of Marcion, who had claimed that the God revealed by Christ had nothing to do with the God of the Old Testament. Further, when, like Irenaeus, Clement asserts the universality of the image of God in man, he is attacking the views of the Gnostics Valentinus and Basilides, who held that only some men are of divine origin, and that these are seeking to return to the heavenly sphere from which they have fallen. Clement attacks the dangerous heresy that there are two distinct types of humanity, and that salvation

is possible only for a select few who are spiritual from the start. Emphasizing as he does the unity of the Old Testament with the New, it is natural that Clement, like Irenaeus, should make much of the doctrine of the image of God in man. For this doctrine, as we have already noted, serves to link the Old Testament with the New, because it is a witness to the one purpose of God in creation, in history and in salvation.

(b) The Unsystematic Character of St Clement's Terminology
There is one rather tiresome characteristic of St Clement's thought which demands our attention at the start. His use of terms is exceedingly fluid. He is by no means a systematic thinker or writer. We must be prepared, therefore, to find no scientific constancy in his use of the terms which we are considering, 'image' and 'likeness'. But, in spite of this appearance of disorder, there is a greater consistency of thought than might at first be evident.

In some passages the words 'image' and 'likeness' refer to two different things. 'Image' refers, as in one strain of the thought of Irenaeus, to that rationality which is universal in man, the power of reasoning, formally considered.[21] Then 'likeness' refers to a real resemblance to God, something going much beyond the formal resemblance of the image.[22] Christ was the first man to possess the likeness,[23] which has in it no physical element,[24] but is an ethical similarity of the soul to God. The task of the logos is the education of mankind, and its elevation into this nearer likeness, which he possesses first himself. And the whole of human history may be considered as the story of the creation, the development and the perfecting of the image in man, a process which will be completed only on the other side of the grave.

But there are in St Clement, as in St Irenaeus, other passages in which no strict distinction between 'image' and 'likeness' seems to be made.[25] In such passages both seem to be considered as the universal endowment of mankind. These are either passages where Clement's dependence on the thought of Philo is clear.[26] For Philo did not make any distinction between the concepts 'image' and 'likeness'. Or else they are passages where, speaking loosely, Clement uses the two terms synonymously in vague reminiscence of the Genesis

passages,[27] as we have already found Irenaeus to do.

There is a third class of passages in which clearly Clement is treating 'image' and 'likeness' as synonyms, and ascribing both to the man who is in Christ.[28]

And there is yet a fourth class of passages where the word 'image' is used for the Christian who has received at baptism the mark of a Christian, while the word 'likeness' is reserved for the Christian who is in process of sanctification.

At this point the reader may well exclaim with some exasperation that there is no possible sense in which at one time or another Clement has not used these terms. But this irritating inconsistency should not hide from us the fact that Clement, however his terminology may vary, at all times relates all men to the divine image. They are described as the image, or as created in it, or according to it. And, secondly, there is a sense in which the Christian is the image or likeness, a likeness which is dependent on divine grace and the sacraments, and which is perfected through sanctification, during the time that the believer is being educated by the logos, who is himself the image and likeness of God. Here then we find indicated the same double structure of the image which we claim to have found in the Bible, and which we shall notice throughout this study. It is true that Clement, like Irenaeus, associates this double structure predominantly with the words 'image' and 'likeness', an interpretation which depends on a wrong interpretation of the Hebrew text of Genesis 1:26. But the claim that there is a double structure does not stand or fall with the legitimacy of the exegesis of this text.

We shall have reason to mention other important aspects of Clement's doctrine of the image in the next two chapters.

3 Conclusion

At the end of this chapter we may note the importance of our doctrine of the image in a day when again an attack is being made on the sacredness of mankind. In these early days of the second century of which we have been treating, the attack was made in the name of an esoteric Gnosticism which held that some men were spiritual by destiny, and others, however hard they might strive, could not possess this high privilege. In our time the attack has come from other sides. The error

we are fighting against is a logical conclusion of any natural-istic philosophy, but in chief it has taken of late two forms, racialism and communism. The first asserts that a man's value depends on his blood, and the second claims that it depends on his class.[29] It is true that the exponents of these philosophies do not talk at all in terms of the divine image but, for all that, the doctrine is a powerful and necessary weapon against them. The power of this weapon against these opponents rests in its emphasis on the unity of the Divine Will in creation and salvation and our further discussions as to the precise sense in which fallen man is still in the divine image are of secondary importance.

The Inward Way to God
and the Need of Historical Salvation

1 Introduction

The second of the problems round which the material of this part of our study is grouped is the problem of salvation. It has always been a fundamental Christian doctrine that apart from Christ 'there is no other name, under heaven given among men, by which we must be saved.' The doctrine of the image of God, which in all its forms represents man as in some way related to God, can thus easily become a danger point for Christian theology. It can only too easily be regarded as the starting point for some alternative way of salvation, by mystical reflection or ascetic purification, or the like. It is clear that where a theologian has left room for such a way of salvation, if logical consistency is preserved, the role of Christ as Saviour must be drastically reduced, and the weight of human sin seriously underestimated.

We shall find that there are in the early theologians a number of places where the limits possible for a Christian doctrine of the image are overstepped in this direction, though such a trespass is not ever intended, and is actually in each case in conflict with the main body of the thinker's theology. By studying some of these passages we shall learn which of the writers are really guilty of such trespass, and we may hope to learn from their error how to avoid the tendencies which have led them into it.

2 St Clement of Alexandria

We must first inquire whether St Clement is guilty of the error which we are now considering. He describes the sancti-fication of the believer as the purification of reason in him.[1] How is this purification to be understood? According to our interpretation of this point, our whole view of the work of Clement on the nature of man and his salvation will differ.

93

R. P. Casey[2] maintains that Clement is really a Neo-Platonist in essentials. If so, the purification of reason in him is to be pictured as a shedding of the passions and a casting away of the attractions of the senses, which are a hindrance to the true reasonableness of man.

If this view be correct, then the place assigned by Clement to Christ and his salvation and the sacraments can only be a small one.[3] If we accept Casey's view of Clement, then we are forced to adopt a Christology in which the Redeemer's place is merely that of a supreme example to mankind, or more exactly, he will have that function of the midwife to human reason which was all that Socrates claimed for himself. He will be one who has shown *to* men the possibilities of their own rational nature.

Mayer, on the other hand, insists that Casey's interpretation is not the right one, though there are passages in Clement which can be cited to support it. In a careful and thorough discussion[4] Mayer asserts that the purified reason which Clement claims for the Christian Gnostic, is a gift of the Holy Spirit, who alone can make man like to God and who alone can give man the vision of God. And Clement's emphasis on the sacraments and on baptism in particular is a proof of this view of salvation as a supernatural gift. There is, of course, a lower reason, which is the possession of all men, but there is no possibility that without the help of grace and revelation this gift should by insensible stages develop into that higher reason which is purified in us by faith in the incarnate logos. Like Philo, Clement held that man's earthborn mind became the image of the Logos through the inbreathing of the Holy Spirit. This was Philo's interpretation of Genesis 2:7: 'then the Lord God formed man of dust from the ground, and breathed into his nostrils the breath of life; and man became a living being.' While accepting this, Clement adds: 'We claim, however, that in addition, the man who has become a believer suffers a further inbreathing of the Holy Spirit.'[5] It is this further inbreathing which purifies the reason in the fuller sense.

It was doubtless a laudable concern of Clement's which led him to describe man's salvation as the purification of his reason. Surely, if Christ be the logos, then his salvation

must make a man more and not less reasonable. And Clement has already described God's providence and salvation in intellectual terms as the education of mankind. It is only going one step further to call salvation the purification of reason in man. In discussing some of the language used by St Irenaeus, which describes salvation in terms of knowledge and vision, Lawson says wisely: '. . . it remains that attainment to knowledge of the truth is a distinct aspect of Christian salvation, even as the mind is a part of the man.'[6]

It must be considered, however, what is the danger of concealing new Christian doctrine under idealistic or Gnostic terms. Where salvation is described in terms of knowledge, it must be made very clear that something new and not a mere addition to ordinary knowledge is meant, and if this is not made clear, irritation on the part of the reader is apt to result, and both he and the writer are apt to become confused. For both are unable to shake themselves wholly free of the old associations and meanings of the terms which are being used. There is evidence that in relation to the use of the term 'impassibility' Clement was actually led astray in the direction of Gnosticism, which also used the term, though with regard to salvation conceived as the purification of the reason we may probably give him a full acquittal.

3 *St Athanasius*

The chief sources for our doctrine in the writings of Athanasius are two books written by him when he was probably only about twenty years old. Their date is therefore somewhere about AD 315. Even the first of them, the *Contra Gentes,* is a remarkable achievement for a man who was hardly more than a boy; but the second, the *De Incarnatione,* is one of the classics of Christian literature.

The *Contra Gentes* ('Against the Heathen') is a piece of apologetic writing directed particularly against worshippers of gods and images, against pantheists and dualists. As A. Robertson says, summing up the argument in the introduction to his translation of the book: 'That God is not Nature is shown by the mutual dependence of the various constituents of the Universe; no one of these, therefore, can be God, nor can their totality, for God is not compounded of parts on

which he depends, but is himself the cause of existence to all. Such a God as this the soul of man can,[7] and, if purified from sin, will[8] recognize; if her imperfections hinder this, the spectacle of Reason and Order in the Universe[9] will assist her to recognize the handiwork of God, and the presence of the logos and through him the Father. The reclamation and restoration of sinful and degraded man can only be effected by a return to the logos.'[10] This restoration can be achieved, according to the *Contra Gentes,* by a process of reflection, of which we shall have more to say later.

In the *De Incarnatione* it is the argument of the earlier part of the book which is relevant to our subject. This argument runs as follows: 'God created the world, and man in his own image. By sin man lost the image, as God had warned him he would do if he transgressed. If the image was to be restored, and God's purpose for man to be fulfilled, no other course was possible than that the word himself should come to earth and make the image visible, so that it might be copied afresh in the nature of man.'

From this summary it would appear that, according to the *De Incarnatione,* no process of reflection or self-discipline would be able to give man such a vision of the logos as would reinstate the image in him, since an incarnation was necessary to do so.

Thus there appear to be very considerable differences, even contradictions, between the teaching of the first book and the second. Since the teaching of the *De Incarnatione* is so very much more profound and true than that of the *Contra Gentes,* one might imagine, from a study and comparison of them, that it was a much later and riper work. But the evidence all goes to show that the *De Incarnatione* was written very soon after the other book, and indeed, Robertson says of the *Contra Gentes,* 'This treatise and that which follows it form in reality two parts of a single work',[11] and Jerome refers to them in terms which show him to have looked on them in the same light. The problem of the contradiction then remains, and no thoroughly satisfactory solution of it is to be found.

It will be of interest, before leaving St Athanasius, to quote one or two passages which expound more fully this unresolved contradiction. First we shall consider two passages from

Contra Gentes, which clearly suggest the possibility of salvation by means of introspection or by the light of natural theology. 'God . . . made,' says Athanasius, 'through his own Son, our Saviour Jesus Christ, the human race after his own image . . . that . . . he (man) might rejoice and have fellowship with the Deity. . . . For, having nothing to hinder his knowledge of the Deity, he ever beholds by his purity, the image of the Father, God the Word, after whose image he himself is made. . . . For when the mind of man does not hold converse with bodies, nor has mingled with it from without aught of their lust . . . then, transcending the things of sense, and all things human, it is raised up on high, and, seeing the Word, it sees in him also the Father of the Word . . . exactly as the first man created, the one who was named Adam in Hebrew, is described in the Holy Scriptures as having in the beginning had his mind to Godward in a freedom unembarrassed by shame, and as associating with the holy ones in that contemplation of things perceived by the mind in the place where he was – the place which the holy Moses called in figure a garden. So purity of soul is sufficient of itself to reflect God, as the Lord also says, "Blessed are the pure in heart, for they shall see God".'[12]

The second sentence quoted seems to refer to man in the state of integrity. The third seems to assume that a state like this can be attained today by those who practise a kind of ascetic meditation, 'does not hold converse with bodies . . . transcending the things of sense. . . .' Such a way of meditation is enough to restore to us the vision of the logos and of the Father in him, which we then can reflect in our own life.

Thus the language is idealistic rather than Christian, and man's capacity to attain salvation by works is implied, as if he were able to make the image shine forth in himself by cleaning up the internal mirror.

A further quotation[13] will make this even clearer: '. . . When it gets rid of all the filth which covers it, and retains only the likeness of the image in its purity, then, surely, this latter being thoroughly brightened, the soul beholds as in a mirror the image of the Father, even the word, and by his means reaches the idea of the Father, whose image the

Saviour is.' Then, as if a little doubtful of the efficacy of this internal way, Athanasius goes on: 'Or if the soul's own teaching is insufficient, by reason of the external things which cloud its intelligence, and prevent its seeing what is higher, yet it is further possible to attain to the knowledge of God from the things which are seen; since Creation, as though in written characters, declares in a loud voice, by its order and harmony, its own Lord and Creator.'[14]

In the *De Incarnatione,* on the other hand, the theme of the image of God in man is treated from a historical standpoint. Here it is said that God created man in his own image, warning him that if he sinned he would incur that corruption that was his by nature. For man's nature was in itself corruptible, but the added gift of being in God's image was given to him to make possible his perseverance in grace. Sin would mean the loss of this grace, and deliverance into bondage and corruption. Man sinned, and as a consequence fell back into his natural corruption. Men began to die, and the divine image in them was wasting. So God was faced with an alternative, either his word was to be made of no effect, and the corruption which he had predicted as a result of man's sin would not come upon him, or else the divine plan for man would be defeated, and that which had been created in God's image would be annihilated.

Would not repentance on man's part be enough to reverse this process? No, for even repentance could not make void the law that he who sins shall die; and, further, man's very nature was corrupted by sin. So the word took a body, and gave it over to death, offering it to the Father, that all might be held to have died in him, and that, whereas men had turned to corruption, he might turn them to incorruption.

The incarnation itself had the work of restoring man to God's image. Men could not do this work of restoration for each other, for they are at best copies of the image. If a portrait has been effaced by a stain, it has to be restored by the painter painting it over again from the original, who must come and sit for him a second time. So the word had to come to earth, that the image might again be visible, and copied afresh in the nature of man.[15]

In Chapter 15 the impotence, not only of the image, but

also of three supplementary means of revelation, is spoken of. Neither the outer law, the instruction of holy men and prophets, nor the splendour of the heavens and the works of creation were sufficient to save man. So God had to send his own image, in visible form. For since men would not look upwards, he had to send the image to earth. 'To this end the loving and general Saviour of all, the word of God, takes to himself a body, and meets the sense of men halfway.'

As we have said, it is difficult to see how Athanasius was able to leave such a glaring contradiction as that between the teaching of the *Contra Gentes* and the *De Incarnatione* on this point. It is probable that he was never sharply aware of the contradiction. This oversight may have been due to a failure on his part to distinguish between the ineradicable relation of all men to the logos, as the light that lighteth every man, and the relation of believers to the incarnate Christ.

St Augustine

St Augustine's doctrine of the image of God in man will be studied in this chapter, for it is the most remarkable instance of a doctrine of the image which appears to offer us a second way of salvation, apart from Christ. This conclusion is of course utterly out of line with the main body of Augustine's teaching.

In his great work on the Trinity, Augustine spends almost half his time in an attempt to discover the divine image in man and see wherein it consists. This effort is not so irrelevant to his main theme as might appear. From revelation it is known that God is a Trinity, and also that man is in the image of God. Augustine is therefore entitled, as far as logic goes, to the conjecture, that the image in man may also be a trinity. And if this conjecture be true, then a study of this derivative trinity may throw some light upon the nature of the God who created it.

It should be noted, however, that the belief that the image of God in man is a trinitarian structure is only a legitimate conjecture, and not a necessary inference. The resemblance between God and man might consist in something other than a trinitarian structure or, again, it might not be a structure within the individual personality. It will be claimed, indeed,

later in this chapter, that the attempt to find the image of God in a trinitarian structure within the self is a very serious error, and that it has caused much trouble to Augustine himself.

A good deal of the treatise on the Trinity is taken up with the examination of various trinities in man's nature, with the purpose of discovering which of these is qualified to be the image of God in man. Before making a brief review of these it will be necessary to quote one passage from the fourteenth book, the fourth chapter, which expresses clearly the criterion by which Augustine judges these various trinities: 'Therefore neither is that trinity an image of God, which is not now; nor is that an image of God, which then will not be; but we must find in the soul of man, i.e. the rational or intellectual soul, that image of the Creator which is immortally planted in its immortality.'

So, if the image in man consists in a trinity like that in God, it follows that it must be one essence with three equal substances. That is, the self must not form this trinity in association with anything accidental to it, such as an outward object of knowledge.

The first of the trinities in human nature examined by Augustine is that which exists in love.[16] 'Well then,' he says, 'when I, who make this inquiry, love anything, there are three things concerned; myself, and that which I love, and love itself.' This is our first trinity, the lover, the object of love and the love which unites them (*amans, amatum,* and *amor*). This trinity does not satisfy Augustine, for reasons which we can guess, the chief being that this trinity is not within the self, since it demands the existence of another self, or another thing, and these are held to be accidental to the existence of the self.

So we find him going on to speak of self-love, where we find the self as lover, and the self also as object of love, and in the third place love itself, which is the bond between the lover and the beloved.[17] Here, at any rate, all that happens takes place within the human subject for the man loves himself, and that of necessity. But a new difficulty appears, for the self who loves is the same as the self who is loved, so that instead of a trinity we have what one might call a 'binity',

the self and its self-love. So the quest must continue.

Augustine now recalls that the self cannot love itself unless it knows itself. And so now we have a third trinity; mind, its knowledge of itself, and its love of itself (*mens, notitia sui,* and *amor sui*). The mind has a direct knowledge of itself not drawn from the sense, and when it thinks of itself there exists the trinity of mind, the thought of self, and the love of self.

At this point there must be given a word of explanation about the knowledge of self, or the thought of self, the second of the substances in this trinity. It is part of Augustine's doctrine of knowledge that when the mind thinks, it begets a word. When the thing thought about is a visible or sensible object, there is an image, but this image is not the essential word begotten. That word is really the concept, which is different both from the mind's image and the audible word which we may utter to awaken the same concept in the mind of another.

When I say the word 'table' there are three entities present in addition to the table itself. They are, first, the word heard; second, the visual or other sensible image; third, the concept of table. It is this last which is the word begotten in my mind. Now when we think of ourselves, although there may be a number of images present to our senses, the true word begotten in our mind is, according to Augustine, none of these. It is the knowledge or concept of the self. The importance of this result for Augustinian speculation is obvious, for the word which is thus begotten is the human analogue of the divine word begotten by the Father.

The third place in the human trinity is taken by the bond of love between the mind and the word, and this is the analogue of the Holy Spirit in the Holy Trinity.

But there is one shortcoming in this human trinity which makes it unfit to act as an analogue of the Holy Trinity. We do not always think of ourselves, and therefore this trinity has still about it something of the accidental, which disqualifies it for the purpose suggested.

So the ground is again changed, and a new, fourth, trinity is introduced. This consists of memory, understanding, and will (*memoria, intelligentia,* and *voluntas*).[18]

In this trinity memory is the chief term demanding explanation. For Augustine *memoria* is a term which has a special

meaning. It does not refer merely to the past, but also to the self. We are not always thinking about ourselves, but we can be recalled to a knowledge of ourselves. Men say to us in a tone of reproof, 'Remember yourself!' They recall, that is, our thought to a knowledge of ourselves which is always there. We have had it since the birth of our selfhood, and we shall have it as long as we continue to be selves. Thus it stands with memory, both when it relates to the past, and to knowledge of the arts or sciences, and when it relates to ourselves. A mathematician does not cease to understand music when he stops thinking about it, and turns his mind to mathematics. And so the memory, which is really the self as a reflective subject, has a perpetual understanding of itself, and love of itself. The fact that the term 'love' has been replaced here in Augustine's formula by the word 'will' is not of great importance, for the two terms are often synonymous for him. There is thus a continual begetting of the word or understanding by the memory, and a continual love of it which accompanies our knowledge of ourselves. Augustine sums up his result by saying: 'Well then, the mind remembers, understands, and loves itself; if we discern this, we discern a trinity, not yet indeed God, but now at last an image of God.'[19]

This then is one strain in the thought of St Augustine on the image of God. But it is not by any means the whole, nor is it his final conclusion. Arguing in the fourteenth book that the image of God cannot consist in the faith of the soul, which has had a beginning, and will some day have an end, when it is replaced by sight, he finds the image in the rationality of the immortal soul. 'It (the soul) is therefore called immortal, because it never ceases to live with some life or other, even when it is most miserable . . . the human soul is never anything save rational or intellectual, and hence, if it is made in the image of God in respect to this, that it is able to use reason and intellect in order to *understand and behold God*,[20] then from the moment when that nature so marvellous and so great began to be, whether this image be so worn out as to be almost none at all, or whether it be obscured and defaced, or bright and beautiful, certainly it always is.'[21] Here, as before, the image of God is placed in the rationality of the soul, but the important point is that it is defined, not in

terms of a memory, understanding and love of *itself*, but as a capacity to understand and behold *God*.

One more short passage may be quoted in this context which sums up this line of argument: 'This trinity, then, of the mind, is not therefore the image of God, because the mind remembers itself, and understands and loves itself; but because it can also remember, understand and love him by whom it was made.'[22]

The only way by which this apparently illogical change of ground can be justified is by assuming that memory, understanding, and love of self are themselves also a capacity for the knowledge and love of God. Does this not further imply that by the interior way of introspection and self-love we can come to know and love God?

It is worth-while to pause for a moment to note the very considerable difficulty in which Augustine has been placed by his search for a trinitarian structure wholly within man, which should constitute the image of God within him.

On the one hand, since it is in a trinity immanent in the individual man that Augustine has decided to look for the image of God, he has been compelled to choose the trinity of self-memory, self-knowledge, and self-love.

On the other hand, his Christian faith told him that man's chief end and true being was to glorify God and to enjoy him for ever. Did he not himself say, 'Thou hast made us for thyself, and our hearts are restless until they find their rest in thee?' What a dilemma for a profoundly Christian writer if his system compels him to describe human nature in terms of an act related to itself in abstraction from God! Would this not be merely to repeat in theology the fundamental sin of man, the desire for independence, the desire to be as God? Could man's likeness to God consist in his loving himself with a love which can only be described as narcissistic? It would have been all very well for Plotinus to believe that the love in God which is the prototype of man's true being is a mere self-love. But it would not do to make this a central point in Christian doctrine. How far away such teaching would be from the New Testament teaching about *Agape*, the selfless love which is given to another! What a difference the doctrine of the Trinity, the very theme of this great treatise

of Augustine, has made to our understanding of God! For the persons of the Holy Trinity love one another with a pure and selfless love of which Plato and Aristotle and Plotinus seem to have had no knowledge.

St Augustine has avoided this pitfall, but at a price. The only way in which he can extricate man from the isolation in which he has set him, will be to show, if he can, that memory, understanding and love of self are a capacity for the memory, understanding and love of God.[23] He will have to show that there is a straight line of development from a love, which seeks, in however refined a manner, its own good, to the love which puts God first.

And yet, if he does so, he will be in the very difficult position of having provided a second way of salvation, an alternative to the salvation provided in history through the incarnation and cross of Christ. This will be a way of interior reflection, a way of remembering our true selves and correcting our affections by setting them consciously on the goal which they are misguidedly seeking all the time. Such a way will have kinship with the way indicated in Athanasius' treatise *Contra Gentes* which we considered earlier. Does Augustine really believe in such a way of salvation?

To this question there can be only one answer. He does not. He has fully declared our inability to save ourselves, and our dependence on the grace of God in Christ. But in his doctrine of the image he has taken over just so much from non-Christian thought as will influence the course of his teaching from time to time, and make him suggest a capacity for self-salvation by an interior process of reflection.

If we wish for confirmation of the evangelical strain of thought in St Augustine, we need go no further than this same treatise on the Trinity. We turn to the chapter entitled 'How the image of God is formed anew in man',[24] and there we read: 'But those who . . . are turned to the Lord from that deformedness whereby they were through worldly lusts conformed to this world, are formed anew from the world, when they hearken to the Apostle saying, "Be not conformed to this world, but be ye formed again in the renewing of your mind," that the image may begin to be formed again by him by whom it had been formed at first.

For that image cannot form itself again as it could deform itself.'

Again, in the next chapter, he says: 'For it is the sentence of God himself, "Without me ye can do nothing". And when the last day of life shall have found anyone holding fast faith in the Mediator in such progress and growth as this, he will be welcomed by the holy angels, to be led to God whom he has worshipped, and to be made perfect by him.'

One final quotation may be given, where Augustine is commenting on 2 Corinthians 3:18: 'And we all with unveiled face, beholding the glory of the Lord, are being changed into his likeness from one degree of glory to another; for this comes from the Lord who is the Spirit.' Augustine says: 'He (Paul) means, then, by "we are transformed", that we are changed from one form to another, and that we pass from a form that is obscure to a form that is bright; since the obscure form too is the image of God; and if an image, then assuredly also "glory", in which we are created as men, being better than the other animals. . . . And this nature, being the most excellent among things created, is transferred from a form that is defaced into a form that is beautiful, when it is justified by its Creator from ungodliness. . . . And therefore he has added "from glory to glory", from the glory of creation to the glory of justification.'[25]

Whatever we may make of this as a piece of exegesis of the phrase, 'from glory to glory', there is no doubt that it expresses an evangelical thought.

It must thus be repeated that if there are in Augustine certain strands of thought which seem to offer an alternative way of salvation to that in Christ, they do not represent the heart of his theology, and are indeed an undigested relic of Neo-Platonism. And it is necessary to defend him from one misunderstanding. When he describes the act of recollection whereby the soul knows God and its own true being in relation to him, he does not think of it as the mere act of realization of a human capacity, but as a happening in which the grace of God is active. As Gilson says in describing the soul's search for God: 'It only tends towards him because he is with it, and gives life to it from within, as the soul gives life to the body which it animates.'[26]

Let us now emerge from the dense and thorny thicket through which we have been painfully picking our way, perhaps not without stumbling. It is good to walk some distance away from the trees in order to have a look at the wood. What are the things that we can learn from St Augustine's doctrine of the image?

5 *Conclusions*

(a) As we have seen in another chapter, the image is defined by St Augustine as rationality. This is a natural enough borrowing from other writers, but it is too narrow a basis on which to found the image of God in man, even when that term receives the fairly wide definition which Augustine gives it. It would have been better to relate the image to man's responsible personal existence before God.

(b) Nor should rationality have been defined by Augustine as it was defined. It will be remembered that in our chapter on the image as rationality we quoted the following passage: 'But the mind must first be considered as it is in itself, before it becomes partaker of God, and his image must be found in it. For, as we have said, although worn out and defaced by losing the participation of God, yet the image still remains. For it is his image in this very point, that it is capable of him; which so great good is only made possible by its being his image.'[27] Here rationality seems to be defined as a quality of the soul in itself, which remains even when the participation of the soul in God is lost. The participation in God is thus an extra, an addition to the soul, which indeed brings the image to perfection. But the soul can carry on some sort of existence without it, and retains the capacity for the participation. The truth is rather surely that the soul is never out of relation to God, and such capacity as it possesses for relating itself to him is merely the continually created power to respond to his act, which holds it in being as a person.

(c) Lastly, the universal image should not have been defined as a power of remembering, understanding and loving God. Having made a wrong start, Augustine was only able to escape by constructing man's memory, knowledge and love of himself as a capacity to remember, know and love God. He did well to rescue the self from the isolation in which he had placed it.

But it was too late. After such a false start it could be rescued only at the disastrous price of making the revelation in Christ seem unnecessary. The universal image is not a capacity for the true love of God, but something wounded which needs to be healed by the divine love in Christ. This Augustine knows well, and can say more powerfully than perhaps anyone else! The image should perhaps have been defined as an endowment which qualifies man for presence before God – a God-given ability to respond to God's special presence and confrontation, and an inability to escape from that urgent presence. Augustine was the first thinker to define the image as a power. This thought was later taken up by St Thomas Aquinas, and there is a real truth in it, especially when it refers to the universal, Old Testament image. Difficulty arises when we try to define and delimit that power. This conception of the image as a power or endowment we shall carry forward with us to use when we attempt to state our own view. There will be many who disagree with this notion of the image as present power, and it is only right to concede that far more important than it is the belief in the underlying purpose and election of God, which destines us for the perfect future image. There will be few Christians who will disagree with the opinion that our creation in the image is a creation by the divine love for an existence that images back God's love to him.

In spite of our criticism of St Augustine, in taking farewell of him we must confess that in the whole history of man there is no one who has contributed more to the substance of man's thoughts about himself. Since apostolic days there has perhaps been no man who has done more to waken in man the sense of wonder at the mystery of his own being and the greatness of God's grace which creates and sustains and redeems us.

The thought of St Augustine is like an ocean on which the ships of our thought can venture. There are in it the whirlpools and quicksands from which we withdraw in revulsion, but there is also the light shining from an infinite cloudland on its wide horizon; there is in it the mystery of the sea, rejoicing continually before its Maker.

CHAPTER VII

Sanctification and Salvation Conceived as Divinization

We have seen in our New Testament study that the notion of salvation as divinization has an extremely slender scriptural basis in 2 Peter 1:4. Some even deny it is taught there. The Fourth Evangelist nowhere teaches this doctrine, and the union of believers with Christ described by St Paul implies indeed that they share not only in Christ's death and humiliation, but also in his resurrection and glory. But nowhere is any crossing by the believer of the frontier between the creator and created being suggested by him, and doubtless the whole notion would have been abhorrent to him.

There is thus a profound union of believers and the Church with Christ by faith, and the gift of the Spirit is a foretaste of what will yet be. But there is no faintest suggestion that even in that day of glory and judgment there will be a fusion of the believer or the Church with God.

We have now the task of examining the early theologians we have chosen as the subject of this part of our study, in order to see whether any of them oversteps in his doctrine of the image and of salvation this barrier which the New Testament, with one doubtful exception, so scrupulously observes.

1 St Irenaeus

In the theology of St Irenaeus there are a number of different strands of thought. There are two main ways in which he regards the office of Christ and the salvation of man. John Lawson says in his fine book, *The Biblical Theology of St Irenaeus*:[1] 'Characteristic of St. Irenaeus is a powerful doctrine of the Saving Work of Christ as the Divine-human Champion of man, "Christus Victor".' But there is another way of conceiving the Saviour and salvation of which account must be taken. 'The dominating conception here is that man is to be

made god, or a son of God. . . . This process of divinization may also be spoken of almost in mechanical terms, as though it were a sort of spiritual inoculation. The conception plainly answers to the notion of the spiritual and the Divine as an ethereal substance, pure and incorruptible. The Incarnate Son is represented as the One who brought down to earth from heaven the metaphysical substance of Divinity, and united it to the substance of humanity. Thus man comes to share in the Divine Nature, and becomes "incorruptible" and "immortal".'[2]

Here the present writer must make some points in criticism and dissent on this subject of divinization.

(a) Lawson says: 'The *general* proposition of "divinization" is not to be rejected. Divinization by "beholding the vision of God", by "seeing the Image of God" in Christ, and by enjoying "the paternal light", etc., are not in themselves objectionable phrases, provided that it be borne in mind that they describe only a single aspect of salvation, i.e. the intellectual.[3] Here a strong protest must be made. The notion of divinization is quite unbiblical, even though it may be found once in Peter, and it is thoroughly objectionable. God is God, and man is man, and only in the incarnation do we find One who is both God and man.

But, on the other hand, the notion of man being renewed in the image of God by looking with faith on the revelation of the Father in Christ is completely biblical, as is the notion of man as adopted into sonship of God, or receiving immortality through the gift of faith. So that our first point is that Lawson has failed to make an essential distinction.

(b) It must, however, be admitted that Irenaeus does use the language of divinization. Among the passages where such language is used is *Adv. Haer.*, IV, 33, 4, where it is said: 'Or how shall man pass into God, unless God has passed into man?' Further in IV, 38, 4[4] Irenaeus says: 'For we cast blame on him, because we have not been made gods from the beginning but at first merely men, then at length gods.'

(c) In spite of this fact, Irenaeus is not so deeply implicated in the theory of divinization as Lawson holds. Even in the two passages last mentioned the context in both cases makes quite clear the difference between God and man, even in his

glorified state. Further there is nothing which goes beyond the Christian biblical hope in such passages as III, 19, 1, 'The Son of God became the Son of Man, that man . . . might become the son of God', while one of the passages cited as most clearly indicating a belief in the divinization of the Christian, surely does not refer to this at all. This is IV, 20, 4: 'Wherefore the prophets, receiving the prophetic gift from the same Word, announced his advent according to the flesh, by which the blending and communion of God and man took place according to the good pleasure of the Father, the Word of God foretelling from the beginning that God should be seen by men and hold converse with them upon earth.' It is clear that this passage does not refer to divinization, but to incarnation.

Further, owing to his failure to make the distinction which we drew under our first heading, a number of the references which Lawson cites as supporting divinization do not in fact support it at all.

(d) While admitting that the language of St Irenaeus does sometimes seem to suggest a mechanical notion of salvation by inoculation with imperishable substance, when we look into his thought more deeply we see that in fact he avoids this pitfall. For example, he says (III, 18, 1): 'When he (Christ) became incarnate, and was made man, he commenced afresh the long line of human beings, and furnished us *en bloc* (*in compendio*) with salvation.' From this statement it might be thought that Irenaeus conceived of human nature as a kind of substance existing in its own right, apart from the human beings who share in it, and that he believed that since Christ had taken hold of it, it was automatically transformed. Such sayings as this do emphasize the truth of the objectivity of salvation, and the fact that something decisive has been done by God to make it available. But the danger of this line of thought is, that if it is carried to its logical conclusion, Irenaeus will have to say that as, owing to our organic connection with Adam, we are all fallen, so by the fact of the incarnation we are all automatically saved. But he never even comes near to saying this.

Further, as Lawson himself notes, the gift of the vision of God and of immortality is almost invariably associated by

Irenaeus with the Holy Spirit, and this is a further guarantee against the danger that salvation shall be actually conceived of as inoculation of a mechanical kind, for the Spirit is always the witness who awakens faith in the heart of the believer — and faith is never mechanical.

Our conclusion is then that while St Irenaeus does on occasion err by conceiving of salvation as divinization, he in fact hardly errs at all in the direction of picturing it as a mechanical process. And, as Lawson says, his conception of salvation as the gift of immortality, as adoption into divine sonhood, as transformation into God's image through the vision of Christ incarnate, are all quite legitimate aspects of the gift of salvation, for which ample scriptural authority can be found, not only in the writings of the Fourth Evangelist, but also in those of St Paul.

2 *Clement of Alexandria*

Baptism means for St Clement not only a crucially important step in the education of man, the act whereby true reason is implanted in him. It is also the gift of the Spirit, and the beginning of a process of growth in the possession of the Spirit, a growth which can be described both as a divine gift and as the fruit of human effort. The tendency of Clement is to emphasize the latter aspect, in opposition to the views of the Gnostics, who held that the man who has the fortune to be in God's image needs to do nothing but to repose on the fact of his divine origin, which at death will be attested by a seal upon him which will automatically secure him entry to the heaven from which he fell.

The process of sanctification is described by Clement in various ways. It is the attainment of immortality and the laying aside of the passions. This latter thought smacks of the Stoic system rather than the Christian, although Clement gives it a Christian seasoning by suggesting that the true expression of this detachment or impassibility (*Apatheia*) is a willingness to forgive injuries.[5] Another term he uses to describe this process is the unification of the soul. But this unification is reached, not through control or sublimation of the desires and inclinations, but through their eradication. The man who is already in possession of God, Clement suggests, does not need any-

thing more. Hope and courage and desire are as unnecessary
to him as wrath and fear. The definition of the impassible
man given in the sixth book of the *Stromateis* is a picture of a
really inhuman being. It is stated that the Saviour, while on
earth, 'ate, not for the sake of the body, which was kept
together by a holy energy, but in order that it might not
enter the minds of those who were with him to entertain a
different opinion of him. . . . But he was entirely impassible,
inaccessible to any movement of feeling, whether pleasure or
pain.'[6] The theory of man that is forced to a docetic interpretation of our Lord's humanity of this type is obviously very
far wrong somewhere, and is clearly drawing its inspiration
from non-biblical sources. Here it is clear that Clement has
not only adopted Gnostic terms, but has been infected with
Gnostic thought.

Upon the soul perfected by grace and effort the word leaves
the 'seal of righteousness'. The receipt of this seal completes
the process begun by the seal of baptism. This second seal is
eloquently described as a 'certain godlike power which stamps
on the righteous soul a kind of spiritual splendour, like the
warmth of sunlight, a visible seal of righteousness'.[7] As Moses'
face shone with a reflection of the divine glory when he came
down from Mount Sinai,[8] so the Christian reflects the selfless
love of God to him. But his soul does not merely coldly
reflect this light. It burns with an inward fire. Such perfection
is perhaps never attained in this life. But he who has attained
to it is the true Gnostic, who knows God as he is known.
This is a fine figure, and the comparison of the light on
the face of Moses with the light on the face of the Christian
who is renewed in the image of God from glory to glory is,
of course, biblical and Pauline.[9]

Less scriptural and less happy is Clement's description of
the soul of the Christian Gnostic as the temple of God, on the
grounds that there is erected in that soul the image of God.
Ancient pagan thought conceived of the image of a god as in
some way penetrated with the divine essence, and thus as itself
divine. So Clement can talk of the Christian in whom the
likeness is perfected as being a god in the flesh. But he does
not really conceive of the process as one of deification, though

the language used might suggest this. He thinks rather of the Christian as being filled with divine power, and as being united with Christ through partaking of the sacrament.

But the connection by Clement of the image of God in man with the conception of man's soul as the temple of God is neither scriptural nor fortunate. These two figures are never associated in the New Testament for the simple reason that the temple at Jerusalem was one in which no image could have been set up without blasphemy, and no Christian writer of the first century could ever have thought of comparing the Christian soul with a heathen temple.

3 St Athanasius

In Athanasius there are frequent references to the divinization of Christians. (The reference is very rarely to the individual.) In nearly every instance, the line of reasoning is the same. Christ must have been, not only man, but God, to have given us the divine nature in salvation. That salvation is the receiving of the divine nature is taken for granted, and from this starting point the argument to Christ's divinity proceeds. Once, in Letter 61, 2, this argument is used in a sacramental context: 'And we are deified, not by partaking of the body of some man, but by receiving the body of the Word himself.'

But one passage above all, which occurs in the third discourse against the Arians,[10] is important, because it defines with some care what is meant by divinization. The Arians, says Athanasius, interpret Christ's saying, 'I and the Father are one', as merely referring to a moral unity of wills and doctrine between God and himself. He rejoins that if this be so, then a great many others, angels and men, would also be sons, 'And that it should be said of them too that they and the Father are one, and that each is God's image and Word.' If we too are called God's image, it is in a different sense from Christ. Forced, therefore, to make a distinction by his opponents, who claim that Christ is no more divine than we are, Athanasius at great length expounds the sense in which he believes believers to be destined for divinization, and how far this status is different from that of Christ.

The Father and the Son are one by nature, and, says Athan-

asius, the unity of believers in the Father and the Son means that their unity is analogous to that of the Father and the Son, which is an example for them to follow.

But Christ in his high-priestly prayer asks something more for his disciples; that they 'may also become one, according to the body that is in me, and according to its perfection, that they too may become perfect, having oneness with it . . . that as if all were carried by me, all may be one body and spirit, and may grow up into a perfect man. For we all partaking of the same, become one body, having the one Lord in ourselves.'[11]

It is clear Athanasius here is referring to the unity of the Church with its head in faith and sacrament. In this manner its members are one with him and with the Father and with each other, sharing in all the privileges of sonship, and membership of God's family.

'For what the Word has by nature, as I said, in the Father, that he wishes to be given us through the Spirit irrevocably. . . . It is the Spirit then which is in God, and not we, viewed in our own selves; and as we are sons and gods because of the Word in us, we shall be in the Son and in the Father, because that Spirit is in us, which is in the Word, which is in the Father.'[12]

The distinction between Christ and his disciples, his Church, is clearly maintained, though it is rather unfortunate that the language of divinization is used. It may be that one of the results of this use has been the development in some quarters of a doctrine of the Church which has not left unassailed the Lordship of Christ.

4 Conclusion

The language of divinization is an attempt to do justice to a real change worked in human nature through union with Christ in his Church. But this union is a union of faith. It is real, and the fruits of the Spirit bear witness to it, but it never amounts to a fusion of the believer or the Church with the Lord. It is a singular union of persons with the divine Person, whereby Christ's benefits pass to his disciples, while his Lordship remains unassailed, and the boundary between creator and creature remains uncrossed. To describe this

union is the real aim of Irenaeus, Clement and Athanasius.
As, in the case of the universal image, man's gifts and
powers depend on the grace of creation in God's relation to
man; so the redeemed nature and gifts of men are dependent
on the forgiving and gracious relation of God to them in
Christ. These gifts never become the possession of men in
such a way that they justify by their own merit.

CHAPTER VIII

The Image as Rationality

In all the Christian writers up to Aquinas we find the image
of God conceived of as man's power of reason. It will not
at this stage be necessary to cover the ground again in detail.
It may suffice to remind the reader that Irenaeus talks of
man being endowed with reason, and in this respect like to
God himself.[1] The rationality described in this passage is wide,
including man's freedom and, indeed, his responsibility, because 'having been created a rational being, he lost the true
rationality, and opposed the righteousness of God'. Here also
we see a distinction which most of the writers make between a
rationality which cannot be lost – the power of thought and
man's accountability for his actions – and a second, higher
rationality, which can be, and has been, lost. This is the rationality of the man who acts not only rationally, but reason-
ably, who is worthy of the gifts that God has given him.

Clement refers[2] to the power of rationality which is identical
with our human nature, and equates this with the image, as
distinct from the higher likeness.

Athanasius does not make the distinction common to the
other writers between image and likeness. While it is clear that
he conceives of the image as a moral likeness to God, a likeness which became visible again on earth because Christ
showed it forth in his life, yet there is one passage where
the image seems to be equated with rationality. Here[3] he says
that God 'has made all things out of nothing by his own Word,
Jesus Christ our Lord. And among these, having taken pity
above all things on earth, upon the race of men, and having
perceived its inability, by virtue of the condition of its origin,
to continue in one stay, he gave them a further gift, and he
did not barely create men, as he did all the irrational creatures upon the earth, but he made them after his own image,
giving them a portion of the power of his own Word; so
that having, as it were, a kind of reflection of the Word, and

116

being made rational, they might be able to abide ever in
righteousness, living the true life which belongs to the saints
in Paradise.'

There is a difficulty here. If the word 'rational' be taken
in its ordinary sense, then sin has made men irrational in
the sense that it has turned them into brutes. But this is inconsistent both with experience, and with the rest of Athanasius'
teaching on the image. The alternative is to interpret 'rational'
here in the other, higher, sense. The only truly rational man is
he who uses his reason to reflect the word, and continue
the true life which belonged to Adam in Paradise. Rationality
is then a quality which can be lost without man becoming a
brute. It is restored by grace, and is in process of restoration
in believers. A usage of this kind by Clement of Alexandria is
recalled.

While this is so, I think we may infer that Athanasius would
hold that rationality is in a sense present in all men. For it is
probable that he held the image was not extinct after the
Fall. *Contra Gentes* certainly implies such a view, and while
De Incarnatione is much more pessimistic about man's natural
state, it also describes the image in fallen mankind as 'wasting'.[4] This implies it was not extinct. And the famous figure
used by Athanasius of an image which has been effaced and
has to be repainted by the artist,[5] is not decisive against our
view. All that it implies is that the image is useless for the
purpose of serving as a portrait of its original, and has to be
painted over again by the artist. Thus we may say that there
are at least indications of the same line of teaching in Athanasius that we have seen in Irenaeus, that man in his state of
integrity was really rational, and in his fallen state is still
rational in a sense.

If we turn to St Augustine, we shall find a very similar
doctrine. In *De Trinitate,* XIV, 4 he finds the image in the
rationality of the immortal soul. 'It (the soul) is therefore
called immortal, because it never ceases to live with some
life or other, even when it is most miserable, so . . . the
human soul is never anything save rational or intellectual;
and hence, if it is made after the image of God in respect to
this, that it is able to use reason and intellect in order to
understand and behold God, then from the moment when that

117

nature so marvellous and so great began to be, whether this image be so worn out as to be almost none at all, or whether it be obscure or defaced, or bright and beautiful, certainly it always is.' Here there is an inalienable rationality consisting of a power to understand and love God, whether that power be used in a right and rational manner or not. As we shall see, Aquinas also places the image of God in the rationality of the soul, in a manner very similar to that of Augustine.

We may ask ourselves why the image was thus constantly conceived, during some thousand years of Christian history?

Firstly, we must see a main reason for it, not in the biblical tradition at all, but in the line of Greek pre-Christian thought, which we have traced from Heraclitus and the Stoics to Philo. All these writers dealt with man's reason as the godlike element in him, and Philo definitely equated human reason with the image. The line from Philo of Alexandria to Clement of Alexandria is not hard to trace, and can be seen in other doctrines as well as in this.

Secondly, these Christian writers were looking for some characteristic which was common to all humanity. If they read in Genesis that, after the creation of plants and animals, God created man in his own image, it was natural for them to ask, what is there in men that animals do not possess, and equally natural to answer, his reason. This is not a wholly false answer, indeed, but it is not, I think, the right one. It is the natural answer for a pagan to give, but it too easily allows us to consider man in isolation from God. Is not the true answer for a Christian to give, that the characteristically human thing is man's presence with God in responsible being? It is true that reason is defined in such a way in the passage quoted by Irenaeus as to indicate that responsibility is not wholly forgotten, but on the whole Brunner's criticism is justified, that Irenaeus' conception of reason is essentially the same as that of the Stoics.[6] In contrast with this whole line of thought, it is surely right, with Brunner, to consider that the primary element in man's being, ontologically, is his responsible existence in confrontation with God.

Thirdly, as we have already noted, the whole terminology of the image tends to concentrate our attention on the intellectual aspect of man's being, and to make us construe sal-

vation in terms of illumination, reflection of the divine light, and vision. This is not wrong in itself, provided that it is remembered that only a part of the truth is seen in this way.

As a result of these three causes, the universal or Old Testament image is regarded in too theoretic a light by the Fathers and by Aquinas. The essence of man's being is in fact not his rationality, even though this be brought, as Augustine brings it, into relation to God and defined, as he defines it in part, as a power to love. The essence of man's being is his responsible existence before God, and his other characteristically human gifts have to be interpreted in the light of this, and not vice versa.[7]

It is probable that this intellectualistic interpretation of the universal humanity of man has led to similar errors in the interpretation of the nature of faith. It may be that this is the origin of the definition of faith as the assent to a body of supernaturally revealed truth, rather than as the turning in gratitude and obedience to the God who confronts man at every moment, and reveals himself in Christ to the believer.

From this short study of the image regarded as rationality, we may take it, then, that the image should rather be regarded in a different light. In so far as it is universal, it is an endowment in virtue of which man stands, whether he will or not, as a responsible person in God's presence. And this endowment is continually given to him by the gift and call of the word of God which confronts him.

CHAPTER IX

The Image of God in Aquinas

In this part of the book we shall give an account of the doctrine in a number of theologians, taking first St Thomas Aquinas.

In his work on our doctrine, what St Thomas did was largely to adopt what Augustine had taught, making it more explicit, and modifying it to fit into his own elaborate system.

The foundation of this theology is the doctrine that God is being, and therefore all created things image him in a certain degree. But his image is not to be found, strictly speaking, in irrational beings.

'Some things are like God first and most generally inasmuch as they exist, some inasmuch as they have life, and a third class inasmuch as they have mind or intelligence.'[1] These last, says Aquinas, quoting Augustine with approval, 'approach so near to God in likeness that among all creatures nothing comes nearer to him. It is clear, therefore, that intellectual creatures alone, properly speaking, are made in God's image.'[2]

Man is therefore in the image of God, because he, like God, is rational. But this rationality is not described in the rationalist manner, as a faculty in man similar to a quality in God, a faculty man can possess in isolation from God. It is certainly a power, but it is defined by Aquinas, just as by Augustine, in terms of relation to God.

When asked whether God's image is to be found in all men, Aquinas answers:[3] 'We must say that when man is said to be made in the image of God in virtue of his intellectual nature, he is chiefly in God's image according as his intellectual nature is most able to imitate God. His intellectual nature chiefly imitates God in this, that God understands and loves himself. Whence the image of God can be considered three ways in man. In one way, according as man has a natural aptitude for understanding and loving God, and this aptitude

consists in the very nature of the mind, which is common to all men.

'In another way, according as man by act of habit knows God and loves him, but imperfectly, and this is the image by conformity of grace.

'And in a third way according as man knows and loves God in act perfectly, and this is the image according to the likeness of glory.'

The first sense of the image is obviously Aquinas' account of the Old Testament image, man's common, universal humanity. The second describes the New Testament image in process of formation, and the third describes it in full and perfect activity.

It is important to note that there is a considerable difference between the first sense of the word image, on the one hand, and the second and third, on the other. The first image is a power or endowment and the second and third describe the man in activity,[4] an important distinction made clearly for the first time in the history of the doctrine. It will be our own conclusion that there is just such a difference between the Old Testament and New Testament images, that the universal image is in fact essentially a gift, the privilege of standing in his presence continually and that all our acts, our decisions, are an answer to the call of God entailed in this confrontation.

In criticism of this passage in Aquinas, it is further to be noticed that he has followed Augustine's illogical step of saying that the image of God in man consists in his power to love and understand God, while the logic of his argument ought to place the image in his power to love and understand himself. Thus, as in Augustine, the relationship to God, so essential for Christian theology, is preserved at the expense of consistency.

Then the definition of the universal image as a power to *love* God is surely also vulnerable, as it was in Augustine. It is certainly a power to respond to him, and response involves some knowledge of that to which we respond. But do all men love God?

Aquinas has left us in no doubt upon this issue. They do. But he carefully defends himself against the suggestion that

such love as is here under discussion can go any way towards
meriting salvation. He has to meet the objection that it is
surely only by grace that men can know and love God, and
that therefore the image cannot in any sense be common to
all men, but only to those who are in a state of grace. The
answer is given as follows.[5] 'The meritorious knowledge and
love of God can be in us only by grace. Yet there is a certain
natural knowledge and love of God as seen above' – and then
we are referred to three passages which come earlier in the
Summa.

The first two passages[6] deal with our natural knowledge of
God, making it clear that all our knowledge in this life starts
from sense, and that therefore we cannot, while on this earth,
know God in his essence. But we can know from the things
of sense that God exists, and is the first cause of all things,
exceeding all things caused by him.

It is, however, the third of these passages which is the
most important, for it describes not a universal knowledge
of God, but a universal love of him. True, it is of the nature
of angels that Aquinas is speaking, with a confidence that
we have lost in these degenerate days; but he brings man into
the discussion too, and it is, of course, with man that we are
concerned. He maintains that angels and all men love God
more than they love themselves. He goes on to cite the
evidence furnished by irrational things. Where the nature
of an irrational thing is to be subordinate to a larger whole,
it instinctively puts itself forward to protect the whole. A
man's hand moves forward instinctively to protect his body,
even at the cost of injury to itself. And this is true also of
rational beings. 'For it is the part of a virtuous citizen to
expose himself to the danger of death for the conservation
of the whole State. And if a natural man were a part of
this State, this inclination would be natural to him. Therefore, because the universal good is God himself, and under
this good are subsumed the angels and men, and since the
whole Creation, inasmuch as it is, is God's, it follows that by
natural law angels and men love God before themselves,
and more than themselves. Besides, if they loved themselves naturally more than God, it would follow that a natural
love was perverse, and it would not be perfected by charity,

ut destroyed.'[7]

There is surely something far wrong here! The organic
relation between an arm and the whole of the body simply
will not do to illustrate the relation between fallen man and
his creator. And it is more than doubtful if it could be said to
be natural for a natural man to give up his life for his State.
The last sentence is particularly illuminating. 'Besides, if they
loved themselves naturally more than God, it would follow
that a natural love was perverse, and it would not be perfected by charity, but destroyed.' This argument is obviously
considered quite final; it is taken as an axiom that charity, the
love of God induced through supernatural grace, should be
related to nature in a purely positive manner, and as its
ulfilment.

Now it may be agreed that 'Grace does not destroy nature,
but perfects it' – if nature be taken to mean that nature which
God gave to man in the first place, human nature as God
planned it. But does sin leave human nature as God planned
it? To accept this view as axiomatic would be to accept the
whole two-storey view of the universe, which teaches that sin
has removed supernatural gifts from men, but left nature
and reason intact. This is the view which Brunner claims to
have had its origin in Irenaeus, and his false exegesis of
Genesis 1:26. But, as we saw, Irenaeus' teaching was not
imply of the two-storey kind in the bare manner that it is
taught here.[8] If this so-called axiom involves the view that
all men love God more than they love themselves, there *must*
be something wrong with it, although on the other hand we
must not define human nature, even in its fallen state, in such
a way as would make impossible the incarnation of the sin-
ess Christ. It is impossible for those who have accepted
the insights of the Reformation to believe that sin has merely
removed supernatural gifts from man, and left nature and
reason intact.

The trouble is that St Thomas has taken over with too
little modification the Aristotelian way of thinking, and added
a second storey of Christian ethic to it. But the Aristotelian
category of organism, of means and ends, is not at all adequate to deal with the matter of ethics. For in the search for
happiness (*eudaimonia*) there is no place for true moral respon-

sibility, and sin becomes merely a mistaken search for means towards the one unquestioned end of happiness. We do not deny that there may be a love of God in the natural man. But if we loved God more than we love ourselves, what need would there be for salvation? And what definition of sin is better than just this, the preference of self to God? Thus the teaching of Aquinas about the Old Testament or universal image of God in man seems unsatisfactory, though he has carefully guarded himself against the suspicion of having offered a second, mystical, way of salvation.

With regard to the second sense of the image, 'the image by conformity of grace, inasmuch as man actually or habitually knows and loves God, though imperfectly', Aquinas contrasts this image with the natural love of God, and calls it the image by conformity of grace. The man who has it loves God with the love of charity. God pours this supernatural grace into the heart of believers, enabling them to love him meritoriously. There appears to be little in Aquinas to tell us how this image is recreated in man, and how this love is awakened. Certain suggestions are given in the *Summa Theologica*. While on earth, all our knowledge comes from two powers of knowing. The first is the act of a corporeal organ, such as an ear, or eye, or hand, which naturally knows things existing in individual matter. Hence our senses know only the singular and not the universal. The second power of knowing is the act of the intellect, which is not a corporeal organ. Through it we understand these objects as universals. Thus while on earth we can never hope to know God in his essence; we have a natural knowledge of him through the objects which are known by sense and intellect. Grace comes to our aid in deepening our knowledge of him through supplying new images to sense, and enlivening the intellect whereby we apprehend the universals in the objects of sense.

This seems a most extraordinarily puny basis on which to found the whole knowledge and certainty of faith, and the witness of the Holy Spirit in the hearts of believers to the word of God and his grace.

But we must remember that powerful as the intellect of Aquinas was, he was able to sound depths in his faith which

his understanding could not fathom. And perhaps we get a more fitting expression of his faith in his great sacramental hymn than we could have imagined possible from the theological statement given above:

> *O blest memorial of our dying Lord!*
> *Thou living Bread who life dost here afford,*
> *O may our souls for ever live by Thee,*
> *And Thou to us for ever precious be.*
>
> *Fountain of goodness, Jesus, Lord, and God,*
> *Cleanse us, unclean, with Thy most cleansing blood;*
> *Make us in Thee devoutly to believe,*
> *In Thee to hope, to Thee in love to cleave.*[10]

Here, more than in St Thomas' theology, we find expressed the evangelical motive of gratitude to God for all that he has done for us in Christ.

We have yet to deal with the third sense of the image given by Aquinas. In glory, by the gift of a 'created light', God will enable the blessed to behold his own essence.[11] For this, an illumination of the intellect is necessary. By this light, the blessed are made like God: '. . . we shall be like him, for we shall see him as he is.'[12] This state can only be reached in glory, and possibly on earth under certain conditions of rapture.

Of those who see the essence of God in glory, some will see him more perfectly than others, for some are made more like him by the light of glory, and are awakened to greater charity which excites desire, and makes learning easier. No created being will ever be able to comprehend God, but those who behold the essence of God will see all things in it at the same time, so that in this truth they will possess all truth, and in this good, all good.

It is strange that in all this teaching of Aquinas, the intellectual element is so prominent, and that from first to last nothing has been said about sonship, a thought so central to the gospel. In spite of all that is noble in the teaching of Aquinas on the divine image in man, it is clear that here we are moving far more in the world of Aristotle than in the world

of Christ, with his gospel of the kingdom and fatherhood of God.

Provisional Conclusions

From the study of the image of God which we have been pursuing, we may now formulate some provisional conclusions. We recall that the Old Testament regards the image as universal – all mankind are in the image, which is not the same thing as man's dominion over creation, but rather the ground of it. Man is in some way like God, and the writer of 'P' probably thought of a physical as well as a spiritual resemblance. It is most probable that the condemnation by the Hebrew prophets of man's inhumanities to man were made because men were defacing the divine image in each other. This image is not to be reduced to a divine purpose of salvation hanging over the head of mankind.

In the New Testament the emphasis is laid heavily on this divine purpose and its embodiment in the believer by means of faith in the redeeming act of Christ, and communion with him in the Church. The relation of the universal image to the New Testament image is not discussed.

In the history of the doctrine prior to the Reformation we have seen in the writings of Clement of Alexandria and Irenaeus the justification for a distinction between the Old Testament and the New Testament image, though Irenaeus' exegesis of Genesis 1:26, on which he bases the distinction, is faulty. We have seen that the universal image has a reality, the image not being extinct, yet the universal image must not on the other hand be defined in terms so optimistic that a second door of salvation is opened apart from faith in Christ's historical revelation, and union with him through the Spirit. We have also seen that the image is wider than rationality, and that it is not a spark of a divine fire. Nor is its renewal by faith a process of divinization.

Nor is the image a natural endowment which remains untouched by the loss of a supernatural grace. And yet the notion of endowment is not wholly to be rejected, provided that it be made secondary to a relation of God to man which cannot be annihilated by sin, though sin on the human side can and does pervert it.

CHAPTER X

The Image of God
in Martin Luther

1 *Introduction*

We come now to the great cleavage in Christian thought
caused by the Reformation, and we shall find that, as was to
be expected, it did not come without leaving its mark on the
doctrine of the image.

But it is important for a moment to consider the problem
which faces us, of giving a theological account of man's fallen
humanity. For those who believe that the Old Testament image
is not exactly the same as the New Testament one, the problem will be how rightly to express the continuity between the
two images and, at the same time, the discontinuity. Some
type of unity there must be behind the things described in
the two cases, for it is not by mere accident that the same
word is used to describe both. And yet there must be a discontinuity, otherwise the devastating effects of sin are altogether discounted, and man's powerlessness to achieve his own
salvation is forgotten.

The eathquake which shattered the carefully built mediaeval
synthesis could not leave the arch of this doctrine uncracked.
The man whose motto was 'Salvation by faith alone' could
not be content with the teaching of St Thomas on this subject, in spite of his careful disclaimer that the natural love
of God was meritorious. It is true that the appearance of
continuity in St Thomas is somewhat deceptive. Both the
universal image and the image by conformity of grace are
described as a love of God. But how far is it right to give the
same name of love to the sinful impulses of man and the
supernaturally motivated charity of grace?

Our criticism however goes deeper than matters of terminology. We are told that grace perfects nature; we could agree
that grace fulfils the divine purposes for which nature was
created; but nature has fallen away from them, and is no
more intact. The men of the Reformation could no longer

accept the simple two-storey relationship of nature and supernature, and therefore some other method of relating sinful
humanity to divine grace had to be found, to replace the
simple relation in which mediaeval thought had placed them,
the one resting like a second storey upon the other.

2 *Traces of a Two-Image Theory in Luther*

Luther was the first writer to attempt the task. In his writings
there are some passages which seem to carry on what we
believe to be the biblical tradition of the twofold image of
God.

In a lecture,[1] commenting on the verse Genesis 1:26, Luther
says: 'There is a double likeness, public and private. Paul
speaks of the private, but our text seems to speak of the
public. "In our likeness"–that is, in governing things. This
likeness remains under sin up till now; the Fall did not take
this likeness from Adam. But Paul goes higher; that likeness
–goodness and justice, sin did remove.' It is clear that the
'public' likeness is so called because it is universal among
men, while the 'private' one is common only to believers. In
short, the distinction here drawn is between the Old Testament
image and the New Testament image. And here Luther says
that the words 'Let us create man in our image and likeness'
refer to the formal or Old Testament image, which is definitely related by him to dominion over animals. There is,
of course, no discussion here as to the relation between the
two images.

Another passage which very clearly points to what we have
called the universal human image is to be found in a sermon
on John 1:4 ('In him was life, and the life was the light of
men'). Here Luther speaks of the way in which all things are
preserved in their being through the word. He continues: 'In
him was life, and the life was the light of men. In him
(John means) was life, not for himself alone, for he gives
all creatures life, but more pre-eminently for men, that they
should live for ever; and he was also the light, that is, the
light of men, that he should give a special light to men. It is
wonderful that the Evangelist St John can speak such homely,
simple words of such high and important matters. He means
that the Son of God comes so near to men that he is their

light, which is a far different light from the light which all unreasoning animals and beasts see. For cows and pigs have the common light of the sun by day, and the light of the moon by night, but man has the specially endowed gift of the glorious light of reason and understanding. That men have invented and discovered so many noble arts, be they wisdom, or skill, or cunning, all this comes from that light, or from the Word which was the life of man. Wherefore this light, Christ, is not merely a light for himself, but he lightens men by his light, so that all understanding, cunning and skill, which is not false and devilish, flows from this light, which is the Father's eternal wisdom. But beyond this light, which is common to all men, bad and good, there is another special light which God gives to his own, on which rests all that John has to say hereafter of the Word, namely, that the Word reveals himself through the Holy Ghost, and through the word of the mouth, and wills to be the light of his people.'[2]

It should be noticed that in these words Luther brings the universal humanity of fallen man into relationship with the logos. The contrast of man with the animals and the contrast of the inner light which is the presence in the soul of the word, with all visible lights, remind us strongly of the passage on memory in the tenth book of the *Confessions*.[3] But it should also be noted that there is no mention of the image of God in this context, although what is being described is what we should call the Old Testament image.

A few lines further on in the same sermon, commenting on the words 'And the light shineth in darkness', we find Luther speaking in the strongest terms about the insufficiency of the light of reason for salvation: 'All men who are not in Christ, are without life before God, are dead and damned. For how should they have life, since they do not only walk in darkness, but are themselves the darkness?'

Strong though these words are, they do not actually contradict what went before; they only express in rather violent terms the inadequacy of the universal confrontation with the logos for salvation.

3 *Equation of the Image of God with Original Righteousness*
Thus far we have seen the traces of a two-image theory in

Luther, and have noted that he does bring the universal humanity of fallen mankind into relation with the logos. But why in the long passage dealing with St John does he not call this humanity in its relationship to God, the universal image? The reason is that the whole drift of his teaching is in another direction. In all his important passages on the subject, he equates the image with man's original righteousness.

In his sermon on Genesis 1:26[4] Luther makes a passing reference to the Augustinian view on the image, and leaves it on one side. He links the passage rather with two others from the New Testament. The first passage is 1 Corinthians 15:48: 'As was the man of dust, so are those who are of the dust; and as is the man of heaven, so are those who are of heaven. Just as we have borne the image of the man of dust, we shall also bear the image of the man of heaven.' The second passage is the one in Ephesians 4:21-4, which tells us to put off the old nature and to put on the new nature, 'created after the likeness of God in true righteousness and holiness'.

We all, says Luther, bear the image of the fallen Adam. He was a sinner, though he was not so created. Christ is the heavenly image, full of light and love, we must bear his image, and be conformed to his suffering. 'So, you see what "image" means, and what "likeness", therefore you must put out of your mind the meaning which the doctors have given, otherwise your understanding will only be still further darkened.' Man must be an image either of God or of the devil, for he is like whichever of the two he copies. Man originally had righteousness, but he did not remain good, and lost the image, so that we have become like the devil.

4 Luther's Rejection of the Augustinian Conception of the Image

In his lecture on Genesis 1:26,[5] Luther refers to Augustine's interpretation of the image as the natural power of memory, understanding and will, while the doctors have interpreted the likeness as the gifts of grace which perfect nature; memory being adorned by hope, understanding by faith, and will by love. He says that he does not condemn these speculations out of hand, but questions their usefulness. They are only

lost at the Fall, when the image remained. The text of Genesis will not bear this interpretation.

(c) We must reject Luther's interpretation of the Genesis image and likeness as referring to man's original righteousness. We base this rejection chiefly on Genesis 9:6.

(d) This is our most important conclusion. We must admit that, once Luther's interpretation of Genesis 9:6 is accepted, his account is a coherent and plausible one. Then the image in fallen man is lost without trace, the relation of sinful humanity to the Logos being accepted as Luther accepts it, but this confrontation being sharply separated from the image. There will now be only one general sense for the term 'image of God' in the Old and New Testaments, if we except the singular sense in which Christ is the image. The image of God is, so to speak, removed entirely from sinful unbelieving man, except in so far as it hangs over him as a divine destiny. It is being restored in believers, and will be perfectly revealed in them at the last. In Luther this view is associated with the belief in a historical Fall, preceded by an original righteousness which clothed man in glory and wisdom. But this doctrine of the image could be held even where a historical Fall was denied. Holders of such a view will be more consistent if they remove from it all references to a relic of the image.

In our opinion, such a view is inferior to our own because it is less true to scripture and less in line with common sense. But it is a live option for those who are convinced that neither the Roman Catholic view nor the view represented in this book is possible for them. To this view which I have just outlined, Luther approximates, more closely than does Calvin, who has more than Luther to say about the relic of the image.

It is probable that in the defence of human dignity against totalitarianism of all kinds this view would be little less effective than the others. For, underlying all other characteristics of humanity, there is the will of God for man's salvation, and that this is present all Christians will be agreed. This divine will is the very foundation and ground, not only of human existence, but of the sacredness of man.

CHAPTER XI

The Image of God in John Calvin

In John Calvin we have a great systematic thinker whose contribution to the doctrine of the image is comparable with Augustine's. In the main he carries on and develops the teaching of Martin Luther.

1 *Knowledge of God and Knowledge of Ourselves Mutually Interdependent, and Dependent on the Revelation in Christ*
At the beginning of the *Institutes*, his chief work, he treats of our knowledge of God and of ourselves.[1] It at once becomes clear how closely in his thought our knowledge of God is interwoven with our knowledge of ourselves. He maintains that the blessings which we owe to God, including the chief blessing of our very existence, should drive us in gratitude to think of him, while our very feeling of ignorance and depravity should remind us of our need of him.

But although a contemplation of our own being should lead us to a contemplation of God, it is also true that unless we have first a knowledge of God we shall never attain to a true knowledge of ourselves, for only then shall we see our own sin and want in their true light. The conclusion to which Calvin later leads us is, that we shall never truly know either God or ourselves until the bond of our ignorance and sin is broken by a twofold action of God. God acts outside of us in his revelation of himself through Jesus Christ, and he acts within us by the witness of the Holy Spirit to that word.

A true knowledge of man is thus confined to those who stand within the circle of Christian faith. But Calvin goes further, and claims that man *is* never truly himself except when he is bound to God by the tie of adoring thanks and obedience for his mercy. From this it can be seen how far Calvin is from any rationalist position. Without the revelation of God in Christ our reason is unable to understand our true

nature. And that nature itself can only be understood in the light of God's purpose in Christ, which it is made to share.

2 *The Image of God to be found in his Creation, and in a Special Sense in Man*

Calvin believes that the image of God is to be found in a sense in all of his creatures. He conceives of God's relation to his world in the following manner. Not only did God at the beginning create all things out of nothing (I, 16, 1) but by his Word alone is the created universe from moment to moment sustained in being. 'The Word of God was not only the source of life to all the creatures so that those which were not began to be, but . . . his life-giving power causes them to remain in their condition; for were it not that his continual inspiration gives vigour to the world, everything that lives would immediately decay or be reduced to nothing.' (*Commentary on John* 1:4)

As God from moment to moment sustains the universe in being, the function of the universe is from moment to moment to image forth God's glory. In his commentary on Psalm 19 ('The heavens are telling the glory of God'), Calvin writes: 'There is certainly nothing so obscure or contemptible, even in the smallest corners of the earth, in which some marks of the power and wisdom of God may not be seen; but as a more distinct image of him is engraven on the heavens, David has particularly selected them for contemplation.' The result of this manifestation is that where anyone has been given spiritual vision, he should be 'ravished with wonder at God's infinite goodness, wisdom and power'.

But there is a special sense in which man is said to be created in God's image. 'It is certain that in every part of the world some lineaments of divine glory are beheld, and hence we may infer that when his image is placed in man, there is a kind of tacit antithesis, as it were, setting man apart from the crowd, and exalting him above all the other creatures.'

Commenting on John 1:4 ('In him was life, and the life was the light of men') Calvin says: 'John speaks of that part of life in which men excel other animals; the life which was bestowed on men was not of an ordinary description, but was united to the light of the understanding. The purpose for

135

which men were created was that they might acknowledge
him who is the author of so great a blessing.'

It is clear that the reference here is to a divinely planned
life for man, which should constitute him God's image in a
singular manner.

3 *The Seat and Character of the Image*

This line of thought leads to one conclusion. It is this, that
the image of God in man consists in the acknowledgment
of God's goodness and greatness. It makes no difference
whether that acknowledgment was given by Adam before the
Fall, or is given by the Christian who is being renewed in
God's image by faith in Christ.

In his commentary on Genesis 1:25, with sure exegetical
instinct, Calvin rejects Augustine's view of the image as consisting in a trinity within the self. He equates the image with
the likeness, and rejects the view that the image can refer to
any physical resemblance, saying further that man's dominion
over nature can be only a very small part of it. He continues:
'Since the image of God has been destroyed in us by the Fall,
we may judge from its restoration what it originally had
been. Paul says that we are transformed into the image of
God by the gospel. . . . Therefore by this word the perfection
of our whole nature is designated, as it appeared when
Adam was endued with a right judgment, had affections in
harmony with reason, had all his senses sound and well
regulated, and truly excelled in everything good. Thus the
chief seat of the image was in his mind and heart, where it
was eminent, yet there was no part of him in which some
scintillations of it did not shine forth.'

It is thus in the mind and heart that the image is principally
seated, and there can be no doubt that according to Calvin's
psychology the image is present when a man truly knows
God with his mind and loves him with his heart. As Calvin
says in a sermon on Deuteronomy 4:10: 'God created us after
his own image in order that his truth might shine forth in
us. It is not God's purpose that men should abolish and
destroy the grace that he has put in them, for that would be
utterly to deface his image in spite of him, but rather,
that as he comes nearer to us and we to him, so he will

have his image known in us, and his truth shine forth in us all the more. Let us understand that it is not the intention of God that we should be ignorant of him, but to utter himself in such a way, that we may be able to distinguish him from forged idols, that we may take him for our Father, and assure ourselves that we are called to the knowledge of the truth, and that we may boldly resort to him to call upon him and seek succour at his hand.'

There is thus a close resemblance between the image of God in the world of nature, and the image in man. In both cases there is a reflection of God's glory back to himself through praise, but inanimate creatures and creatures without reason do this unconsciously, while men do it in gratitude and humility when they acknowledge their complete dependence on God and give him their obedience. It was for this that they were given the light of reason.

Calvin pictures God as all-powerful creative activity. It is therefore natural that he should conceive of man, who was created in God's image, as also being, in his measure, a dynamic being. Therefore it may be said that man is in God's image in so far as he reflects back God's glory to him in gratitude. As Torrance has pointed out,[2] the picture of a mirror is the governing one in Calvin's mind, though he occasionally uses the figure of an engraving.[3] The figure of the mirror has, of course, New Testament authority.[4]

This whole line of thought in Calvin brings him very close to modern Christian existentialism, which pictures man's being as a life of decision in response, obedient or disobedient, to God's act of creative and sustaining love.

4 The Image in Sinful Man

Calvin followed Luther in his equation of the image with man's original righteousness and restoration in Christ. He has, therefore, chosen the New Testament sense of the image as fundamental, and he thus is faced with the problem of relating it to the Old Testament image, which is common to all mankind. The problem arises for him in the shape of the question, 'Was the image of God lost at the Fall?' The answer that one would expect Calvin to have given would certainly be that the image was lost. How could it in any degree remain

if it consists in the kind of reflection which we have described? In that case there would be no universal image today. And there are passages where Calvin seems to speak of a total destruction of this kind.[5] But he rarely commits himself to this viewpoint without reserve. The reasons for this hesitation lie, as we shall see, in the difficulty and complexity of the subject as much as in anything else. It is instructive to consider passages in his commentaries where verses of scripture important for our doctrine are discussed.

In the passage dealing with man's creation in the divine image and likeness (Genesis 1:26-8), Calvin says indeed that the image in man has been destroyed by the Fall. But a page later he expresses himself more cautiously: 'But now, although some obscure lineaments of that image are found remaining in us, yet they are so vitiated and maimed that they may truly be said to be destroyed. For besides the deformity which everywhere appears unsightly, this evil is added, that no part is free from the infection of sin.'

In his commentary on Genesis 9:5-7, Calvin has to express himself still more cautiously. For the passage, it will be remembered, deals with the sacredness of fallen humanity, which was created in God's image at the first. It is because man is sacred that the life of the man-slayer, be it man or beast, must be forfeited. Calvin argues that God is not solicitous for human life rashly and for no purpose. Men are indeed unworthy of God's care, if respect be had only to themselves, but since they bear the image of God engraven on them, he deems himself violated in their person. Thus, though they have nothing of their own whereby they obtain the favour of God, he looks upon his own gifts in them, and is thereby excited to love and to care for them. Should anyone object that this divine image has been obliterated, the solution is easy; first, that there exists some remnant of it, so that man is possessed of no small dignity; and secondly, the celestial creator himself, however corrupted man may be, still keeps in view the end of his original creation, and, according to his example, we ought to consider for what end he created men, and what excellence he has bestowed upon them above the rest of living beings.

In this admirable comment there are four things worthy of

note. First, Calvin's insight into the fact which seems to
escape some modern theologians, that there may be a dignity
in man which constitutes no ground for moral boasting, since
it is purely a gift given to man by the grace of God.

Second, Calvin distinguishes two such grounds for reverencing the persons of men. The first ground for reverence consists in something which is actually present in man. One might,
although with some danger of misunderstanding, call it part of
the very structure of his being as man. And then there is a
further ground for reverencing man – the divinely planned end
of his creation, which God keeps in view in spite of human
sin.

Thirdly, we must note that neither of these two grounds for
reverence can be described as any actual response of man
to God's creative word, and yet these gifts and that divine
purpose both go to constitute the divine image in man. It
would appear therefore that while it is true to say that man
is in God's image in so far as he reflects back in gratitude
God's glory, this definition is not exhaustive.

And, fourthly, the elements of the image spoken of in the
passage under consideration are not to be described as belonging to that wider image which is common to creation, for
Calvin here is explicitly referring to an 'excellence he (God)
has bestowed on them (men) above the rest of living beings'.

In his commentary on Psalm 8, Calvin says, in reference
to the words, 'thou hast made him little less than God': 'I have
no doubt that he (the Psalmist) intends by the first (man's
being a little lower than God, and crowned with honour) the
distinguished endowments which clearly manifest that men
were formed after the image of God, and created to the hope
of a blessed and immortal life. The reason with which they are
endowed, and by which they can distinguish between good and
evil, the principle of religion which is planted in them; their
intercourse with each other, which is prevented from being
broken up by certain sacred bonds; the regard to what is becoming, and the sense of shame which guilt awakens in them,
as well as their continuing to be governed by laws; all these
things are clear indications of pre-eminent and celestial
wisdom. David, therefore, not without good reason, exclaims
that mankind is crowned with glory and honour.'

In a curious passage which follows, Calvin claims that these blessings belonged to the state of integrity, though it is clear that some of them, such as 'the sense of shame which guilt awakens' could not do so. 'He goes on to say that by the Fall 'we were reduced to a condition of wretched and shameful destitution. In consequence of this corruption, the liberality of God, of which David here speaks, ceased, so far at least, that it does not at all appear in the brilliancy and splendour in which it was manifested when man was in his unfallen state. True, it is not altogether extinguished, but alas! how small a portion of it remains amidst the miserable overthrow and ruins of the Fall!',

One has here the strong impression that Calvin has been made uncomfortable by the emphasis of the Psalmist on God's gifts in human nature, although, as we have seen, Calvin can himself speak eloquently of these. His attempt to refer the psalm to the days of man's integrity is an indication of this discomfort. But is it wholly Calvin's fault that at one time he wishes to emphasize the destruction of the image, and at another the fact that it is not wholly obliterated by the Fall? For there is something paradoxical in the situation which he is describing. The image is indeed something very complex, which from one point of view, as God's gift to man, has certainly not been obliterated by man's sin, while from another viewpoint, regarded as the integrity of man's response of heart and will, it certainly is obliterated. The gifts of God to man, the continued relationship to himself, the possession of reason and the other gifts which flow from that relationship; these are wonderful things, and yet, when one considers that this relationship is not only the source of man's continued human existence, and the condition of his salvation, but also that it has been perverted by sin to a relationship of guilt on our side and of wrath on God's; the complexity and the paradoxical nature of the reality Calvin is trying to describe become very evident.

If we might put it crudely, without incurring the suspicion of Pelagianism, when Calvin talks of what God gives in the image, then he says it is not wholly lost, but when he speaks of what we contribute, then he must talk of it as obliterated

in the natural man since the Fall. This distinction must also be kept in mind in dealing with Calvin's doctrine of total depravity which we shall have to consider later.

5 *A Universal Confrontation of Man with God*

As we have seen, Calvin teaches that we do not only owe our creation to God, but also our continued existence from moment to moment. In addition to this he says that all men are in a special relation to the logos, the second person of the Trinity, a relation which modern philosophy describes as confrontation. This becomes clear from his comments on John I:4, 9: 'In him was life, and the life was the light of men. . . . The true light that enlightens every man was coming into the world.' He says: 'There is therefore no man whom some perception of the eternal light does not reach' – even though the light of reason which God implanted in men has been obscured by sin, and all save a few shining sparks has been utterly extinguished. This light is quite different from the light of the Holy Spirit which shines only upon the elect, and creates faith in them, bearing witness to the revelation in Jesus Christ.

There is a somewhat different emphasis in the commentary on Genesis 2:9, where Calvin approves Augustine's suggestion that the tree of life was a figure, or sacrament of Christ to Adam. Here he says: 'For we must maintain what is declared in the first chapter of John, that the life of all things was included in the Word, but especially the life of men, which is conjoined with reason and intelligence. Wherefore, by this sign was Adam admonished that he could claim nothing for himself as if it were his own, in order that he might depend wholly on the Son of God, and might not seek life anywhere but in him. But if he, at the time when he possessed life in safety, had it only as deposited in the Word of God and could not otherwise retain it, than by acknowledging that it was received from him, whence may we recover it, after it has been lost? Let us know, therefore, that when we have departed from Christ, nothing remains for us but death.' From this latter passage it might be inferred that after the Fall, the relationship of man to the logos was entirely lost, save for those who have had it renewed by faith in Christ. It

is, however, better to think of Calvin's view as being that the relationship is not lost, but perverted on the human side.

The original purpose of the light given to Adam was that he might reflect the image of God 'by depending wholly on the Son of God, and might not seek life anywhere but in him'. After the Fall, the sparks of that light which still remain serve a different purpose. They make man inexcusable for his sins; there is no way back by their guidance to man's lost integrity. This is a favourite doctrine of Calvin's.[6]

It is clear that he thinks of the relation of sinful man to the word not as merely one of election, but as an actual bond of confrontation. We have seen this from his commentary on Genesis 9:5-8, where the relic of the image is said not only to consist in God's purpose of grace for man, but also in certain sparks of the divine light present to all men. Here Calvin is in line with Augustine and most other commentators, and indeed with the Bible itself. Karl Barth is the first who has tried to regard the universal relationship of men to the word as one of election alone. Calvin, indeed, would have had an added difficulty in accepting such a view, for he expressly rejected the view that election is universal, and in view of John 1, he had to accept the tenet that the light lighteth every man.

This relationship to the word through confrontation must necessarily in some way be reflected in man's knowledge, and Calvin gives a more thorough account than any other theologian of the scope and effectiveness of the knowledge of God and the world which the remaining sparks of the image can secure for man in his fallen state. In the diversity of skill and wisdom which men possess, he says 'we can trace some remains of the divine image distinguishing the whole human race from other creatures'.

He agrees with Augustine that man's supernatural gifts were withdrawn after the Fall, and his natural gifts corrupted. Among the first are faith, love to God, charity towards our neighbour, the study of righteousness and holiness. Of natural gifts a residue of intelligence and judgment and will remain, but soundness of mind and integrity of heart were withdrawn. Still some sparks remain in man to show that he is a rational

animal, different from the brutes, but this light is almost smothered by clouds of darkness.

But especially with regard to inferior objects, the natural man's reason makes progress. 'In policy, economy, mechanical arts and liberal studies, in the regulation of human society by laws and the principles of these laws, there is advance. There is universal agreement in regard to such subjects, both among nations and individuals, the seeds of them being implanted in the breasts of all without a teacher or a law-giver.' And this holds true in spite of lawless persons who try to deny and turn upside down such principles. Men are often found to accept general moral principles even when denying their applicability to their own cases.

Further, the admirable light of truth displayed in profane authors should remind us that the human mind, however much fallen and perverted from its original integrity, is still adorned and invested with admirable gifts from its creator. To reject or condemn truth, wherever it appears, is to insult the Holy Spirit. There follows a noble passage, too long to quote here, about the gifts which God has given to mankind, through ancient lawgivers and philosophers, in their exquisite researches, and skilful descriptions of nature, and so forth.[8]

Whatever of reason we retain, Calvin continues, ought to be ascribed to the divine indulgence. Had God not so spared us, our revolt would have carried along with it the entire destruction of nature.

But with regard to higher things, the knowledge of God, and of his paternal favour towards us, and the regulation of our behaviour in accord with divine law, men are blinder than moles, and such glimpses of the truth as they have are like the flashes of lightning on a dark night, which vanish before the traveller can take a step by its light.[9] This is at least true of the knowledge of God and his paternal favour towards us. With reference to the divine law, men can know something of it by the light of reason. But on the whole all that this knowledge suffices for is to make our sin inexcus-able. A striking sentence says: 'But since the sinner, when trying to evade the judgment of good and evil implanted in him, is ever and anon dragged forward, and not permitted

to wink so effectually as not to be compelled at times, whether he will or not, to open his eyes, it is false to say that he sins through ignorance.'[10]

6 Calvin on Total Depravity

In connection with the image, something must be said about Calvin's teaching on the subject of total depravity.[11] Is this not clearly inconsistent with things that he has to say about certain sparks of the image of God which are left even in fallen man? Our argument will be, that when it is seen what Calvin means by depravity, it will also become clear that there is no necessary contradiction here, though Calvin is sometimes led into inconsistency, and interprets man's perversity in such a sense that the dignity and sacredness of human nature appear to have perished with the Fall.

It is clear from a consideration of many passages that when Calvin talks of man's corruption, he does not mean that sin has severed the connection with God altogether. It is further worthy of note that those passages where the darkest picture of man is painted, all deal less with the gifts God has bestowed on human nature than with the use to which they are put by man. Not that the gifts remain untarnished by sin, even apart from man's sinful use of them. But it is always with this sinful will that Calvin is concerned when he speaks most harshly of corruption and perversity, and always his thought is of our inability to justify ourselves before God, and our need of salvation from beyond ourselves. Two quotations from a long list of passages will serve to make this clear:

'When I say that all mankind is polluted, my meaning is, that we bring nothing from our mother's womb but mere filthiness in our nature, and that there is no righteousness in our nature which can reconcile us with God. Man's soul was indeed endued with singular gifts at the first, but there remaineth in it no drop of pureness any longer, therefore we must seek for cleanness without ourselves.'[12]

'The gifts which God has left to us since the Fall, if they are judged by themselves, are indeed worthy of praise, but as the contagion of wickedness is spread through every part, there will be found in us nothing that is pure and free from every

144

defilement. In us all these things (sc. natural knowledge of God, and the power of distinction between good and evil, etc.) are completely polluted in the same manner as the wine which has been wholly infected and corrupted by the offensive taste of the vessel loses the pleasantness of its good flavour and acquires a bitter and pernicious taste. Thus in the whole of our nature there remains not a drop of uprightness. Hence, it is evident that we must be formed anew by the second birth.'[13]

In general, the argument is that these gifts of God do no good to us, they are perverted by the use we make of them, they serve but to make us guilty and inexcusable before God. Our whole will is in a contrary direction to God's will, and in this perverseness we are unable to lift a finger to save ourselves, unless God helps us. If the doctrine of total perversity means this, then it expresses a truth which the Bible assumes, though Calvin, by continually hammering at it, gives a picture of God and human nature subtly different from that of the Bible.

But there are times when Calvin writes in a way which makes it seem that for the moment he has forgotten the distinction between the perversity of man's will and the continuing dignity of God's gifts in him. 'When man is considered in himself and his nature, what can one say? Here is a creature cursed of God which is worthy of being rejected from the rank of all other creatures, worms, lice, fleas, and vermin; for there is more worth in all the vermin in the world than in man, for he is a creature where the image of God has been effaced, and where the good which he has put in it is corrupted. There is nothing in him but sin; we have so gone to the devil, and he does not only govern us, but has us in his possession, he is our prince.'[14]

It might be claimed that this passage begins, 'When man is considered in himself', and thus refers to man in abstraction from his essential relation to God, referring to perversion of his will, and not to his nature, which is not quite the same thing. But it does read strangely inconsistently with a passage from the *Institutes*,[15] where Calvin says: 'The Lord enjoins us to do good to all without exception, though the greater part, if estimated by their own merit, are unworthy of it. But

145

scripture enjoins a most excellent reason when it tells us that
we are not to look to what men themselves deserve, but to
attend to the image of God, which exists in all, and to which
we owe all honour and love. . . . In this way we attain to
what is, not to say difficult, but altogether against nature,
to love them that hate us . . . remembering that we are not
to reflect on the wickedness of men, but love the image of
God in them, an image which, covering and obliterating their
faults, should by its beauty and dignity allure us to love
and embrace them.'

7 *Importance of the Relic for Calvin's Theology*
Calvin thus does not hesitate to use this notion of the relic
of the image in sinful men to drive home on us the duty of
honouring them and treating their persons as sacred. It is
hard to see how this can be consistent with the notion that in
them the divine image is wholly extinct. And further, it is
hard to see how such advice can be reconciled with the belief
that there is not a genuine universal offer of salvation. To be
consistent, Calvin would have had to base his moral advice
to us on the *possibility* that our neighbour, however improb-
able it may seem, is really one of the elect. For an image, or
the relic of an image, whose *sole* purpose is to make its bearer
inexcusable before God, can never supply an adequate ethical
motive for another man to treat him as if he were Christ in
person. There is only one belief that will justify us in treating
another as 'my brother for whom Christ died'. And that is
the faith that Christ actually died *for him*, that God has a
purpose for him, that in salvation he should be eternally
united with Christ. And our motive will be still stronger if we
can believe also that this purpose of God has its own embodiment in the life of the man from moment to moment, since
the man is confronted, in however paradoxical a manner, with
God's claim, and God's sustaining grace. If we regard our
neighbour as less than lice, fleas, and other vermin then, unless
we can be sure that God wills to save him through Christ,
shall we not be very strongly tempted to disregard him entirely,
if not to liquidate him when he opposes us?

Thus, however tempting it may be to treat as an inconsistency Calvin's doctrine of a relic of the image in fallen man,

he does not hesitate to make considerable use of that doctrine on occasion. And his own teaching on the perversity of the will is not necessarily, but only accidentally, in conflict with what he says of the relic. Nor can this image in fallen man be described as merely an instance of that image which is shared by the universe in general, so far as by its excellence it declares God's glory. It is something far more paradoxical than that, and more tragic, though in the last instance, by the insight of faith, we can see that it promises good and not evil.

8 *The Relic and the General Revelation*

It will already be clear that the relic of the image does not enable man to come to a full knowledge of God, or in any degree to love him. The knowledge of God which the natural man attains is self-contradictory. 'Still, though seeing, they saw not. Their discernment was not such as to direct them to the truth, far less to enable them to attain to it, but resembled that of the bewildered traveller who sees the flash of lightning glance far and wide for a moment, and then vanish into the darkness of the night before he can advance a single step. . . . Besides, how many monstrous falsehoods mingle with those minute particles of truth scattered up and down their writings as if by chance. . . .' To the great truth, what God is in himself and what he is in relation to us, human reason makes not the least approach.[16] The knowledge of the believer who is 'firmly persuaded that God is reconciled and is a kind Father to him' is not attained by anyone unless he has faith in Christ.[17]

As we saw, Calvin has no doubt that there is an evident revelation of God's glory in nature. This appears from his doctrine of the image of God in the natural world. The glory of God is there visible, but it is only rightly seen and interpreted by the man of faith, whose eyes have been opened by the word and the inner testimony of the Holy Spirit. But 'had Adam stood upright' all men would have had a right understanding of this revelation in nature. Calvin's witness to a general revelation cannot be questioned.

But equally without hesitation he rejects the notion of a valid natural theology. He does not use the word, but he consistently denies that there is any true system of knowledge of God built up by natural reason on the basis of the divine revelation in nature and the relics of the image in man. That revelation is like wine made bitter by the impurities of the cask into which it is poured. God has endued all men with some idea of his godhead, the memory of which he constantly renews, but though experience testifies that a seed of religion is divinely sown in all, scarcely one in a hundred is found who cherishes it in his heart, and there is not one in whom it grows to maturity.

There is one difficulty to be noticed at this point. Calvin maintains that the natural man is quite unable to come to a true knowledge of God through the use of the relic and the general revelation. And yet this general revelation and the relic serve the purpose of making man inexcusable. It is hard to see how man's ignorance could be culpable and inexcusable had there not been a possibility of attaining to a true belief which he had failed to seize. But this difficulty does not only attach to the teaching of Calvin, according to which some men are predestined to damnation and yet are to blame for their sin. It attaches to the teaching of all orthodox Christians. For we all maintain that men are to blame for their sin, for their disobedience to general revelation. And yet we maintain that without Christ none could have been saved. We maintain, that is, the inadequacy of the same general revelation which is the ground of our guilt because we have disobeyed it.

9 The Renewal of the Image by Grace

Calvin teaches that there is a sheer break between the natural man and the man who is in a state of grace, in so far at least as there can be no gradual transition from the one state to the other. 'Hence it appears that the grace of God is the rule of the Spirit in directing and governing the human will. Govern he cannot without correcting, reforming, renovating. Hence we may say that the beginning of regeneration consists in the abolition of what is ours.'[18]

Commenting in the *Institutes* on the words 'A new hea[rt] also will I give you, and a new spirit will I set within you', h[e] says: 'If it is like turning a stone into flesh when God turns us to the study of rectitude, everything proper to our own will is abolished, and that which succeeds in its place is wholly

of God. I say the will is abolished, but not in so far as it is will, for in conversion everything that is essential to our original nature remains. I also say that it is created anew, not because the will begins then to exist, but because it is turned from evil to God.'[19]

The problem of the 'point of contact' is not raised in so many words by Calvin, and one cannot say whether he would have denied its existence. Certainly a will whose sign has to be reversed from rebellion to obedience can prove to be no point of contact. Nor can the supernatural gifts of 'faith, love to God, charity towards our neighbour and the study of righteousness'[20] serve, since they were lost at the Fall. What is left to fallen man is a weakened reason and a power of distinction between right and wrong. These, as we have said, are powerless of themselves to lead to a true knowledge of God, and yet their presence may serve as a necessary precondition for the testimony of the Spirit. Calvin does not discuss this question. The very fact that these gifts have remained even in fallen man may be argued to indicate that God chose to use them in a subsidiary way together with the word and the testimony of the Spirit, although he might do without them.

The image is renewed by a twofold agency, that of the word and the testimony of the Holy Spirit. Commenting on John 6:44, 'No one can come to me unless the Father . . . draws him', Calvin writes: 'Did not Christ descend into the world that he might make the will of his Father manifest to men, and did he not faithfully perform the office? True, he did, but nothing is accomplished by his preaching unless the inner teacher, the Spirit, open the way into our minds. Only those therefore come to him who have heard and learned of the Father.' This doctrine of the testimony of the Spirit, so important to Calvin's thought, cannot be discussed at greater length here. It is enough to say that the witness of the Spirit within is always given to the word without, and gives illumination of it and an assurance superior to reason[21] that God's promises are true. This special work of the Spirit is distinct from his other work in men's lives and hearts, which work is not confined to the elect. Though Calvin does not draw attention to it there is a parallelism between the inner relic of the

image in all men which bears ineffectual witness to the revelation of God in nature and the world, and the image restored by the Spirit's testimony which bears effectual witness in the hearts of the elect to the revelation in Jesus Christ, the word.

The manner of the Spirit's working in the elect is that he creates faith in our hearts, so 'that the image of God, which had been effaced by sin, may be stamped anew upon us, and that the advancement of this restoration may be continually going forward in us during our whole life, because God makes his glory shine forth in us by little and little'.[22] Therefore, as the image of God constitutes the entire excellence of human nature as it shone in Adam before the Fall, but was afterwards vitiated and almost destroyed, so now it is partly seen in the elect so far as they are regenerated by the Spirit. Its full lustre, however, will be displayed in heaven,[23] and the image will shine in greater glory in the elect there than it did in Adam.[24]

10 *Conclusion*

Such is Calvin's teaching about the image. It is a theme to which he has given greater attention than any great theologian since Augustine, and his contribution is even greater than Augustine's. Indeed, little that is radically new and important on the subject has been said since Calvin. He conceives the image dynamically, and brings it into relation to God as Augustine does, and as every sound doctrine of the image must do. He defines it better than Augustine and Aquinas, and in line with the insights of the Reformation. His apparent contradictions on the subject are at least in part due to two aspects of the reality with which he had to do. He did draw the right distinction between them, but perhaps not with sufficient clarity and persistence. His use of the term 'relic' is not wholly fortunate, but it is hard to find an adequate term to describe the very singular reality with which he is dealing. The relation between what we have termed the Old Testament image and the New Testament image – between the relic and the image in the wholly regenerate blessed – is not clear. And it is here that Calvin's peculiar views on election have done damage to his doctrine. For the real link between the universal Old Testament image and the New

Testament image, which is the hope of men in Christ, is the loving purpose of God to all men through him. Now, on Calvin's doctrine of a limited offer of salvation it is extremely hard, if not impossible, to maintain that there is such a universal purpose. Hence for some men the Old Testament image is a prelude to salvation, while for others it is, and has been from the beginning, only a prelude to damnation. The middle term which gives unity to the image is thus faulty or missing in Calvin's theology. If it be urged that if we reject Calvin's view of election, then we must either accept universalism, or believe that God's will for man may in some cases be finally thwarted, the point will have to be conceded. There are great difficulties in the way of any view of the last things.

CHAPTER XII

The Image of God
in Emil Brunner

1 Development of the Controversy with Karl Barth

Brunner is the theologian whose work on the image of God has perhaps made the most impact on the thought of our time. His study is the outcome of a very wide range of reading, and the resultant richness of matter, combined with his philosophical grasp, makes his great book, *Man in Revolt*, a piece of stimulating reading.

It was in reaction against Brunner that Barth's views on this subject were developed, first in violent opposition in his pamphlet, *Nein*, and then in a modified and much more considered form in his *Church Dogmatics*, Vol. III, 1 and 2. The controversy continued for over fifteen years, and up till 1945, the year of the publication of *Church Dogmatics*, Vol. III, 1, the course of the argument seemed to provide yet one more instance of the futility of theological discussion. But since then there occurred changes in the thought of both disputants. With Brunner it was chiefly, if not wholly, a matter of modification of terms. Barth both developed his thought in great detail and richness, and moved nearer to Brunner.

In the final stages of their thinking there was a surprising amount of common ground between them, though certain decisive differences still remained.

The chief source of Brunner's teaching on the subject is *Man in Revolt* (1939), which was searchingly criticized by Barth in his *Church Dogmatics* Vol. III, 2. Brunner in his turn replied to Barth's criticisms in an article to the *Scottish Journal of Theology*.[1]

2 The Word as source of Christian Knowledge of Man, and also as Source of Man's Being

In *Man in Revolt* Brunner starts by distinguishing his doctrine of man from its non-Christian rivals.[2] It is impossible, he claims, to have a coherent doctrine of man which does not

rest upon presuppositions. For man is too complex a phenomenon to be understood as a totality unless some characteristic of his nature be singled out as fundamental and used as
a key principle of interpretation. So, various keys have been
tried in the attempt to unlock the human mystery. If, for
example, the key of natural causation be used, a naturalist
view of man results; if the idea of Spirit be chosen, an idealistic doctrine is the outcome.

Brunner claims that the true principle of interpretation is
the word of God. This does not just mean that we must let our
understanding of man be moulded by what the Old and New
Testaments say of him. It means that only in faith in Christ
the Son of God, the revealer of God in history, shall we
understand our own nature. And for this understanding to
arise in us, it is necessary that the witness of the Holy Spirit
be heard in our hearts, creating faith in Christ, to whom the
witness of both Testaments points.

Brunner does not, of course, deny that the various sciences
have an authoritative word to say, each in its own domain,
about man and his nature. Indeed, it is a first principle with
him that the Christian report on man may not conflict with
common sense experience, or with the legitimate statements
made about man by any science which keeps within its own
recognized territory. The principle to which he holds in general
is, that the nearer any discipline of knowledge approaches
to the kernel of man's nature, the more possibility there is
that it should make statements which are in conflict with the
legitimate statements of Christian theology. There can indeed
be no Christian geography or mathematics, but there is a
Christian psychology, if by psychology we do not merely
mean a science that deals with sensation or other elementary
processes, but a science of the nature of the human soul as
the bearer of personal life.[3]

But the word of God is not only the source of our Christian
knowledge of man; it is also the source of man's being, as it
is the ground of all being. But the case of man is singular.
His being has a quite singular relation to the word of God:
because in man being and knowing stand in a quite singular
relation to each other. All things are created through the
word of God, and "without the word was not anything made

that was made". But only of man is it true that this word is also the light, "the true light that enlightens every man".'[4]

'It is no figure of speech or parable, but a sober account of fact to say that man lives by the word of God. Just as the new man is begotten by the word of God, so in the original divine creation[5] man is begotten by the word of God. But just as generation in the word of God implies hearing and believing the word, a spiritual relation to the word of God, so also the original creation of man in the word of God is such that man is made, not only the product, but the receiver of the word of God.'[6]

It is obvious that the word of God is spoken in two senses in this last paragraph. The new man is begotten again by Jesus Christ the word of God, but the original relation of man to the word is not for Brunner a relation to the incarnate Christ, but to the pre-existent logos. Brunner makes this clear in a passage on 'The forms in which the Word of God is expressed',[7] where he says that the revelation of God in Jesus Christ is alone the source of our power to speak of God's word. He himself is the word, and the Bible bears witness to him as the word. 'But the word of God revealed in the flesh is identical with the word in the beginning, with the word in which all that is was created, with the light that "enlightens every man, that cometh into the world." The revelation in Christ refers back to the revelation in Creation, to the word "by which all things consist", in which man also, in a very special way, has the ground of his being.'

Thus this relationship to the word which constitutes human personality can only be rightly known through faith in Jesus Christ, but it exists even where it is not understood, and where Christ was never heard of. This gift and call of God, and the power and necessity of man to respond to it, one way or the other, is the common element in all humanity. It may be worth quoting another passage in order to make the matter clear beyond doubt. 'The work of God in which the being of real man is created and maintained is the word and work of creation and preservation: but the source of our knowledge of this first work is a second work, the work and word of reconciliation and redemption, the historical word of revelation which discloses eternity. In God's second work

we acknowledge his first work as his first, as that in which
we possessed our life from the beginning.'[8] It is this first relation to God which makes man man; it is, consequently, this
which makes him morally responsible. Without it he could
not even sin, but would sink into nothingness. In this word,
though in a perverted relation to him, the heathens live
and move and have their being; and of this relationship to
God which distinguishes him from the other animals man is
somehow aware even in his blindness.

The doctrine of man set forth in this passage is questioned
by Barth in *Church Dogmatics,* Vol. III, 2, § 44. 2. Barth
is not quite clear whether Brunner holds to the view that
has been here expounded, or whether he is stating a view
similar to Barth's own, which admits of no universal confrontation between man and the pre-existent word. Barth hopes that
Brunner holds the same view as he himself does, but fears
that he does not. I would not hesitate to say that Brunner
holds the view that Barth attacks, though there are occasional
passages in *Man in Revolt* which might be interpreted in a
sense similar to Barth's own view.[9]

3 *Man's Being as Gift and Task. Faith Knows that Man's
   True Being is a Love responsive to the Creative Love of
   God*

To continue our exposition of Brunner's teaching; it is important to emphasize that the word of God spoken to man in
creation is primarily a gift and not a demand. Brunner says:
'But this responsibility . . . is not first of all a task, but a
gift; it is not first of all a demand, but life; not law, but
grace. The word which – requiring an answer – calls man,
is not a "Thou shalt" but a "Thou mayst be." The primal
word is not an imperative, but it is the indicative of the
divine love; "Thou art mine." '[10]

'This word, moreover, is given to man in such a fashion
that he must receive it, though it is not thrust on him, for that
would result in man's having a character like that of the
animals, "ready stamped". But God calls this word to man,
and man must repeat it, not making a word of his own, but of
his own initiative repeating it, "Yes, I am thine." '[11]

Since the word spoken in Creation is a light that enlightens every man, there is a certain knowledge of it present even in sinners. What remains in sin of that knowledge is an awareness of moral responsibility, though man does not rightly know to whom he is responsible, or what that obligation calls him to do.

Only Christian faith knows the true meaning and content of moral obligation, and Christian faith alone truly knows the God to whom it is due. For faith knows that in Christ God is revealed to man as love. Faith knows that that love is not a mere accidental character of the divine nature. His heart is love, for he is revealed as a trinity, whose persons love each other with an eternal love. It was the eternal will of God to create men to answer in love to the divine love for them. This response is indeed man's true nature, the destiny for which he was created. And as he fulfils this destiny, man is changed into the same image as the Lord, answering in love to God in Christ, who first loved him.

4 *The Human I-Thou Relation also Constitutive of Our Humanity*

But this responsibility in love which is the true nature of man is not expressed only towards his Maker. There is also the command to love our neighbour, and in this relationship of man to man the image of God is expressed as well as in the relationship to God. But here too the prior thing is not the command, but the gift.[12] For God does not only give himself to us in the word; he gives us our neighbour also. With the divine 'Thou' there is also given to us the human 'thou', as the condition of man's existence as a self. For man cannot be man in isolation, he can only be human in community. And this human 'thou' is thus not something accidental to our humanity, but it is the very condition of our being men. Thus we get a new definition of humanity, which finds its kernel not in the creative power of freedom, nor in cognitive reason, but in fellowship as fulfilment of responsibility.

In his own being, the triune God is love; he is creator in his relation to the world. And man's true being, when it corresponds to God's own being, as God's image on earth, is a being bound to his fellow men in love.

This thought of the image in the human I-thou relationship

is not dealt with in anything like the detail of the treatment in the case of the I-God relationship. For example there is no statement of what the formal image amounts to in the human relationship. In other words there is little definition of what constitutes the real or actual man in distinction from the true man. Sentences referring to the one alternate with sentences clearly referring to the other.[13] It is not probable that Brunner wishes, like Barth, to give a positive moral content to the universal image in the human relationship, when he has been content with a formal definition of that image in the I-God relationship.

We saw that in the I-God relationship Brunner holds that the universal image consists in man's inalienable standing before God so long as he is man, as a responsible being. We may then infer, though we are not here directly told, that the universal image *vis-à-vis* men consists in man's inalienable confrontation with his fellow men, and moral responsibility for them, a responsibility which continues even though a man should deny it or misinterpret it in a legalistic sense. And as man was made for love to God, so he is made for love to men. This is the true meaning and goal of his existence.

In the Barthian theology the relation of the man to the woman and the wider relation of the 'I' to the human 'thou' takes a larger place than in Brunner, perhaps because of Barth's exposition of Genesis 1:26, where the relation of the man to the woman is made the basis of the doctrine of the image. One may, of course, say that a great deal of *Man in Revolt* deals indirectly with this theme, and Brunner, in an article[14] can speak of his delight and surprise at finding Barth's agreement with 'one of the central thoughts of my anthropology'. This central thought is the linking of the divine-human I-thou relation with its human counterpart.

5 *The Importance of the Body for the Image*

While it is as a responsible, created being standing before God and his fellow men that man is in the image of God, the image is not *merely* spiritual, but has reference also to the body. Brunner says[15] that for many centuries exegetes of Genesis 1:26 have debated whether the image referred to man's soul or to his body. The purely spiritual conception

of God in the New Testament seemed to decide in favour
of a purely spiritual likeness. But this was only because the
thought of the exegetes was Greek rather than biblical. In
reality man in his totality as soul and body is God's image,
and in the erect posture, beauty and free glance of the human
body there is a symbol of man's spiritual nature. To hold this
is not to fall into the error of certain Christian theosophists,
who believe that God has a body. Our bodies are both a
sign of our created and limited nature, and a means whereby
we express our limited creativity and dominion in the world.

This teaching is little different from that of Calvin, who
says that while the chief seat of the divine image was in
Adam's mind and heart, yet there was no part of him in
which certain scintillations of it did not shine forth.[16]

6 Content of the Christian Revelation about Man

We have spoken of the Christian revelation as the source of
our knowledge of man. How does it speak to us of human
nature? Brunner says that it affirms three things, whose
truth we acknowledge in faith. Firstly, it tells us that man
was created by God in his own image. Secondly, it tells us
that man is in opposition to God and the image through
sin. And, thirdly, it tells us that his whole existence is qualified
by this contradiction between his origin and his opposition
to it.

We must therefore say something about Brunner's views on
Creation and the Fall. Unfortunately – and probably inevitably – these views are not altogether clear, and there is a
resultant slight ambiguity about the image.

(a) The Creation

Brunner believes that the early Church made a mistake in
taking the Old Testament story of man's integrity and Fall
as literal historical fact, the Fall being supposed to have
followed in time the life of our first parents in integrity in
Eden. Brunner claims that this picture has been made impossible by the advance of science. There is no sign at all in
primitive history of such a state of integrity, and any attempt
to push it further and further back into the past, beyond the
times about which historical evidence may be forthcoming,

s a pitiful stratagem. Nothing is lost, and much is gained,
f we give up the belief in a historical state of righteousness
and a subsequent Fall.

Thus for Brunner the terms 'origin' and 'creation' do not
refer to a date so many years BC in the case of mankind, or to
a date so many years AD in the case of the individual. He
quotes the famous passage in Psalm 139, where the writer
speaks of his own creation, and says of the Psalmist: 'He
knows of his empirical beginning; that is, his conception in his
mother's womb. But he also knows of his origin; that is,
the thought, will, and creative act of God. . . . The Christian
doctrine of the Creation . . . is the doctrine of the invisible
divine origin behind, above, and in this visible and earthly
beginning.'[17]

From this passage it might appear that the divine gift in
creation is just the gift of life itself, seen as coming from
the hand of God, and bringing us into confrontation with the
logos, a life where the primary element is the divine gift and
not the divine demand. Original righteousness would then
be the whole given element or endowment of our lives, regarded as a gift and favour of God to us from moment to
moment. Without this gift and this favour, we could not even
disobey God, we would not exist at all.

But a careful study shows that Brunner takes a different
view of original righteousness. As we have said, he is always
clear that original righteousness does not lie in the empirical
time-series somewhere in the past. Speaking of creation and
Fall together, he says, 'As we ask in vain, in relation to the
creation: How, where and when did this occur? So also is it
in the case of the Fall. Creation and Fall both lie behind the
historically accessible reality as its presuppositions which are
always present, and are already finding their fated expression
in the sphere of history.'[18]

If this be so, then inevitably original righteousness will be
spoken of as a 'past' event, though we know that when we
use this term we are not speaking literally. And if this be
true, then it is not merely the case that in our sinful moral
decisions from hour to hour we fall away from the state of
integrity which is offered to us by God, but we 'have revolted'
from God by the Fall, 'before' we make these sinful daily

decisions. And if this be so, the gift of original righteousness is regarded differently. For in this case it includes not merely the gift of God to us in our life, but also the true response of our being, which we 'once' made in harmony with God's creative word, but now can no longer make.

(b) The Fall

We must now pass on to speak in more detail about Brunner's teaching on the Fall. All men, he says, see something of the fact of the Fall, but only the Bible takes it in deadly earnest. The Bible asserts two things about sin that seem contradictory; first, that we cannot avoid sin; secondly, that we are to blame for it. Sin is a cleft that runs through our whole nature, a cleft between our original constitution and our sinful wills. This opposition is not one which we can overcome by our own efforts from day to day, as if today we could disobey God, and tomorrow obey him. Thus, behind the various sinful decisions we make from day to day, there lies a total sinful decision, which is the Fall. It is our own decision, and not something imposed on us.'[19] The view that Adam, our historical ancestor, made a sinful decision in the past which involved us in guilt, could not but rouse a sense of indignation in the ordinary man. This indignation the theologians tried to disarm by theories of the seminal presence of Adam's descendants in his loins when he sinned, and other similar devices. But the truth is that we are all our own Adam. This total decision does not determine the particular decisions of our daily acts in the manner that a logical ground determines its consequent, or as a cause determines its effects. It determines them rather in the manner that the constitution of a state determines the acts of statesmen who put that constitution into action, while they are left by it still morally responsible.[20] Brunner claims that the reality which the Church calls the Fall and Original Sin is to be found, not in the region of the empirically ascertainable, but 'behind' it, not indeed in a timeless existence, or an existence above time, but in a created original existence which, like the Creation, can only be 'seen' from the standpoint of the word of God, and not from that of experience.

(c) The Contradiction and Its Cure

But whether original righteousness be still a gift to us day by day, as Brunner sometimes seems to hint, or whether it be a gift now lost, as he explicitly states, one thing is certain. The sinner does not know of this grace or this lost integrity until he believes in Christ. And when he believes, the split in his being is both revealed, and its healing is begun. For to see the contradiction in our nature is itself the beginning of the cure, the beginning of faith.[21] And faith is only given as we acknowledge that God has removed through the cross the barrier between himself and me. In faith my relation to God is transformed, and since my very being is identical with that relation, my very being is also transformed by faith.

Faith is thus the birth of a new self. Other religions have seen something of the need for rebirth, but the fact that the cross was necessary shows that the contradiction of our nature is more radical than they understand. By faith in the cross, the contradiction is overcome, but only in principle, and fragments of the 'old man' stick to us, as fragments of its shell stick to the day-old chick.[22] But the essential 'new man' is there, and will be revealed in his perfection in eternal life.

7 Brunner's Review of the History of the Doctrine of the Image and Its Conclusions

Brunner feels that there are certain theological problems which are posed to us by the biblical teaching on the image, which have not yet received a satisfactory solution. In order to know what in his opinion these problems are, and in order to consider the answer which he offers, we must first give a short review of the doctrine, as he traces its history from its foundations in the Bible through the centuries of the Christian era. This needs not be done at great length, since this book has to a large extent followed Brunner in his analysis, and in his opinions, so that what he has to say will be familiar to the reader. When we have made this review we shall be in a better position to see how far in our opinion the problems which he grasps are the real problems, and how far his answer is the right one.

He tells us that the main problem concerning the image of God in man arises from the fact that in the Bible there are two senses in which the term is used.[23] Following von Oettingen, he makes the distinction between the formal image and the material one.[24] The first is certainly that of the three passages where the Old Testament directly mentions the phrase (Genesis 1:26-7; 5:2; 9:6). Brunner says that whatever the varying views of modern scholars may be about the meaning of these words, they are at least agreed in this, that in the Old Testament 'the term *imago dei* is always used to describe man as he now is, and never a mode of being lost through the Fall'. This sense of the phrase is, however, not confined to the Old Testament; it is also found in two passages in the New (1 Corinthians 11:7 and James 3:9).[25]

But in the New Testament there are some passages of decisive significance 'which give to the concept of the image an entirely new meaning'. There is brought into relation to the characteristic New Testament ideas of sonship of God, and likeness to him, and particularly into relationship with the doctrine of Christ as express image of God. And thus it is brought right into the centre of the New Testament message. Thus '. . . the concept of the image has been torn out of its Old Testament structural or morphological rigidity, and a basis has been given for the interpretation of the image as act, as an existence in the word of God through faith, which is fundamental to my whole work.'[26]

Brunner goes on to point out that 'the presupposition of this new, New Testament *imago* doctrine in contrast to the Old Testament doctrine, is that man's existence in the image of God is lost; that man must be restored to it, so that the whole reconciling and redemptive work of Christ can be comprehended in this central concept of renewal and perfection of God's image in man.'[27]

What is to be done to relate these two conceptions of the image? It is impossible to make a simple appeal to the Bible, and ask what it teaches, for it is clear that both doctrines lie together in it, even in the teaching of St Paul, and that no attempt is made either to reconcile or relate them. Such a relation of the concepts to each other is, Brunner believes, a necessary and important task of systematic theology. It is really the problem of the theological significance of man's humanity and, as Brunner says, 'In interpretation of the phrase "created in God's image" was decided from the first, and is decided still today, the precise relation between reason and revelation, Church and culture, faith and humanity.'[28]

For example, he continues, the answer given by Irenaeus decisively influenced the structure of Catholic theology for the next thirteen hundred years, and the Roman Church still stands on the foundation then laid. Brunner says 'Supported by the double expression "image" and "likeness" . . . the first great theologian of the early Catholic Church distinguishes a double element in man: the *image of God*, which consists in the freedom and rationality of his nature, and *the likeness* to God, which consists in his self-determination according to the divine destiny in the original righteousness as a special divine gift, the gift of supernatural communion with God. While sin has destroyed this second element, which was added to nature, man has retained the first, the human element.'

The result of this interpretation is the construction (not to be found until much later than Irenaeus) of a two storey view of the universe. It is then claimed that reason, unaided by faith, is able to build up a true natural theology, or, at least, to acknowledge it as convincing on purely rational grounds. To this rationally discovered structure there is added the supernatural second storey of revealed truth and supernatural grace. In this way there is achieved a synthesis between Christian faith on the one hand and the thought of Plato, Aristotle, and the Stoics on the other.

It was Luther who broke down this synthesis. He saw that the words 'image' and 'likeness' in Genesis were a Hebrew parallelism, and could not refer to different things. He took them both to refer to man's original perfection, and so asserted that the image as well as the likeness was lost.[29] But if we believe with Luther that man's original nature is destroyed, what have we to say of his actual corrupted humanity? Only two possibilities remain. (1) That we should refuse to regard this fallen humanity as having any relation to the original creation and image of God. (2) That we should in some way or other acknowledge the relation between the original humanity and image, and fallen man.

The Reformers took the second course, adopting the highly dubious concept of a 'relic' of the image which was held to have survived the Fall. This relic, while insufficient to enable man to perform any works that would justify him before God, yet did enable theologians to give a theological significance to the universal humanity of man, that singularity of our race which distinguishes us from the animals. And on this basis the moral responsibility and guilt of man before God were given a theological foundation, and the whole of human culture, civilization and art, were held to be a flowering from this slender root.

But this dubious doctrine of the relic, says Brunner, says both too much and too little. Too much, because it indicates that there remains in our nature an undamaged spot; and too little because it forgets that even in our sin we bear witness to our original relationship to God. It forgets that precisely in sin man manifests himself as *the* theological being, the being who 'stands before God' and is related to him: 'It was also precisely at this point that in the time of the Enlightenment, the whole Reformed Front was penetrated and rolled up.'[30]

The other alternative is the radical one which no theologian until Barth has dared to take. The Reformers, in spite of their fight with the humanism of their day, were humanists enough to know that the difference between a man and a cat[31] is no banality, but a concern of the highest theological importance. However much they emphasized the fact of the 'corruption of all man's nature', they refused to cut the cord between man's humanity and his relationship to God, and conceded that a relic of the image was left in him, Karl Barth has cut the cord.[32]

Brunner finds both these ways of dealing with the problem unsatisfactory, for the reasons given above, and claims that we must take up the problem afresh, where the Reformers left it, seeing that more recent theology has not advanced the question at all.

8. *Three Outstanding Problems: Brunner's Answers*

The problems which Brunner conceives to be outstanding at the end of this historical development are three.

Firstly, 'What is the theological significance of fallen man's humanity?' This question may also be formulated in terms of the image of God: 'What is the Old Testament image?' To ask this question is not to ask what the Old Testament writer meant by the term in Genesis 1:26, but to inquire what the reality is which he was trying to describe.

Secondly, 'What is the relationship of this universal image to the man whom God designs, the man perfected in Christ?' This question also may be differently formulated: 'What is the relation of the Old Testament image to the New Testament image?'

Thirdly, it will be seen that a subsidiary question arising out of this one is the inquiry about a point of contact: 'Does a point of contact exist in the natural man for the preaching of the gospel of grace, or is there no such point?'

We are agreed that these are three very important questions, and shall consider them in brief, asking here merely what are the answers which Brunner gives to them. Criticism of these answers will be reserved for a later chapter.[33]

(a) We have already noted that Brunner has rejected both the view that the image of God has entirely disappeared from fallen man, and the view that a relic of it remains. His own solution is as follows: 'I teach with Barth that the original image of God in man is destroyed, that the *iustitia originalis,* and with it the possibility of doing, or even willing, what counts before God as good, and consequently the freedom of the will, is lost.'[34]

But 'Even as a sinner, man can only be understood as one created originally in God's image – he is the man who lives in contradiction of that image. We must not forget that when we speak of an "image of God" and its destruction we are using a figure of speech. What we can say in clear terms is this, that the relationship to God which determines the whole being of man is not annihilated by sin, but perverted. Man does not cease to be a being responsible to God, but his responsibility is changed from a life in love to a life under the law, a life under the wrath of God.'[35]

This then is the theological significance of fallen man's humanity, this is the formal or Old Testament image, a responsible existence, a guilty existence before God. Man could not escape from this confrontation without ceasing to be man, and by his own efforts he cannot return to original righteousness, or move forward to salvation.

In a well-known and often-quoted passage Brunner writes: 'We must in fact speak of God's image in man in two senses, in a formal sense and in a material sense.'[36] The formal image signifies the superiority of man within creation, a position based on the fact that God has created man to bear his image. 'The function or calling as a bearer of the image is not only not abolished by sin, rather indeed it is the presupposition of the power of sin, and our sin itself bears a living witness to it.'[37] 'We make a distinction of category; formally the image is not infringed upon even in the least degree; – whether he sins or not, a man is a subject, and responsible. Materially, the image is completely lost, man is a sinner through and through, and there is nothing in him which is not stained by sin.'[38]

(b) The second question which is outstanding is: 'What is the relation of this formal or universal image to the material image – the man whom God designs, the man perfected in Christ?' It is clear that the answer to this question may be given by a description of what happens when a man passes from unbelief to faith, from the one image to the other. Before we discuss these matters, it is worth noting that Brunner does not for a moment believe that any of his utterances in any way infringe upon that central evangelical doctrine which Luther expressed in two words, *sola gratia,* salvation by grace alone. It is precisely on this issue that Barth criticizes Brunner, and tries to show that his doctrine, especially on the subject of the 'point of contact', vitally endangers this central truth of the gospel. We shall later have to go into this discussion, and see whether we agree with the criticism of Barth.[39]

In an impressive passage dealing with the rise of faith in the believer, Brunner argues that, in our case, faith must always include penitence for the past. Faith and penitence, however, alone are not sufficient, for faith cannot remove the barrier between God and myself which my sin has built up. My faith depends on the knowledge that what I could not do, God has done. He has removed the barrier in Jesus Christ the crucified, who comes to me, and in order to reach me, must take on himself the curse which my sin has created. The more seriously a man takes himself the more he takes his past seriously. The cross shows that God takes our past more seriously than we do ourselves. Hence, for the image to be restored in us by faith, our self, our longing for independence, must be broken. But modern man is unwilling to undergo humiliation, to pass under the Caudine Forks. And yet he must do it, must be humiliated and confess before the cross his sin, must turn right about, since there is no smooth way forward from sin to salvation, no evolution from the formal image to the material one.

And yet, when the word of God comes to a man, it comes not as a sheerly new word, but as the word that was in the beginning. So faith is never a new beginning from nothing, but a *renewal* of God's image in us. For grace, and its counterpart, faith, are the impartation of a word and the understanding thereof, a miracle, but not magic. This faith is the act of the new man, but while the new man is real, the old man remains, and has to be mortified from moment to moment, and faith is an act which needs to be renewed from moment to moment. We look forward to the day when that which we now possess in faith and in faith alone, will be ours by sight, and faith itself will be perfected and transformed in love.[40]

Such is Brunner's account of the renewal of the image, and it would appear to be essentially true to the New Testament and to reformed doctrine. It remains to give a short account of Brunner's teaching on the point of contact.

Brunner's views on the point of contact do not appear to have changed since 1933, when he expressed them clearly in *Natur und Gnade.* There he says:[41] 'No one who agrees that only human subjects, but not stocks and stones, can receive the word of God, can deny that there is such a thing as a point of contact for the divine grace of redemption. This point of contact is the formal *imago Dei,* which not even the sinner has lost, the fact that man is man, his *humanitas* in two senses . . . capacity for understanding speech (*Wortmächtigkeit*) and responsibility. Not even sin has done away with the fact that man is a being receptive of words (*Wortempfängliches Wesen*), that he and he alone is a being receptive even of God's word (*Auch für das Wort Gottes empfäng-*

liches Wesen). But this receptivity must not be understood in the material sense. This receptivity says nothing as to his acceptance or rejection of the word of God. It is the purely formal possibility of his being addressed.

'This possibility of being addressed (*Ansprechbarkeit*) is also the presupposition of man's moral responsibility.' It is only by reason of a misunderstanding, a confusion between the formal and material image, that men are able to deny the existence of such a point of contact. Just as, materially, the image of God has been destroyed, while formally it remains, so materially, there is no point of contact, but formally it is a necessary presupposition. 'The word of God does not have to create man's capacity for understanding words (*Wortmächtigkeit*). He has never lost it, it is the presupposition of his power to hear the word of God. But the word of God itself creates man's ability to believe the word of God; that is, the power to hear it *in such* a way as is only possible to the believer. It is evident that the doctrine of *sola gratia* (salvation by grace alone) is not in the least endangered by such a doctrine of the point of contact.'

In short, Brunner's teaching on this point is that this capacity of man for understanding discourse is a necessary presupposition for his belief in the word of God, but that in addition thereto there is necessary the word of God to speak to him, and the inner witness of the Holy Spirit. Man's capacity for words – or as Baillie has called it, his verbicompetence, is not at all a capacity for revelation, or for the word, and no contribution made by man to his own salvation. It is a gift of God still left, even in sin, from the gifts of creation with which God endowed man, and it is the presupposition of his moral responsibility and his guilt before God. There is in man no wholly sound element of belief or knowledge on which God can build a superstructure of faith; just as there is no act of the sinner which can in any way prepare him for the justification which God gives him by grace.

As Brunner four years later added (in 1937) the point of contact includes everything in man on which the word of God takes hold, in order to give us faith. He lays claim to that which he created, our outward presence and our outward hearing, our power of understanding logic and grammar, our rational personal existence, and above all, its centre, our knowledge of responsibility.[42]

But this situation is complicated by the fact that at the very point where contact is made, we offer the greatest resistance. For we misinterpret our responsibility to God in a legalistic manner and think that we can satisfy his claims upon us, until at last our resistance is broken, and we confess our dependence on his grace. How this happens is always a mystery. It is on God's side his gift alone, but on our side, not passivity, but the act of faith, which is the only act in which the whole of our personality is involved.

CHAPTER XIII

The Image of God in Karl Barth

1 Growth and Development of Barth's Views

The main source for the teaching of Karl Barth on the image of God in man is to be found in the third volume of his *Church Dogmatics,* and therefore our discussion will deal mainly with the two large books which constitute this volume. But Barth's views have passed through two earlier stages, and it will be worth-while briefly to mention these in order to prevent confusion.

In his *Commentary on Romans,*[1] Barth speaks of man's unity with God in the state of integrity, a unity in some respects like the unconscious unity of the child with its mother in the womb. All this is lost since the Fall, which does not belong to our time series. Sin is a lapse from man's immediate unity with God; and the world as we know it, in its various contrasts of spirit and nature, the ideal and the material, soul and body, is a result of sin.[2] Later, in the second stage of his thought, Barth equated the condition of original right-eousness with the image of God. But in the *Commentary on Romans* the term 'image of God' is not used, and it is not necessary to criticize further the very strange picture of original righteousness given above, for the good reason that Barth himself later repudiated it in no uncertain terms.[3]

The second stage of his thought is represented in the first volume of his *Church Dogmatics*[4] and the Gifford Lectures.[5] In *Church Dogmatics,* Vol. I, 1, Barth is speaking about the word of God and faith, and comes to discuss the question of the 'point of contact', a theme which was the subject of a long and rather acrid controversy, particularly between him and Emil Brunner, in the thirties. This is a question which we shall later have to treat in greater detail. At this point it is only necessary to summarize Barth's line of thought on the matter in the first volume of his *Church Dogmatics.*

Here he says that faith is not a human possibility, but a pos-

sibility lent to man by God. In faith there is a conformity
of man to God, and this is the point of contact about which
there has been so much debate. 'This point of contact is what
theological anthropology calls the image of God, with reference to Genesis 1:27. But in this connection we are unable
to understand with E. Brunner the humanity and personality
which even sinful man retains in virtue of his creation. For
the humanity and personality of sinful man can certainly not
constitute a conformity with God or a point of contact with
the word of God. In this sense, as a possibility for God
belonging to man *qua* creature, the image of God is not only,
as is said, destroyed with the exception of a few traces, but
annihilated. . . . Man's capacity for God has really been
destroyed, whatever may be the case with his humanity and
personality.'[6]

The image of God which is the point of contact is the
new-created righteousness (*rectitudo*) which is awakened by
Christ from real death to life and *thus* 'restored'. And it is
only real in faith. Man's power to hear the word of God
is a property of the image lost in Adam and regained in
Christ. And we can only say that it is a possibility because
we know in faith that it is an actuality.

In the Gifford Lectures, Barth takes as his text the Vulgate
Version of Genesis 1:27, '*Ad imaginem et similitudinem
ipsius*'. God created man 'to be the image and likeness of
himself'. This image was not some quality of man, such as
his reason or humanity. It was, rather, the divinely fixed purpose of his existence, a life of gratitude and praise to the
creator. Man has fallen away from that life in the divine
image; his very being is out of harmony with the divine
purpose, and each of his acts is a further expression of this
fundamental rebellion. The Gifford Lectures are a free commentary on the *Confessio Scoticana* of 1560, and Barth comments on the words of the Confession, 'the image was utterlie
defaced in man'. He says that the image has become a
tarnished mirror in which the glory of God can no longer be
reflected. To be man now means to be an enemy of God, and
that means to be the destroyer of our own proper glory.
'It is impossible for man to undo or make amends for his
sin' – to restore the image in himself. God's revelation in Christ

does restore man in the image, and at the same time shows the impossibility of man's doing it for himself.[7] There is no contradiction between the last two views here represented. They rather supplement each other. From *Church Dogmatics* Vol. I, 1, we gain three propositions. In brief we learn, firstly, that the image is wholly lost as a result of the Fall; secondly, that there is no point of contact for God in fallen man, and thirdly, that in faith the image and the point of contact are miraculously restored by God's word.

And in the Gifford Lectures we find emphasis laid on the fact that man was made for the image, which, since its destruction, men cannot restore. But God purposes that it should be restored, and does so in Christ.

This thought of God's continued purpose of salvation for man becomes even more central in the third and latest stage of Barth's teaching. The chief difference between it and the earlier stages is that Barth no longer holds that man's existence in the image has been lost. To anticipate for a moment the more detailed exposition on which we are about to embark, man's existence is now declared to be 'constituted by the very existence of man as such and as a creature of God. He is God's image inasmuch as he is man.'[8]

The question may be asked: Does this change mean that Barth acknowledges that he was previously wrong on a major theological issue, or is the alteration mainly one of affixing new labels? Our conclusion will be, that the change must necessarily be a massive one. General revelation seems still to be denied, but there are already considerable signs of what can only be called a point of contact for the gospel in the natural man's knowledge of himself. And Barth himself, in one of the most profound and brilliant parts of the book, engages in a task which he used to regard as outside the legitimate sphere of theology, the task of apologetics – an interpretation on Christian presuppositions of certain metaphysical views of man, with a view to showing their truth and their limitations.[9]

The fundamental change in Barth's teaching is that he now holds that the nature of man remains unchanged by his sin, since sin cannot recreate man, making him bad where he was originally good. It can, and does, conceal the real nature of man from himself and his fellows, but his true nature is not concealed from God.[10]

As the old interpretation was based on an exegesis of Genesis 1:26-7, so also the new interpretation is based on a new exegesis. Since the subject is very difficult, it may help towards clarity if Barth's new position is summarized in a number of theses. The image is seen by Barth to exist in two relationships of man, the man-woman relationship, taken as the supreme example of the relationship of man to his fellow human beings; and the man-God relationship. Let us consider first the man-woman relationship.

2 *Barth holds that man is in God's image because his relationship to the woman is like the harmonious confrontation between the Persons of the Holy Trinity*

Expounding the text above mentioned (Genesis 1:26-7),[11] he bases his new exegesis on the fact that *tzelem*, the Hebrew word for 'image' and *demuth*, the word for 'likeness', refer rather to the original than to the copy made from it. When God said 'Let us make man in our image, after our likeness', he meant that there should be in man a harmonious confrontation like that which exists in the Godhead.[12] This analogy of relation holds good in spite of all the immense differences due to the fact that man and woman are two individuals, while God the uncreated is but one individual.

What is this partnership of co-existence which has its being in God and its created analogy in man? Its nature in God is indicated by the words ascribed to him in Genesis 1:26, 'Let us make man in our image.' Here he is clearly not speaking to a heavenly council of mere angels or Elohim-beings, for the persons addressed share in the act of creation, and their likeness is the image and likeness of God. So this verse *points*, at least, in the direction of the Trinity, in which there is a divine movement to a divine other, a divine call and a divine answer. This is the creative ground of man's existence.

And what is it in man that corresponds to this call and answer within the Holy Trinity? Here Barth makes much of the fact that both in Genesis 1:27 and 5:2 the statement that man was created in God's image is coupled with the words, 'Male and female he created them.' We are comparing God and man. God is able to say that man is in his image because, as in the Deity there are an 'I' and a 'Thou' confronting each other, so also man does not exist as a solitary individual, but as two persons confronting each other. Later on Barth gives a much more precise definition of the content of the man-woman relationship, which fits it to be an image and parable of the divine nature.

3 *Man is also in God's image because he stands over against God in a way analogous to that in which the Persons of the Holy Trinity confront one another*

'Neither heaven and earth,' says Barth, 'nor water and land, nor yet the living creation from the plants upwards to the land animals, are a "Thou" which God could confront as an "I", nor could they stand to each other in the relationship of "I" and "Thou", or enter into this relationship. . . . But according to the first account of Creation man exists as such in this relationship from the beginning.'[13]

It will be noticed, if this passage is read carefully, that while man is here described as standing in the relation of confrontation to the woman, from the beginning, his relation to God is merely described as being that of one whom God could confront as an 'I'. The actual confrontation of God and man as 'I' and 'Thou' universally is not asserted, and it will later be seen that a universal present confrontation is denied. This agrees with Barth's assertion that there is no general revelation.[14] God is only known to the man to whom he is revealed in the incarnate Christ.

4 *The image of God in man is universal*

Barth says that 'the image does not consist in any particular thing that man is or does. It is constituted by the very existence of man as such, and as a creature of God. He would not be man if he were not God's image. He is God's image inasmuch as he is man.'[15] Every man is in the image of God in respect of his relationship to the woman, and every woman is in it in respect of her relationship to the man. Further, we are all in the image in respect of a certain relationship to God, which will be more particularly described later.

A result of this universality of the image is that the long discussions about 'the real man' which occupy many pages of *Church Dogmatics*, Vol. III, 2, are discussions, *ipso facto*, about the image. Indeed, generally speaking, the theme of the first three hundred and ninety pages of Vol. III, 2, is the image of God. In adopting this view of the universality of the image in man, Barth has been forced to give up the doctrine of the Reformers, according to which the image was lost at the Fall. We shall later have to inquire how he interprets the universality of the image.

5 Barth speaks from the standpoint of the Christian revelation, and his doctrine is Christological

In the first place, he refuses to accept any doctrine of man which claims to discover the essential truth about man from direct intuition or introspection. For he is convinced that sin has made man incapable of knowing the final truth about himself until he submits to be told it by God revealed in Christ.[16]

But we must define his starting point more closely still. It is in a special sense Christological. Starting from our knowledge of Jesus Christ, the Son of God, who was also man, Barth gains from a study of Christ's humanity certain criteria whereby we shall learn what human nature really is in its relations both to man and to God. And this study, he claims, will give us a norm whereby we shall be able to judge other, non-Christian, doctrines of man. It may be noted that this is not the only approach to the study of human nature which has the right to be called Christological. Any anthropology which holds that man was created for the glory of God through union with Jesus Christ by faith is also a Christological doctrine of man.

Barth's method has certain acknowledged difficulties. Apart from his divine Sonship and Nature, Christ's human nature is not identical with ours. It is indeed the same human nature which he shares with us, but in his case it is held directly from God, and, as we shall later explain more fully, our human nature is constituted by our relation to God in Christ.

175

Further, his human nature is different from ours because it is untarnished by sin, and also by the fact that in him it is revealed, while our human nature is concealed.[17]

6 *The divine image in man, in man's relation to God, must correspond to Christ's human nature in its relation to God*

For us to be sharers in Christ's humanity, there are certain qualities which our human nature must possess. If it did not have them, it would not be the same human nature as his at all, and he could not be our Saviour. (We must remember that Barth is here dealing with our human nature in its Godward relation.) He next makes an examination of Christ's human nature in its Godward relation, and gains six criteria which can be shortly summarized as follows: 'In Jesus God works in history to assert his own sovereignty and glory in such a way that Jesus' action and God's action are one. This man is for God, and has no aim but to do the Father's will.'[18]

7 *The image in man's relation to God consists in man's election in Christ, and in his faithful and obedient hearing of him as God's word, and in his willing service of God*

If our humanity is to have the necessary correspondence with Christ's, Barth asserts that it also must satisfy six criteria, which I shall summarize as follows: 'Every man belongs to God, and is the object of Christ's redemptive act wrought in history. Every man is destined for the glory of God by sharing in this redemption, and his whole being consists in the active service of God.'[19]

To say less than this about our common humanity in its Godward relation would be to make us men of a different human nature from Christ.

In all things we are dealing with man's nature, not in its relation to human beings, but in relation to God. We have indeed been speaking about every man's relation to the man Jesus Christ, but this is because God meets man through Jesus Christ. It is the special characteristic of Barth's doctrine of man, that he will have nothing to do with any thought of the relation of man to God through the unincarnate logos in a general revelation such as Brunner postulates. If man is to be related to God at all, it must be through the *incarnate*

Son, Jesus Christ.

It will be seen that there is a difficulty here. Crudely put, it is this: If man is to be defined as the one who is in relation to God through the incarnate Christ alone, then what about the men who died before he was born? Were they not men?

Barth used two notions here to explain his thought, and the first goes some way towards clearing up the matter. It is the notion of election.[20] Man's being depends on his election by God in Christ, long before any man came into existence. And one must agree with the soundness of this thought, admitting that the reason that we are men today is that God thought of us long ago, and planned that we should be united in blessedness with Christ. Thus all men are brought into relation with God through Jesus Christ, though for many it is an unconscious relation. Each is 'my brother for whom Christ died'. But a number of other difficulties arise. If man can only be related to God through God's election of him in Christ, and if, as is obvious, nothing of this election could be known to men who lived in the past or who live today beyond the reach of the gospel, then how are we to interpret the sense of moral obligation which such men certainly felt and feel? That they did and do feel obligation, Barth will not deny. Nor will he deny that their obligation is seen by the Christian to be an obligation to God. Yet of this God, *ex hypothesi*, they could know nothing, and their sense of a transcendent reality or person to whom it was due was purely illusory! There is some lack of clarity in Barth's views on the matter of a knowledge of God among the heathen,[21] but there is a passage in his *Church Dogmatics* which probably represents the main drift of his teaching.[22] Here he says: 'The highest responsibility to which a man can be called outside of the revelation in Christ is the responsibility of taking himself seriously.' This position is almost too paradoxical to be taken seriously.

But there is a further, and much graver, difficulty ahead. The real man is he who is not merely elect and the object of the salvation in Christ, but the man whose whole life is service of God. Surely this service implies a knowledge of God. Barth says[23] that both the creatures and the human race are called upon to praise God. We do not know *how* the other creatures praise him, and we do not know of any other creature which is *responsible* for praising him. But man's gratitude, 'and his alone, consists not only in his obligation and submission to his divine Benefactor, but in his binding and submitting himself to him, and finding therein his life'. But if God is known only in the revelation in Christ incarnate, then those who live outwith the reach of it in space and time cannot be real men.

The difficulty becomes even more clear when Barth introduces the second notion by means of which he hopes to make clear the picture of the real man. The real man is he who hears the word of God in Christ. And when Barth mentions this, he will allow of no hearing that would leave the man an alternative choice of not listening or not obeying. The real man is not a cave-dweller who might choose instead to go fishing or hunting. Hearing is the hearing of faith, and this entails glad obedience to the word.[24]

But surely, to press an obvious point, those men who have heard with their outward ears the preaching of the word, and have not obeyed, are real men. Do they not share in human nature? If the image be universal, as Barth has conceded, how can they be men, and in the image?

This is a great difficulty, and I cannot be satisfied that Barth has met it. In his long discussion the argument seems to be as follows.[25] Sin, however much power it has to hide our nature, cannot destroy it, or recreate it in a perverted form. Therefore what men really are, is not what they appear to be, but what God sees them to be. And since they are all elect in Christ, God sees them as such, as responding to Christ in faith. Sin, which is not a part of nature, has *actually* come in, and therefore grace, which is also not a part of nature, is necessary to reveal our true being and bring it to perfection.

Now this teaching surely confuses the *real* man with the *true* man. Every Christian theologian would agree to the proposition that the true man is he who is renewed in the image of God through Christ, and loves God and his neighbour.

178

But Barth asserts these things not of the true man, rather of the real man. The title of the sub-paragraph which we are considering is 'Real Man'.[26] Thus nothing is left to say of the man who does not love God, save that he is unreal. This teaching seems in danger of making sin, not a monstrosity – it does not need to be *made* that – but a logical monstrosity, which Barth is forced to express by such phrases as 'Godlessness is consequently not a possibility of human existence, but its ontological impossibility.'[27] Surely an ontological impossibility is sheer nonsense.

And further very strange inferences must be drawn from this position. Here is one of them. 'In the free fulfilment of his responsibility before God – and this is his being as a creature, man is actually good and not bad. Even his sin cannot alter this. . . . If the real man is hidden from us . . . if we cannot recognize his traces in ourselves and in others and in the whole of human history, yet is it in God's sight as if he were not lost. . . . We have let God's word say to us who and what the real man is.'[28] Now if we say this of the real man, and not of the true man, we must assume that though no trace of him can be seen in us or in anyone else, he is really there in all men. And this real man is one, who by definition both knows and loves God. Yet he lives in the same skin with the man we see who, unless he is a believer, knows nothing at all of God. Surely paradox cannot go this length without landing in absurdity![29]

8 *The image of God in man in his relation to the woman, and his human neighbours in general, consists in a bond of willing helpfulness which is man's by nature and not by grace*

We must now deal with the second relationship in which man's nature exists and consists. Man can sin, and does, but there can be no absolute dualism between his nature and his divine destiny; there must be at least a correspondence between them, or God's creative act would have been foiled by sin. So once more we must find out what constitutes man's human nature. But this time we shall be considering man's relation to his fellow men, and not his relation to God.

Again we must build on a Christological foundation, so we must again consider the humanity of Jesus; this time in its relation to other men.

A theological doctrine of man must show that Jesus is the man who is wholly dedicated to other men. A superb piece of New Testament theology here follows.[30] The humanity of Jesus is the image of God. We cannot, however, find God's image in other men as it is in him.[31] For, even were some other man sinless, there could come to no other man the call to be the redeemer of all men. And yet the nature of man for whom Christ died cannot be wholly other than Christ's human nature. What is the humanity which makes all men capable of the covenant of grace? Be it noted that it is no merit of man's, and no contribution towards man's salvation. That depends wholly on God's free grace in Christ. Barth at last defines this humanity common to all men. It must be noted that it is wholly of nature, and not of grace. It entails four points:

Firstly, that I should see my neighbour as a real man.

Secondly, that I should speak to him, and receive his answer as a real answer.

Thirdly, that I should help him.

And, fourthly, that I should do these three things gladly.[32]

Since all this belongs to nature and not to grace, we must not be surprised that many unbelievers are more human than many Christians; though grace does repair human nature, and makes men more human than they were before. This human nature is in fairly good repair, even after the Fall, though sin does pervert it.

A number of recent theological writers have taken a certain delight in saying that all natural love, and all love outside of the Christian revelation and its sphere of action, partook of the nature of *Eros,* a hunger for satisfaction and the stilling of desire, whether this hunger was earthly and sensual or refined and spiritual. With this they contrasted *Agape,* the miraculous love which descends to sacrifice itself for the sake of the worthless; a love that only entered the world with the revelation that culminated in Christ.

It will not do, says Barth, to divide all love into these two kinds.[33] There is a third possibility, which is natural, and not supernatural, the love constituted by our common humanity. Nor, indeed, is *Eros* so black as it has been painted.

We have not the time to go into this discussion, but it is worthy of a careful study, and is indeed one of the most liberating things in the whole book, showing Barth as a great humanist and liberal, in the best sense of the word. That there has always been this side to him is shown by the wonderful essays on Novalis and Rousseau in his strangely entitled book *Protestant Theology in the Nineteenth Century*.[34]

Barth continues his argument thus: sin perverts humanity and Christian love is needed to restore and perfect human nature. In this relationship of man to woman and man to man the universal image of God does in fact visibly function to some extent. And we must not be disturbed by the fact that non-Christians like the heathen Confucius, the atheist Feuerbach and the Jew Martin Buber, have said things about man's humanity which sound very like the statements of Christian faith.[35]

There are certain difficulties caused by Barth's determination to choose the relationship of the man to the woman as the constitutive relation of our personal being. He says: 'Man is alone among animals and in the whole creation in this, that he stands continually and will stand in his life-relationship (as man and woman) before God.' And again: 'A human being will in any case only be such before God and among his kind upon these conditions, that it is as a man in relationship to the woman, or woman in relationship to the man.'[36]

Now, it is too obvious to need emphasis that the distinction between male and female is not something peculiar to mankind. And if it be argued that it is not this distinction which Barth has in mind, but our whole responsible existence as man in relation to woman, then we may surely still object that it is the personal element in this situation and not the sexual which is distinctive, though admittedly the two elements are singularly fused.[37]

Barth does himself later admit that women in a nunnery can have a real personal existence, while Goethe with his ocean of mistresses failed to achieve a fully personal relation with others. He explains that the relation of man to woman of which he speaks is not confined to the relation between man and wife, but covers all the relations between men and women, such as that between mother and son, or father and daughter, or brother and sister. While the relationship is at its highest and most difficult and dangerous in the bond between husband and wife, it is also at its most rewarding, and the whole nexus of personal relations between one sex and the other is an example of personal relations *par excellence*. This we may be willing to grant him.

He will also certainly claim that here he is not spinning an airy piece of speculation, but writing solid biblical theology, interpreting, in fact, Genesis 1:27 and Genesis 5:2, where the image is in both cases defined further by the words 'male and female he created them.'

The reader may be inclined to doubt whether this sequence twice repeated, is more than accidental; whether the writer had in his mind the idea that the image consists in the mutual confrontation of the man and the woman before God. But we would do well to concede that the singular honour of man described in these passages does in fact consist in such a confrontation of persons with each other and with God, together with all that is implied by that confrontation. It is however rather difficult to harmonize this passage in Barth with what seems to be the main drift of his teaching, that there is no general revelation, and no universal confrontation of man with God, and no knowledge of God for man save in the incarnate Christ.

Whatever the interpretation that the author of 'P' placed on his own words, we will probably be right in holding that St Paul saw in these verses a prophecy of the union of Christ with his Church. Barth draws our attention to this. In the relationship of the man to the woman, Paul sees a great mystery. For our destiny is to be united with God through Christ. As united with him we are not isolated individuals, but members of the Church, the Bride of Christ. Thus, together with him, united to him by faith, we are the image of God, and he is the image of God, but not alone, not in isolation from his Church. He is also God's image along with

182

the woman that belongs to him, that is, along with the community of the redeemed.[38]

Thus the relation of man to woman, and of man to man, is a parable and earnest of the relation of the Church to God in Christ. The subject of the analogy, Barth says, is not a being, or a capacity, like the capacity of reason which the Roman Catholics assert to be the image of God in man. We compare two inalienable relations, the man-woman relation, and the man-God relation. The first is a bond of nature, and the second a bond of grace, and the first is an image of the second. And the communion of the Church with God in Christ is an image of the communion between the persons of the Holy Trinity. So that indirectly the natural communion of man with woman, or of man with his friend, is an image of the nature of God himself, and this image is universal. And, unlike the image in the Godward relationship, it is more or less open to men's sight, being neither concealed nor wholly destroyed by sin.

9 General Criticisms

There are one or two points of criticism which must be made here. There are long passages in the book on the image in the manward relationship, which are among the noblest things that have been written in theology for many years. But one feels inclined to ask why does Barth speak so generously of men in their actual relations to each other? It would indeed have been an immense impoverishment of the book had he not done so. But he might have spoken of the image in the man-woman relationship as being concealed wholly by sin in the man-woman relationship in somewhat the same manner as he believes it to be concealed in the Godward relationship. Perhaps he feels the more entitled to speak in this generous manner about man's love even in these days of Nazism and Stalinism, because he does not believe in a general revelation of God. If he did believe in such a general revelation he might not find himself so far away from the position of St Thomas, who spoke of a natural human power of remembering, loving and understanding God, although this was not to be taken as any contribution on man's part towards his own salvation![39] But still we must ask the question: How is it that 'the wiser among the wise of this world'[40] can see so much of the reality of human nature without any insight into man's relation to God? How can that nature be so largely revealed in the one relationship, and so wholly concealed in the other? Is this consistent with a doctrine of man which holds that human nature cannot be rightly understood save when seen in its relation to God?

10 *Comparison of Barth with Brunner*

It will be worth-while in closing this chapter to draw attention to the resemblances and differences between Barth's views to-day on the image and those of Emil Brunner. There is a startling amount of agreement between them. They are agreed on the following points: Firstly, the image is not to be looked for in the isolated self, but in an active relation of man to his neighbour and to God. Secondly, the image is universal, in the sense that it is not destroyed by sin. In a manner of speaking, therefore, Barth and Brunner agree that every human being is in the image, though they do not mean quite the same thing when they say so. For Brunner it is the formal image or, as we have called it, the Old Testament image, which is universal. It is so in both the man-man and man-God relationships. For Barth too the image is universal in both relationships in which man stands. In the man-woman relationship it exists in a different manner from the manner in which it exists in the man-God relationship. Thirdly, both start from a Christian standpoint, and neither of them indulges in natural theology, or tries to build up his doctrine of man on insights available to the intuition or introspection of the natural man. Further, both hold a Christological view of man, although their approach is not the same. Brunner holds that man was essentially created for the glory of God through union by faith with Christ in the Church. Barth agrees with this, but has a Christological standpoint peculiar to himself, not so much because he defines Christ's human nature and then defines man's essential human nature as necessarily corresponding thereto, but because the definition given to man's real human nature in its Godward dimension is such that it is very hard to see how it can be brought into any relation with human nature as it actually exists in the world.

This is the most striking feature, and also the greatest difficulty, in his teaching on man.

In discussing the resemblances between the two thinkers, we have already been forced to mention one or two of the differences. Further differences are as follows:

Firstly, Brunner believes that every man has a direct relation to God in the general revelation, or as he calls it in his later work, the revelation in creation. This is a relation to the word, the light which enlightens every man. We may call it a relation of confrontation, though Brunner does not use the word. It is this relation which makes man man. It is the ground of human responsibility, though outside of the revelation in Christ incarnate it is not truly interpreted or understood.

Barth will not consider such a view for a moment, holding that a relation to a so-called word like this, which would leave man the freedom to choose obedience or disobedience, would make the possibility of human sin have its ground in God's word, which is unthinkable.[41] Secondly, Brunner believes that man's relation to God in creation gave him freedom, and that this freedom has not been utterly destroyed by the Fall. Though man has no longer the freedom or power to avoid sin, there remains to him a certain power of alternative choice. Barth will not allow any theological significance to such a freedom. For him the only freedom worthy of any consideration at all is the freedom to do God's will.

Thirdly, Brunner sees in the Bible two senses of the image, the formal or Old Testament image, and the material or New Testament image. The formal image is universal, and the material one peculiar to those who have faith in Christ.

For Barth there is but one image. But in the relation between the man and the woman, where there is actual confrontation and human love, he sees a parable and promise of the other relationship of men to God in Christ, of the church, the Bride, to the Bridegroom. In both relationships the image is universal.

Fourthly, Barth lays a special emphasis on the man-woman relationship, while Brunner speaks rather of the relation to one's neighbour, without laying emphasis on the sex difference.

Where the original work is so long and complex as Barth's it is difficult to give a condensed account such as has been here attempted, without conveying an impression of aridity. But it is only fair to say that the impression the book itself makes is one of great freshness and richness, for all its immense length and frequent obscurity. It will probably be the verdict of later times that this is one of the great theological works of the last half-century.

CHAPTER XIV

Theological Conclusions

Having reached the end of our long historical inquiry, we must now attempt to give our own conclusions. It will make a good starting point if we try to reach a theological definition of the Old Testament image, the universal humanity of man.

1 *Our Agreements and Disagreements with Barth about the real Man*

In Genesis 9:6 we are told that 'Whoever sheds the blood of man, by man shall his blood be shed; for God made man in his own image.' God made man in his own image, and, even in a sinful world, that image still exists, and every man is in God's image. We have seen that Karl Barth now agrees with this view. He says of man's existence in the image, 'It does not consist in something that man is or does. It exists because man exists himself and, as such, exists as God's creature. He would not be man, were he not God's image. He is God's image by being man.'[1]

We have not, however, been able to agree with the way in which Barth develops his theory. While admitting the image to be universal, he so defines it, and the nature of the real man, whom he equates with it, that all men who do not obey Christ's call to faith in him are inevitably implied to be unreal. This is a result of defining man's existence *vis-à-vis* God exclusively in terms of a relation to the incarnate Christ; a relation, not merely of election, but of actual glad obedience and faith.

Therefore we shall be forced to go back and seek a definition of the image, the universal humanity, which is in accord with the passages in Genesis which we have so often discussed.

While we disagree with Barth's own definition, there is, however, much that we can learn from a long interesting passage called 'Phenomena of the Human' in *Church Dog-matics*, Vol. III, 2.[2] This passage is a study and criticism of the various criteria brought forward by different writers as the distinctive marks of human nature.

Barth here claims that no thinker who, by a process of abstraction, severs the connecting link between God and man, and looks at man apart from this relationship, will ever have a right understanding of human nature. An example of such abstraction is to be found in the writings of the theologian Polan, who defines man as 'an animal gifted with reason'. It cannot be denied that Polan brings in God at a later stage, declaring him to be man's creator and God. But it is too late. The impression is left that the relationship to God is an afterthought, and thus not of essential importance.

The subject of Barth's search is something that marks man's special character, something which distinguishes him from all other creatures. We are looking for the real man, who 'cannot be drowned in his world', and this man is in fact only to be found when we consider him as the subject of history which has its ground in God's revelation to us.

All other criteria, though interesting, do not describe the real man, but only phenomena of humanity, or possibilities of our human nature. The singularity in man which they disclose is only a relative singularity. Only when we know already the real man can we understand these phenomena rightly. Then they become for us 'symptoms of humanity'. Barth elsewhere speaks of them as commentaries which can only be truly understood when we are in possession of the text which they set out to interpret – the real man. He further describes man's real being as a historical being, and we have already seen how he more particularly defines it; the real man is one who, confronted with God in Christ, loves and obeys him. We have seen cause to reject this conclusion, and have given our objections to it above.

But we can accept much of Barth's reasoning here, especially the assertion that the various sciences take as their subject matter certain powers and aspects of man's nature. When we make man the subject of chemical, psychological, or logical inquiry, we make certain abstractions. In all these disciplines we attain a certain and varying amount of success without taking into consideration man's relation to God. We may even, as existential philosophers following Jaspers, study man in his relation to the transcendent, without filling in the form of that concept with the content of Christian belief about God.

But we must never forget that we are making abstractions, and that man is not merely a body where chemical processes are going on, nor a physical being where psychological processes are happening, nor is he merely a reason that follows the laws of logic. In short we would say that the real man is a historical being, as Barth does, but we would define a historical person as 'one who is faced by God and has to make responsible decisions before him'. And we would not confine that confrontation to a meeting with God in Christ incarnate, nor would we say that the decision is necessarily one of love and obedience. We would claim that every man is a historical being, inasmuch as, possessed of certain powers and endowments, he stands inescapably before God, and must respond to him in the acts of his will.

It is true that the various disciplines which deal with aspects of man's nature tell us things of importance which are not the direct concern of faith. But the personal relation to God is more essential. Brunner made this point when he wrote: 'Man's relation to God is not to be understood as a function of his reason, but his reason is to be understood as a function of his relation to God. Responsibility is not to be added as an attribute, as an enrichment, to the rational man, but reason is from the first implanted in man for the purpose of receiving God's Word.'[3]

Faith sees man as a responsible person in God's presence; biology may consider him as a metabolic system, and the philosopher as a reasoning being. These are aspects of the real man. How are we to know that what faith sees is the result of a deeper insight than that of biology? We may say that many of man's other functions are shared by other members of the animal kingdom, while moral responsibility is, so far as we know, the possession of man alone. But this fact does not entitle us to think of it as more real and central in man's being than anything else. Our judgment is a judgment of faith, which cannot expect to be convincing to those who do not share the Christian view of God and man.[4]

But when we have thus described provisionally the real man, we have not finished with him. Just as man is confronted by God in a special manner, so also he is related to God's purpose in a special manner. His real being is related in a singular manner to his true being. There is no doubt a certain parallel here with other creatures, which may and do fall short of their true nature, though in a different manner from man. But faith sees man's actual being continually in the light of a special destiny, which is shared, so far as we know, by none of the other earthly creatures. This destiny we assert to be the union of man with God in Christ by obedience and faith. Only in the light of this destiny can actual, real man be fully understood. ⎟ START

2 Barth's definition of human nature in its relationship to God fails to face the problem of sinful man's relationship to God

It may be asked by advocates of the Barthian theory of the image, why we are not satisfied with his view. He admits that the image is universal,[5] but refuses to speculate on its character as Troeltsch and others have done, 'without further considering the text, by means of concepts snatched out of the air, according to the requirements of their contemporary anthropology'.[6] Why should we not be satisfied, like Barth, to allow the biblical definition of the image to stand, 'male and female he created them',[7] and define the image accordingly, as 'quite simply the existence in confrontation of I and thou'?[8]

If this really were Barth's view, we would give it our hearty assent, for it is almost exactly what we are trying to say. The universal image is a relationship of confrontation between 'I' and 'thou', existing, so to speak, in two dimensions, between man and God and between man and his human counterpart. But one must remember that every man stands in this double relationship, the sinner as well as the saint. And so one would have to consider the existence in confrontation in what must be called a quite formal way, irrelevant of its content, irrelevant of the question whether the man loves God and his fellow human being.

190

But it is clear, even in *Church Dogmatics,* Vol. III, 1, that more than such a formal relationship is meant. This man is 'capable of dealing with God and making covenant with God', he 'stands in natural communion with God',[10] and later we are told that 'This is the God who as creator is free for man, and the being that corresponds to God is the man who as creature is free for God.'[11]

In short, it is not every man who is here regarded as existing in the image. The image is no longer pictured as universal in the humanity of a sinful world. That man is in the image who loves God and obeys his call in Christ gladly. Thus Barth escapes the whole difficult problem of the Old Testament image. Like Luther, he starts in fact from the New Testament image, and fails to face the problem which the existence of the image in sinful man poses to theology. Thus Barth does not have to worry with such devices as the relic of the image or the formal image. He escapes the need by the desperate device of asserting that the New Testament image is present in all men though wholly concealed by sin. Luther came to the conclusion, it will be remembered, that, since the Fall, the image has disappeared without trace in sinful man. Barth used to hold this view, which has the disadvantage of contradicting the clear evidence of the Old Testament.

3 *Discussion of the Concepts of the 'Relic' and the 'Formal Image'*

In talking as we did a short time ago about the real man, we were in fact describing the Old Testament image; the humanity which we share with all men. Since Barth's attempt to solve the problem of the Old Testament image is as useless as Luther's, we must now go on to consider two theological concepts used to describe that universal humanity: Calvin's doctrine of the relic and Brunner's concept of the formal image. Both these terms attempt to describe what binds fallen man to God. Calvin believed in a historical Fall in the past; Brunner does not, but holds that we must talk of it as if it were in the past, while recognizing the inadequacy of the analogy, since the Fall is not a fact on the historical plane at all. Calvin taught that there remains in man today a relic of his original humanity, while Brunner teaches that the form of the image of God remains, while its original content has entirely disappeared. Both these concepts have been sternly criticized.

Let us first consider Calvin's belief that a relic of man's original endowment remains after the Fall, and that this is what constitutes his humanity. Brunner is right in saying that this notion is dangerous, both because it says too much, and because it says too little – too much because it suggests that there is some kernel of man's nature which remains uncorrupted by sin; and too little, because it forgets that, even in his sin, man stands in relation to God, and is the theological being *par excellence*.[12]

But it should be remembered that, in point of fact, Calvin did not forget either of these dangers. Indeed, the doctrine of man which he expounds is extremely like Brunner's own. He was certainly in no danger of thinking that there was some area of human nature which was untarnished by sin; and in general, he hardly ever forgets that, even in his sin, man stands in personal relation to God. Perhaps there is a hint of such a lapse in the passage where he says: 'There is more worth in all the vermin in the world than in man, for he is a creature where the image of God has been effaced. . . . There is nothing in him but sin, and we have so gone to the devil, that he does not only govern us, but has us in his possession, he is our prince.'[13]

Brunner himself has suggested the use of the terms 'form' and 'content' as a substitute for Calvin's doctrine of the relic. The content of the original image of God is entirely lost since the Fall, though the form is not in the least influenced.[14] John Baillie's criticism that you cannot have form without content is perhaps a little facile,[15] since Brunner would not deny that there is a certain content given with the formal image under conditions of sin.[16] He would only claim that the original content has been wholly lost. In both cases we may say that man, whether in a state of original righteousness, or as a sinner, is in the presence of God, and that his life is inescapably related to the word, as an answer to a creative call.

Baillie is quite justified in asking whether the terms 'matter' and 'form' are suitable to the reality which we are here describing. We must, of course, remember that no figure we choose will be adequate to the reality, for there is nothing else quite like personal being. But it would appear that the outcry which has been raised against Brunner has hardly been justified, for, like Calvin, he does not seem to have been misled by the terms which he has used. Like Calvin, he has kept his eye on the reality which he is seeking to define. He has not been misled by the admittedly inadequate figure which he uses to describe our fallen humanity, but has kept his eye on the scriptural picture which is painted in the revelation.

It was, of course, Barth's contention in *Nein! Antwort an Emil Brunner* that Brunner's doctrine of the formal image still retained by fallen man was not nearly so harmless as Brunner thought, and that it implied a 'capacity for revelation'. And this 'capacity for revelation' either meant that man was a man and not a cat,[17] or a lump of lead or a tortoise,[18] in which case it was a harmless and theologically insignificant remark; or else it meant that a man could contribute to his own salvation, as a swimmer who was being rescued might help the man who was saving him by a few strokes of his own.[19] Barth thus claims that Brunner's doctrine of the formal image does mislead him, since it endangers the principle that we are saved by grace alone and not by works.

With this criticism I cannot agree. The fact that a man is a man and not a lump of lead is precisely what Brunner teaches by his doctrine of the retention of the formal image. And this is a precondition of salvation, but no contribution of man towards his own salvation. Thus it is no theological bagatelle, as Barth would make it. Barth is led to his error in thinking man's humanity to be either utterly unimportant or else a contribution to salvation, by his failure to accept the fact that there is such a thing as grace of creation. It is this grace which, in spite of man's sin, keeps man human, and its purpose is, not merely to keep man human, for were this its aim, it might well be intended merely to preserve man for future damnation: as Barth puts it, 'It might be our condemnation to a kind of antechamber of hell.'[20] The purpose of grace of creation is to retain man in God's presence and in existence as man, so that he may have the chance of sharing in God's salvation. And this is the purpose of the universal image and confrontation.

Thus, in spite of Barth's criticism, it must be held that Brunner's doctrine of the formal image, whatever its limitations and defects may be, does not lead him any further into heresy than Calvin was led by the doctrine of the relic.[21]

4 *Our Own Attempt to Define the Universal Human Image in Its Relation to God*

Our agreement, it will be seen, is with Brunner and Calvin rather than with any other writers. We may now try to consider further the nature of man's sinful humanity and its relationship to God. We shall try to keep our eyes on scripture to save us from error. We shall be using some concepts which are not given us by scripture, but we are trying to do justice to the truth shown to us by scripture.

There is a further danger here that in venturing out on such a dangerous minefield a writer whose philosophical armour is thin may be blown up and injured, if nothing worse befall him. However, though the attempt must be inadequate, it seems right that someone should try to make it, and any mishaps that may happen in the next part of this chapter do not invalidate what has been said thus far.

In defence, we may say that even Barth in his work of the doctrine of man is not perhaps so severely dependent on scripture as might seem. Had not Martin Buber written *I and Thou, Church Dogmatics*, Vol. III, 2, might have had a different shape. Further, the four criteria which Barth sets up as the minimum requirements for a humanity of which Jesus Christ could be the Saviour might be criticized as 'arbitrarily chosen out of the air' rather than deduced from the fact that Christ is to be the Saviour of mankind, and that to be saved by him man must possess these qualities at least. One is glad that Barth has painted so generous a picture of mankind, but could not Christ have saved a humanity whose fallen state was less attractive?

In speaking as we have done of man's original righteousness, it is not necessary to assume that man once lived, at some time in the historical past, in such a state of integrity. Nor is it indeed necessary to assume, as Brunner does, that we must talk as if the Fall were in the past, though we know that it did not occur so many thousand years ago, but 'was' an event on, so to speak, a different plane.

We may contrast the image as it exists in sinful men, first, with that existence which God willed for men in the beginning, which our sin has prevented us from attaining. And, on the other hand, we may contrast the image as it exists in sinful men with the image which God renews through grace and faith in Christ. In both cases we shall be making the same contrast, for Christ comes to restore us to our place in God's original plan of salvation.

It appears that the Christian existentialism of Brunner helps us to understand the nature of man, and therefore we shall adopt a great deal of his account in our reflection upon man. It will be a help to clarity if we number the points in our discussion, remembering all the while that we are looking at the nature of man with a view to defining the Old Testament or universal image of God.

(a) Every man is in relation to the logos, and that relation is one of confrontation. This confrontation involves an act of response on the part of man. We have already seen that as Christian students of the doctrine of man we must think of him as a creature bound to his maker. And we have biblical authority for bringing man into relation with the logos. Every man is indeed in relation to Christ, not only in the sense that God plans to save him through faith in Christ, but also in the sense that his very being is confronted by the second person in the Holy Trinity. Each human being stands continually in the presence of the logos in a manner of which the presence of one human being to another is only a feeble analogy.

The prologue to the Fourth Gospel speaks of the word who was in the beginning, who was with God, and was God, through whom all things were created. He is the light of men – a light that has shone through the ages, and has not been overcome by the darkness. And this word became flesh in Jesus Christ.[22]

In the first chapter of Colossians, St Paul is obviously pursuing a similar line of thought, though he does not use the term 'word' to describe either the pre-existent or the incarnate

Christ. In this chapter he says that all things were made by
Christ, and for him, and all cohere in him.[23]

This confrontation is compatible with a very profound
ignorance of God on the part of man, and also compatible
with a will opposed to God. Thus when Christ saves us, he
saves what had always been his, though it had fallen from
him, and he saves what had been in his presence all the
time, though as Augustine says, 'Its misfortune was not to be
with him as he was with it.'

Brunner takes up the clue given by John and Colossians,
and amplifies the hint here given. God creates us all through
the word, he maintains, and our relation to the word is a
singular one, unlike that of things, which are also created
by him. Our life itself is an answer to that creative word of
God, a word spoken in response to that divine word, a deciding, responsive, responsible existence. Thus a Christian existentialism is built up on the basis of a New Testament doctrine.

It will be seen that while we have biblical authority for the
belief that man's very being is created through the word, the
unincarnate logos, who is spoken to us by God, as on the
day of creation, there is no direct scriptural authority for
regarding man's being as an answering word.

But, as Brunner says, something of the kind is implied by
the teaching of the New Testament. 'Through the word God
creates man, but, as all the passages in the New Testament
which treat of this *imago dei* agree, he creates man in such
a fashion that a claim is made in this very act of creation
on man's active reception, his hearing, understanding, and
faith. . . .' Man's being is essentially of the nature of a
response to God.

Brunner remarks further that among the created beings in
the universe there are two very different kinds. First, there
are those whose nature is, as it were, stamped upon them as
an image is stamped upon a coin. These are turned out of
the creator's hand complete; they are what they should be,
and they remain so, even though they may go through a
course of natural development. And, secondly, there are
God's human creatures, whose existence is not a passive one.
These the creator holds by him in his workshop, and in his
hand.

The peculiar mode of existence of persons is well described in a further passage, where Brunner says that man is a sinner, but because this 'is' refers to man, it must not be confused with any other 'is'. Man's being never ceases to be a 'being in decision'. Even as a sinner, man is not a psychological or rational object qualified in this manner or that. Man 'is' not a sinner in the same manner as the elephant 'is' a mammal, or the sum of the angles of a triangle 'is' a hundred and eighty degrees. In the copula of this predicate, in the word 'is', there lies concealed the whole problem of humanity, while the philosophers and theologians have sought for it mostly in the predicate. To be a sinner means to be involved in revolt against God. Sin never becomes a quality or a substance. Sin is, and remains, act. It is worth-while to say, what Brunner does not mention, that there must be some analogy between the act whereby a person is, or exists, and the act whereby a thing exists, or else the same word 'is' could not be used of both.

(b) While man's mode of existence is his act of response to God's creative call, man's being is not reduced to act or relation. As endowment, man's being is a substance which exists in responsive act to God, and in personal confrontation with him.

The claim is sometimes made by theologians influenced by existentialism that man's being is nothing but act, and that if we think of it in terms of substance, we are thinking of persons in terms only suited to our thought about things. It seems clear from the following quotation that Brunner does not belong to this school of thought: 'The necessity of decision, the inevitability of deciding in every moment, is the distinguishing feature of man's being. It is, therefore, in contrast to all sub-human being, being-in-action, self-positing, thinking, and willing being, the kind of being which is being-for-self. But at the same time in contrast to all divine Being, it is not *actus purus*, not self-sufficient, not originally self-positing, but "answering" responsive, responsible being. . . . It is posited by God as the creaturely counterpart of his divine existence for himself, the counterpart which can answer God, and only in this answer fulfils God's creation, or destroys it.'[25]

Yeago

Brunner indeed rejects the conception of man as a substance which can exist independently, and to which a relation to God can be added as an accident. But to claim this is not to deny that man can be truly a substance. The proper antithesis here is not between substance and act, but between persons and things, or between person-substances and thing-substances. If personal being is reduced to decision or act or relation, the objection is perfectly justified that one cannot think of a decision which is not the decision of a subject, and that relations are meaningless without related terms. This does not mean that the terms can always exist outside of the relations. It will be remembered that our contention is that in the God-man relation, man cannot exist as man outside of his relation of confrontation with God. In response to God's creative act, he exists. But were our life nothing but decisions following the one upon the other, there would be no personal continuity. Our being would be like a pearl necklace without a thread. We must admit that this figure of the self as continually responding to God's call, while true, is not exhaustive. In dealing with matters of this kind one figure must be used to correct and complement another. There is perhaps even an element of error in Brunner's figure, since we do not, as he claims, actually decide in every moment. But we are responsible for every waking moment, and our being is essentially a being in decision. But there are other aspects of our being to which A. Farrer has called attention in his remarkable book, *Finite and Infinite*. There are long-term projects of the human self, which God makes possible by the gift of freedom and there is also an element of creativity in the human self. This forces us to say that, while God destines us for union with himself in Christ, the detail of the picture is in part left to our own creativity. If this aspect be left out of account, then the existence of man is too much reduced to a soulless, responsible dependence like that of a stenographer on her employer's dictation. In these other aspects, where the self is regarded as a creator and as the fulfiller of a project, the substantiality of the self is also to be discovered, as well as in the act of moral decision. But the confrontation with God runs on, in all our projects, and in all our creativity.

(c) The self may be regarded as endowment in action, or

as gift and response. Because endowment is actual in response, we can see the link between views like those of Augustine and Aquinas, which regard the image as a power, and the modern views, which regard it as an existence in confrontation between persons.

There is general agreement that in the self of every human being there is something which comes to the man from without, something which he did not create, and also something which he does, and must, create from moment to moment. In his acts he both draws on that which is given him, and at the same time expresses and creates himself. We have seen that man's being exists in his decisions. And yet, in a sense, it transcends them, for my decisions do not exhaust my being. The self has a reality which envelops its decisions; they are not all equally characteristic of it. In speaking thus of endowment it is hard to avoid the supposition that it has a separate existence like that of an object. This tendency is probably due to the fact that our bodies are a very important part of our endowment. And they, particularly in the state of sleep, do seem to have an existence very like that of a thing. There is, or appears to be, no element of active decision present. We must say, that while there does appear to be an existence in sleep, in which our bodies approximate to the existence of objects, yet the significant way to look at them, for our present purpose, is to regard them, with the rest of our human nature, as endowment for the act of responsive decision.

The ontological status of endowment and its relation to the act of decision can be indicated by language, but not described in terms of anything else, for it is quite singular. When we speak of it in terms of potentiality, it is probable that our very notion of potentiality is a generalization from our immediate awareness of our endowment, and our power to create an act expressing it. Our freedom is grounded in our endowment and is not a bare liberty of choice. A man of great powers can face a difficult situation with a far richer freedom of choice than a man of lesser powers. But there is also a noble inability which results from noble endowment.

We must realize that in calling this power which lies behind our freedom of decision our human endowment we are using an inadequate figure of speech. For all other endowment is given *to* the self. But this endowment is the self in one of its two inseparable aspects. The same kind of inadequacy is evident when we call our decisions 'my response'. For the response to God is myself, myself in action. Our language 'my endowment' and 'my response', may lead us to image that we stand outside of our endowment and response, as a kind of transcendent point of unity of action and thought. But we *are* endowment in response. Be this as it may, it is possible for us to make the distinction in thought between endowment and response.

And it is not a meaningless question to ask whether in any sense the image of God is to be found in the one or the other.

It is a tempting suggestion which Brunner has made,[26] that the endowment is nothing less than original righteousness. In it God gives us himself, and ourselves. In our sinful decisions and responses, and in that mysterious decision which somehow lies behind our other decisions, we fall, and have fallen, from the original righteousness. Thus an attempt is made to translate the old orthodoxy into a language not dependent on the notion of a historical Fall. We must agree that the endowment and the relation to God in which it enables us to stand, are a divine gift, and not a mere demand. But surely we ought to distinguish this gift from original righteousness. For surely that righteousness and the righteousness for which we hope through Christ, ontologically involve not merely a gift but also response. The righteousness of the blessed is a grateful mirroring back of God's love. And this response is missing in our endowment, which is only a gift which conditions our response, even when that response is one of opposition and rebellion. If endowment were original righteousness, then we might say that the endowment was the image of God in the full New Testament sense, for the New Testament image is the restoration of original righteousness. If we do not believe in a past original righteousness, we can say that the New Testament image is the fulfilment of God's purpose in us and through us from which in fact we have fallen away.

Are we then to conclude that the image in the lower, Old Testament sense is to be found in the natural man's endowment? We must confess that the natural man does not find it there. If he reflects, he is aware that his gifts and powers do not come from himself, but from beyond him. He has not, however, the insight to see that these powers in some way relate him to God. This might, of course, be the result of the fact that the very act of thought whereby he reflects upon his endowment is involved in a measure of revolt against God, which blinds him to the truth about his endowment.

But it appears that the endowment itself is altered for the worse by our rebellion. We know as a matter of experience that our sins from day to day change and diminish our spiritual endowment, and limit the freedom and choice of our actions. It is surely a part of the dealings of persons with each other that as other men deal differently with us, so we deal differently with them. And so to change our responses to each other is not necessarily a sign of sin in us. A man who shows himself unworthy of responsibility is given less privilege by those who are set over him. Is it not reasonable, then, to suppose that our endowment as men, which is God's gift to us, should be dreadfully less than what it would have been if sin had not intervened? The argument of the first chapter of Romans means nothing if it does not mean this.

But in spite of this, we maintain that God does hold us continually in his presence, and that our endowment, though lessened by sin, is still sufficient to enable us, standing in that relationship, to make our response to him. Thus our endowment does go some way to constitute our continuing likeness to God; and this is purely an act of his grace to us.

If we look at the act of the will whereby we respond to the creative gift of God and posit ourselves in the world by our decisions, shall we find there also the image of God? There is one difficulty in the way of such a conclusion. The Christian must believe that every decision of the human will, apart from faith, is in some degree rebellious against God. We are talking here of the natural man. That which is in rebellion against God cannot be like him, and therefore the image of God cannot appear directly in the decisions of the natural man. Yet the image of God in the wider sense is borne witness to in every decision of man, and this because it is a response to the creative call which brings him with his

201

endowment, not without his response, into existence. The universal human endowment enables us to make an answer to God in our decisions – indeed, it compels us to do so. We are all in his presence, and cannot escape from it. This human existence is a life lived before a God who both loves us and is angry with us. But faith can see that the real goal and meaning of our life is salvation. The universal image of God is a grace which is given along with our humanity and this image is seen in our endowment and borne witness to by our response. And the fact that it is thus given does not mean that it becomes something at our disposal, or ceases to be a gift of God's free grace. For he could at any moment withdraw our life from us. The meaning of the continuance of our life is that God's patience is not exhausted and man ought to recognize this fact. It was to men who forgot this fact that St Paul wrote: 'Or do you presume upon the riches of his kindness and forbearance and patience? Do you not know that God's kindness is meant to lead you to repentance?'[27]

It will be seen that this conclusion about the universal image is very much like Brunner's although differing in some details. Man is in the universal image of God because he stands in an inescapable relation of responsibility to God and man. I have developed in line with Aquinas and Augustine the thought of the power which enables man to make that response. His responsibility does not change, though the form of his response may change to an almost infinite extent. Hence it is properly called a formal image, though we have chosen to call it the Old Testament image.

5 *The Universal Human Image in Its Relation to Man*
So far we have spoken of the universal image in the relation of man to God. Now we must speak of its manifestation in the I-thou human relationship. Here again, to be consistent, we would do well to define it as our inalienable confrontation with our fellow men, and our moral responsibility for them to God. This definition is purely formal, and we can safely say that so long as a man is a man he will be covered by it. This responsibility continues, however boldly a man may deny it, or however cunningly he may misinterpret it. And we shall be ready to look for its reflection, even though dis-

torted, in a man's conscience, in his desire for human love, and in other symptoms. Here again it will be seen that we are following very closely what we believe to be Brunner's view.

Barth has developed a quite different view of the image in the human I-thou relationship. He claims that humanity in the sense in which he speaks of it is an inescapable fact of our existence, and no mere ideal. He gives it a positive ethical content. The natural universal endowment of man entails four things:

(a) That I should see my neighbour as a real man.
(b) That I should speak to him and receive his answer.
(c) That I should help him.
(d) That I should do all these things gladly.

The objection may be raised that this surely cannot be a humanity active and universal among men, for if it were, we would be very nearly in Paradise. And as we read on, we see that Barth holds we can deny and misuse this humanity,[28] our life may be lived in greater or less consistency and perfection according to our nature, and as man sins, his humanity too, without simply disappearing, becomes sick, confused, perverted, destroyed, unrecognizable.

Barth here seems to be in a difficult position. For he has described our common nature as something which even our sin is not able to destroy. That which was good and God's creation cannot be changed into an evil nature by our act. Therefore our human nature must be intact. It is no ideal but the ground-form of our being.[29] Is it then obscured and overlaid and so ineffective? This might be the answer, but unfortunately, the image has been described in terms of act, seeing, hearing, helping and doing so gladly. Where I do not, or cannot, do these things the only correct inference would be that I have lost, or damaged, the nature from which they spring.

These powers are inferred by Barth to exist in man's nature, quite apart from grace; because to be saved by Christ man must be a sharer in his humanity, and unless this endowment entails at least these things, then man is not such a one as could be saved by Christ. But the artificiality of this construction is evident when we reflect that many men who are saved have had (before their salvation) not any one of these powers,

The implication of Barth's view, however, is that though none of the powers were in evidence, they must all have been there in order for the man to be saved.

There is much that Barth has written on man's natural endowment that is both wise and fine. It is much to the point to remark as he has done that we should not blacken human nature in order to make grace appear greater, for God is not praised when we are dishonest in facing facts, or when we decry his good creation.

But it appears that this attempt to give moral content to the universal humanity will not succeed when so obviously there are many men who cannot satisfy its conditions. Brunner's formal definition is surely much sounder.

Perhaps we could accept Barth's statement about the four-fold capacity which he claims constitutes universal human nature, if we were to take it as his meaning that on occasions man can do all these four things without the divine grace received through the Christian revelation. And Barth certainly does not claim that the man who has lost these powers can regain them by his own efforts; his suggestion is that grace, if it does not restore human nature, is able to make it shine forth unconcealed again, and that for this achievement nothing less than that grace is actually needed.

But we still have the objection to make, that for all his existentialism, Barth describes man's nature far too much as if it were the nature of some other part of the world. He tells us that the characteristics of the lower creatures are shared by man and that in addition he has an openness towards his fellow men. In addition he is destined for the covenant with God. But Barth's denial of a universal confrontation with God surely allows man too much independence of God; it seems to screen off the whole nature of man, apart from those who are believers, from the divine grace. Only if this tent-roof, so to speak, could be erected over humanity could we specify as closely as Barth does, what human nature alone can achieve, and what is beyond it. Barth's denial of the confrontation of every man as man by God seems to lead him in the wrong direction here.

Would not a modest scepticism about the positive content of human nature be more in place? We know that in God's

plan it was good; we know also that the natural man may
sink to extreme depths of degradation, and may rise to great
heights. Why should we not think that the good in the
greatest achievements of the pagan world are in some way
due to the gift of divine grace? But our chief certainty will
be that in God's sight all men are sinners, and that there is
no other name under heaven given among men than Christ's,
by which we must be saved. So that all who in the end are
saved, will be saved by faith in him.

6 *The Christian Doctrine of Man demands a general revelation. Barth's attack on general revelation criticized*

One more conclusion would appear to be suggested by our
study. If we are to have a satisfactory doctrine of man, we
must relate him in two ways to God; first by means of a
general revelation, or revelation in creation, which continues
even under conditions of sin, and secondly, by means of a
divine purpose for man – the purpose of salvation by union
with Christ. It is not necessary here to enlarge on the importance of the divine purpose for man, for no Christian will call
it in question. Were there not this purpose, then man would
never have come into being, and the whole grand story of
salvation would never have begun.

In speaking of a general revelation, it is not claimed here
that a passage by inference is possible from the existence of
the natural world to the existence of God, but rather that
in human experience God, by the continual invasion of his
grace, confronts man. Thus there is in all man's existence
a relationship to the infinite Thou, misinterpret it as the
natural man may, and does.

Karl Barth is the chief opponent today of such a doctrine
of general revelation, and it is therefore worth our while to
ask what his teaching is. This teaching is made harder to
understand because Barth persistently confuses general revelation with a valid natural theology. The doctrine of general
revelation is that God does reveal himself in some sense
to all men; the doctrine of a valid natural theology is the
claim that man, outside of faith in Christ, can have a true,
though perhaps truncated, knowledge of God.

Barth defines natural theology as 'The doctrine of a bond

The Image of God in Man

with God which exists apart from God's revelation in Jesus Christ'.[30] This exactly covers what we mean by the doctrine of general revelation, except for the fact that we claim that God's general revelation is also a revelation through the word – the light that enlightens every man. Barth's general argument is that if Christian theology allows a place to the doctrine of natural theology, all is lost. For natural theology is the natural man's self-interpretation and self-justification. To admit it to Christian theology is then to allow the natural man a place inside the Church. The strength of such a natural theology is not broken, but only strengthened by the admission of a theology of revelation alongside of it. In such a struggle the natural man always wins, the natural theology is determinative, and the Lordship of Christ is finally denied. So Christian theology must have nothing to do with it for 'the truth of man's existence is this and this alone, that Jesus Christ died and rose again for him'.[31]

We must not, Barth continues, however, take the natural man as seriously as he takes himself. Are we afraid that unless we allow him some knowledge of God outside of Christ, he might not know the divine law and the divine judgment, without which he cannot receive the salvation which is in Christ Jesus? As if there were another law and judgment than this, that in Jesus Christ God has taken man's concern out of his own hand and made it his own concern!

Barth does not state that natural theology ought to be opposed by us in general. We only deny it a place in the Church. Provided that we concede that humanity constitutes an independent sphere, within that sphere, natural theology is a necessary undertaking. Man uses his capacities to assure himself and others – even God, whom he does not know – that even in that state, outside the grace of God, he is not godless, but fears and honours God. It would indeed be unkind to try to rob the natural man of his natural theology. 'One should be merciful and understand – the fact itself which we must here understand is merciless enough – that natural theology is the natural man's only consolation in life and in death.'[32] Further, it is vain to try to argue the natural man out of natural theology. Only God's grace in Christ can reveal its futility.[33]

It will be noted how Barth's use of the term 'natural theology' slips over from the meaning 'general revelation' to 'natural theology' in the terms of our definition – the construction of a system of belief about God claimed to be valid on the basis of general revelation as seen by the natural man.

There are many points of criticism that could be made about this passage of Barth's *Church Dogmatics*. But it will perhaps suffice to refute Barth's arguments if we can show the falsity of his exegesis in one decisive passage of scripture, the passage in the first chapter of the Epistle to the Romans, verses 18-21.

These are the verses in question: 'For the wrath of God is revealed from heaven against all ungodliness and wickedness of men, who by their wickedness suppress the truth. For what can be known about God is plain to them, because God has shown it to them. Ever since the creation of the world his invisible nature, namely, his eternal power and deity, has been clearly perceived in the things that have been made. So they are without excuse; for although they knew God they did not honour him as God or give thanks to him, but they became futile in their thinking and their senseless minds were darkened.'

Barth starts his comments by saying: [34] 'Doubtless in this passage a knowledge of God is ascribed to man in the cosmos. . . .' (This is the term used by Barth for the natural man, outside of the revelation in Christ.) 'And were these verses, say, a fragment from a Stoic writer of the time, we might assume, not knowing their context, that man in the cosmos was an independent witness of God's truth. But this passage stands in the context of the Epistle to the Romans. The righteousness of God mentioned in the previous verse (1:17) is God's righteousness revealed in the gospel of Christ. And his wrath, mentioned in verse 18, is the reverse side of that righteousness. God's revelation always comes as judgment on those who reject it. The Jew confronted by Jesus Christ is the man mentioned in Chapter 2 as inexcusable and the Gentiles who are spoken of as judged in Chapter 1 are inexcusable too because they are confronted by Jesus Christ. Thus the knowledge of God which renders Jew and Gentile alike inexcusable is no knowledge gained from any general revelation, but from the revelation in Jesus Christ.'

Now, we will agree that the cross and resurrection of Christ reveal as nothing else does the sin of both Jew and Gentile. And it is clear that in 1:16 and 17 it is the gospel which is spoken of. But it is equally beyond cavil that verses 19 and 20 do not refer to Christ, but to the general revelation. 'Ever since the creation of the world his invisible nature, namely, his eternal power and deity, has been clearly perceived in the things that have been made. So they are without excuse.' The proof of the correctness of this exegesis is that this revelation of God was prior in time to the judicial blindness and idolatry of the heathen. The knowledge of God was offered to the Gentiles – indeed, forced upon them ('they knew God', verse 21) – and was rejected by them, long before the incarnation. Were Barth's exegesis correct, the absurd result would follow that Gentile idol-worship and moral decay did not begin until after Christ was rejected by the Gentiles. A case which demands such an exegesis must be a poor one indeed. So poor is it in fact, that on the next page we find Barth giving it away with both hands. Here he says:

'From the same Golgotha, where it was revealed that the Jews never kept their own law, it is clear that the heathen also have sinned against God no less guiltily. Sinned against the truth which was well-known to them too! God was always known to them. The world which was always round about them was always his world; it spoke of his works, and therefore of himself. Objectively judged, although they refused to give God the honour and thanks, although they were sunk in the emptiness, darkness and madness of idolatry, they were always men who knew God.'[35]

If this be conceded, why was Barth at such pains to deny that a Christian theologian can speak of such a knowledge, or that Romans 1 and 2 state its existence?

He goes on to say: 'All this (knowledge) is not elicited from the heathens in the manner of a catechism containing knowledge which they already have before they come to the gospel. . . . All this is as new for them as the judgment that the Jews never kept the law, but always transgressed it, is new to the Jews, a truth of revelation proclaimed by the apostle of Jesus Christ.'[36] But it is not really possible to have it both ways. We are agreed that the gospel reveals man's guilt to him as nothing else can, and that in order to do this, it does not browbeat him into a confession of guilt and sin against the light previously available to him. But we must assert that there was either a certain actual knowledge, or at least a possible knowledge of God, which made the heathens guilty before the coming of Christ. For if there was no knowledge, and no possibility of it, then there can have been no guilt. If the special revelation reveals men's guilt, then there must be a general revelation to which it appeals. Otherwise it does not *reveal* guilt but *creates* it.

It is the denial of this obvious fact which has led Barth to give an exegesis of the first two chapters of Romans which, I believe, has never been put forward by any earlier scholar. He is, however, not quite able to make up his mind. As we saw, he admits in one passage that the heathens were always, objectively judged, men who knew God. But this is not the main drift of his thought. This drift is represented in another passage,[37] where he says that the so-called God of natural theology is not the God of the true revelation. The knowledge of the god or the gods encountered in natural theology has nothing to do with the real God. It only serves to make us blind to him. The highest responsibility to which a man can be called outside of the revelation in Christ is the responsibility of taking himself seriously. And the consequence of thus taking himself seriously is that he withdraws himself from confrontation with the real God.

It is curious to see how near Barth's standpoint, as far as the non-Christian is concerned, is to that of Sartre! In short, if we are to judge him by this passage and many others, Barth believes that there is no possibility of a theological interpretation of moral obligation, for there is no universal confrontation of man with God. Surely such a violent tearing apart of the being of the natural man from God is not true to the Bible. We have seen how Romans 1 contradicts it flatly, and it appears to be equally foreign to the spirit of the Old Testament. Is it not the teaching of the prophets that not only Israel, but also the Gentile peoples are punished by God for their sins against him? And does not such sin imply he had in some sense revealed himself to them so that they either actually knew him, or could have known him, however much they may have shut their eyes to his glory and fallen down to worship gods that were no gods? Barth's is a theological position held neither by Calvin nor by Luther, and even Barth is unable to hold consistently to it.

7 *The attack on general revelation is also fatal for the Christian doctrine of God*

But, further, the denial of a general revelation causes theological difficulties not only in our framing of the doctrine of man, but in the sphere of the doctrine of God. If God had been unable or unwilling to reveal himself to what Barth calls 'man in the cosmos', there would in either case arise a very grave problem for faith. We would have to conceive of the history of man as continuing for thousands of years in a world belonging to God where yet God had been either unwilling or unable to reveal himself to the many millions of men and women who had therefore to live and to die without any ray of light from heaven. Such a God would either not be the gracious God who is always seeking man, the God who wills to be with his people, and at the last takes human nature upon him and dies for man. Or else he would not be the God of power on whom his people can rely. Had evil so prevailed against his power as utterly to thwart his goodness, how could he be the God and Father of Jesus Christ? Therefore a general revelation is not only clearly borne witness to by both testaments, but it is necessary both to the Christian doctrine of God and the doctrine of man.

Having asserted the necessity of general revelation for the doctrine of man, we must hasten to add that this does not imply a belief in the existence of a valid natural theology. In this we shall be adhering closely to Emil Brunner's position as expounded in his *Dogmatics*.[38] There he asserts the existence of a general revelation, or as he now calls it, a revelation in creation. But there he also denies that the reason of the natural man, unillumined by Christian faith, is able to build up a true system of knowledge about God on the strength of this general revelation. There is not space at our disposal to defend this view at length. But it is worth-while reaffirming that this is the position presupposed in this study.

As Brunner says, there *is* without question a natural theology.[39] There are, in fact, many such systems. The pantheons of the heathens bear witness to the vitality of natural theology. And, further, these religions bear witness to the existence of the one God whose revelation in creation lies behind them all, the source of whatever truth there may be in them. But there is no way upward through the religions to a knowledge, unmixed with error, of the truth that is behind them. Only Christian faith, which knows the revelation of God in Christ, can see that truth which is behind the mingled truth and falsehood of the religions.

The objection has naturally been made that this is a strange, even monstrous revelation, if it never succeeds in being known by the men for whom it is meant. Has not Brunner himself said: 'Revelation is a transitive event which started from God and ends with man, an arc of light with these two poles'?[40] Granted, the objectors continue, that this is said of the revelation of God in Christ, yet it must also be true of general revelation if it is to bear the same name.

8 *A Denial of the Validity of Natural Theology*

But Brunner never denies that God is known in the general revelations. All that he denies is that man builds up a true system of natural theology. In commenting on the first chapter of Romans, he notes that it speaks 'not only of a possibility of knowledge of God, which was once present, but now is lost, nor yet of a present possibility of knowledge of God, but of an actual knowledge, which in consequence of sin is changed at once into illusion. It is, thus, a knowledge which does not take effect as knowledge but is transformed, as it were, into idolatry through the ferment of sin.'[41]

It is this continual flashing of the knowledge of God into the heart of man to which the Bible bears witness, and which is necessary for the theologian to give him the basis for a universal moral responsibility. Without doubt, as we saw, this is the teaching of Romans 1, which implies a true knowledge of God in flashes in the heart of the natural man, but denies a true natural theology. 'Their senseless minds were darkened.'

And is the experience of converts from heathendom not sometimes a confirmation of this? There are indeed those who find the gift of faith as a release from something which was without qualification horrible. 'I was delivered from two million demons to serve the one God,' said one aboriginal. But others have been found to say, 'God was always speaking to me, but I refused to understand.' Is it not in that earlier speaking of God that we shall be justified in seeking for the so much disrupted point of contact?

Certainly some systems of natural theology are less idolatrous than others, as certain religions are less idolatrous than others. But if a valid natural theology exists, it is hard to account for the fact that so many men are not aware of the universal confrontation with God. It is also hard to account for the fact that there are so many false interpretations of the nature of the moral imperative. This is also, admittedly, a difficulty for the belief in a universal confrontation, although a less extreme difficulty than it is for those who believe in a valid natural theology.

9 *Transition from the Old Testament Image to the New Testament Image*

How do we picture the change which occurs when a man passes from disobedience to faith? We have spoken of man's nature as endowment in response. We shall have to consider briefly the change in both these aspects of human nature. But, further, we must think of God's purpose for the man, and also of God's act of confrontation which creates him and holds him in being and elicits his response. Thus there are four things to be considered, God's purpose, God's confrontation, man's response and man's endowment.

(a) When a man begins to believe. God's purpose remains unchanged. It is a purpose of love – God wills that all men should come to a knowledge of the truth and be saved.

(b) There is a change in the act of divine confrontation. Inasmuch as the man believes, this becomes a confrontation of pure love. Before, it was a confrontation of love mingled with anger. It was love because of God's own nature and because man is a created son of God, even in his disobedience. But it was anger because of that disobedience. The love was primary, and longed to overcome the anger, but the anger was real in so far as the man refused to respond in love. Had the disobedience persisted fatally, the love might never have been able to break through as it did. But now that the man has begun to believe, the love which in Christ broke through and overwhelmed the great barrier between God and a sinful world, has broken through the barrier of this man's will, and he knows that God loves him, and surrenders his life to God.

(c) The human response is simply changed from one tainted with fear and disobedience to one of love and obedience.

(d) The endowment up till this moment has been a curious mingling of the good original gifts of God and of the evil into which sin, corporate and individual, has changed them. Now it is changed in its nature, as the divine relation of confrontation is changed. God's overruling power begins to work on it, using it for the perfecting of the man in the community of believers. Faith in the supremacy of God means that there is no element in this endowment which cannot become wholly translucent to the divine light, and wholly malleable to the divine grace. It is surely wrong to assert, as some do, that when God forgives he does not ever remit penalty, but turns it from a punishment to a fatherly discipline. We do not know, and cannot limit the action of God's grace. We cannot but thank him for what he does to us, and trust that he is not only loving, but also supremely wise.

CHAPTER XV

Karl Marx's
Conception of Man

In the last hundred years three writers have made outstanding
contributions to thought about the nature of man. They are
Charles Darwin, Karl Marx, and Sigmund Freud. The present
study accepts, as do most Christians today, the scientific
teaching of Darwin about human origins. It is therefore not
necessary to say anything about him in this part of our book,
whose aim is to set forth modern views about human nature
for comparison and, if need be, for contrast with the Christian
view. Darwin's work is strictly scientific, in the sense that it
limits itself to what can, in principle, be confirmed or falsi-
fied by appropriate scientific methods, and does not entail a
general world-view. The same cannot be said about the work
of Marx, or Freud, as it stands. It is not necessary, or indeed
possible, to agree with all that they say, but to speak or
write as if they had never existed, is to brand oneself as being
out of touch with reality. Their work has made such an
impact on man's understanding of himself, that things can
never be the same again.

For those who hold the Christian view of man, that his
being is not rightly understood unless in terms of his relation to God, his creation by God, his relation to Christ, his
response to God, and his place in God's plan for the universe,[1]
there could at first sight hardly appear a greater contradiction
than the Marxian view of man, for Marx's doctrine of man is
in fact bound up with an aggressive form of atheism, and he
holds that religion in all its forms is, in the last resort, a
pernicious and invalid projection. Yet to reject Marx's contribution outright would be a grave error. Further, as we
approach our special task, of expounding and criticizing the
Marxian conception of man, we cannot help feeling a certain
apprehension. As Helmut Gollwitzer has written, 'The analysis
of Marxist atheism is unavoidable, but it has this danger . . .
that it reduces it to principles whose dictates govern not it

alone, but equally the behaviour of the Christian who encounters it in pure reaction.'[2] This danger is inherent not only in
the criticism of the Marxian atheism in general, but also in
setting forth the Marxian doctrine of man which is so closely
allied with it. In doing so it is hard to avoid the suggestion
that we are satisfied by setting down in parallel and contrasting
columns the two doctrines of man and, having done so, are in a
position complacently to write off the whole Marxist challenge.
A study leading to such conclusions would celebrate a
barren and smug victory. The truth is, that nowhere is 'our
Christian civilization', 'the Christian self-understanding' exposed today to such a searching challenge as that made to it
by Marx and Marxism. Much has been made of the challenge
of Freud, and his thinking has undoubtedly been a powerful
corrosive agent, but it has today less dynamism than the
challenge of Marx. For if Freud has shown us that reason
and consciousness play a much less dominant part in the life
of the individual than had been thought, Marx has opened
our eyes with even more disillusioning results to the way in
which social background and membership of a class can
pervert men's judgments, and turn them into mere smoke-
screens for private and class interests. The result is that any
statement of 'the Christian doctrine of man' will be met
with a justifiable cynicism until its effective expression in
action can be estimated. Further, Freud's individualist thinking never had a political outreach, and could never be imagined
as contending for the loyalty of hundreds of millions of men
today, and offering to satisfy their hopes of a better society.
But this is precisely what the system of Marx does.

So, in spite of hesitations, the task of inquiring what view
of man underlies the thought of Marx is one of the first importance. In this chapter we shall have to limit ourselves
to Marx himself, leaving out the writings of his famous
contemporary and ally, Engels, and subsequent Marxists
almost entirely. And we shall deal only with those aspects
of Marx's thought which seem to have special relevance to
his views about man.

1 *Marx's Materialism*

A good point of entry to Marx's thought is to give a brief

description of the type of materialism he advocated. As
Bernard Delfgaauw[3] points out, the word materialism can be
used in at least two senses. It can be used to describe the
view that there is only one reality, the reality which we can
perceive around us, and that no transcendent or divine reality
exists. It can also be used to describe a philosophy which
holds that the reality which we do perceive is in fact only
matter, that is, that there is no essential difference between
lifeless matter, plants, animals, and man.

It was the first of these two types of 'materialism' that
Marx advocated, and he vigorously repudiated the second.
He was indeed an atheist, but those who are accustomed
to use the term 'materialism' in yet another sense, as the outlook which disregards everything spiritual, should realize
that by 'materialism' Marx meant an outlook (his own) which
was opposed to *philosophical* idealism, and was, in fact, a
type of philosophical realism. He was both indebted and
opposed to the great German idealist philosopher Hegel,
and much of his writing becomes clearer when we realize
this context, and this love-hate relationship.

'In opposition to Hegel, who made the "Idea" the active
element in history, Marx put forward the view that history is
determined by the relations of production, which are in their
turn dependent on . . . the forces or means of production.
On these relations, Marx argued, hangs the whole development
and unfolding of human history. All ideas and theories which
find expression in the spheres of science, art, philosophy,
religion, law, and politics are determined by the productive
forces.'[4] Here in a nutshell, we have Marx's theory of historical
materialism. The theory that everything is 'matter' is of no
relevance here at all; but what is important is that material
needs determine the development of society, and so also the
history of mankind.[5]

Thus Marx was in reaction from Hegel. But we have now
to indicate his main debt to Hegel. Hegel had taught that
the march of history as well as the processes of thought proceeded according to the 'threefold rhythm' of dialectic. First
there came thesis, then antithesis, and lastly, transcending and
incorporating both thesis and antithesis, synthesis. Hegel's
dialectic was one of thought. Marx also believed in a dialectic,

but one of opposing social forces out in the world. He determined to start, not with ideas, but with concrete historical realities. Beginning with a primitive condition of communism, the history of mankind had followed a scheme of dialectical tension and development. Today the world was drawing near to a final struggle between the two classes of capital and labour, the bourgeoisie and the proletariat. The irrationality of the present situation found expression in the fact that while production had become a vital concern of the whole community, and was accordingly social in character, the ownership of capital and the means of production was not social, but in the hands of a numerically ever-decreasing minority. The situation could be transcended only by the victory of the proletariat, the expropriation of the capitalists, and the abolition not only of them, but of both classes, and the introduction of the classless society, with which true history would begin, and the reconciliation of man with man, and of man with nature, would take place.

2 *The Concept of Alienation in Marx*

We must look a little closer at this picture of the present and the future of man. According to Marx, under present conditions, man is alienated from his true self, and this alienation must be overcome. Hegel had also in his philosophy made use of the concept of alienation.[6] 'Man has been alienated from himself – this was a central theme in Hegel. Man is a spirit who expresses himself in nature. In understanding nature – which, for Hegel, was the purpose of philosophy – man finds himself back in nature, and so transcends and abolishes his self-alienation. Marx also thought that man had been alienated from himself, but that this was due to the structure of society. Thus man does not "come to his senses" again merely by understanding this structure, but only if he succeeds in changing it. This cannot be achieved by the individual, but only by the mass which most suffers from the existing structure – that is, by the proletariat.'

We shall later have to deal with Marx's use of the concept of alienation to dismiss man's belief in God as an illusion, a projection, and a 'mystification'. But first we must consider how he uses it in the economic and social field. He pictures man as expressing, and indeed finding and realizing his own nature through his dealings with the world around him, of which he is an integral part. This is what for Marx 'production' means, man realizing his potentialities through his interaction with nature, man in society creating himself as he goes through life, through his domination and development of his natural environment. Thus the concept is much wider than what is customarily known as production, though it includes production in the industrial, commercial sense.

Under the capitalist system, while production is social, the appropriation of wealth is private. Since man's production creates wealth, and in a sense creates man himself, the private appropriation of wealth by a minority is not only unjust, but it leads to a distortion and crippling of human nature, not only in those who by their labour produce the wealth, the workers, but also in those who appropriate it, the capitalists. The labour itself which, as man's labour, should be used to develop the world for the common good, becomes frozen into an independent entity as capital, and stands over against man as a power and an idol, and man becomes increasingly enslaved to economic forces which should be under social control. But under capitalism, they operate ever more inhumanly and capriciously. In this machine age 'The alienation of work in man's production is much greater than it was when production was by handicraft and manufacture. "In handicrafts and manufacture, the workman makes use of a tool; in the factory the machine makes use of him." '[7]

Further, under capitalism, what is produced is not what is humanly and socially most needed, but what will keep the creaking competitive economic system moving, and while true world-needs are disregarded, false needs are stimulated to keep the machines active. And a further evil results, that a false system of values is encouraged, in which what is authentically human is subordinated to money and what it can buy, and man is alienated, not only from his true nature, but also from his fellow man.

Marx believed that to overcome this alienation private property must be abolished.[8] He wrote, 'Communism is the *positive* abolition of *private property*, of *human self-alienation*, and thus the real *appropriation* of *human* nature through and for man. It is, therefore, the return of man himself as a *social,* i.e., really human, being, a complete and conscious return which assimilates all the wealth of previous development. Communism as a fully-developed naturalism is humanism, and as a fully-developed humanism is naturalism. It is the *definitive* resolution of the antagonism between man and nature, and between man and man. It is the true solution of the conflict between existence and essence, between objectification and self-affirmation, between freedom and necessity, between individual and species. It is the solution to the riddle of history and knows itself to be this solution.'[9]

It is in this context that Erich Fromm writes, 'It should be clear by now that according to this concept, socialism is *not* a society of regimented, automatized individuals, regardless of whether there is equality of income or not, and regardless of whether they are well fed and well clad. . . . Quite clearly the aim of socialism is *man.* It is to create a form of production and an organization of society in which man can overcome alienation from his product, from his work, from his fellow man, from himself and from nature; in which he can return to himself and grasp the world with his own powers, thus becoming one with the world. Socialism for Marx was, as Paul Tillich put it, "a resistance movement against the destruction of love in social reality".'[10] It is not too much to say that there is a strikingly 'personalist' aspect to Marx's thought.

While it is true to say that alienation is a prominent concept in Marx and in Hegel, the notion is, of course, and has always been, common property, since from the beginning of time men have been aware that they were not living up to what they had it in them to be – not fulfilling their true nature. And in particular the biblical view of man, in its teaching about sin and salvation, lays great emphasis on the difference between the true man and the actual man, and the impossibility of man's achieving his true nature without the help of grace.

In terms of the image of God in man, we have seen this doctrine reflected in the difference between the Old Testament image and the New Testament image, or, in Brunner's terms, between the formal and the material image. And we have

seen reason to criticize certain of the earlier Christian writers
on the grounds that they seem to suggest that by an effort of
reason or will man could 'purify the image' in himself.[11]

Must we not then here find grave grounds for criticism of
Marx, who suggests that man's alienation from himself can
be overcome by a revolutionary social act, as a result of
which men will be reconciled both with nature and with
each other? Strictly speaking, this criticism is valid, and can
be urged against over-enthusiastic and exaggerated statements about the beneficial results of the revolution and the
end of the class-war.

However, there is a danger that Christian thinkers should be
landed in a sterile denial of the whole Marxian challenge by
saying 'Here is a blatant piece of attempted self-salvation, of
man taking into his own hands what God alone can do for
the individual and for society.' For the Marxian theme can
be restated, as it were, in a lower key (as Thilo Ramm has
suggested).[12] If it is not possible for men or society to become
wholly righteous in God's sight, it yet remains true that a
relative righteousness and justice can be achieved, and it may
well be that in a society where *institutional* exploitation had
been overcome, the morally good life would be much easier,
and men would behave much more justly and humanely.
Christian thinkers should accordingly be very careful not to
reject the whole Marxian argument because it has painted its
Utopia in too brilliant theological colours.

3 Marx's Claim to Represent Humanism
Today, largely in reaction against misunderstandings of Marx
as interpreted by an orthodox Marx tradition, which looks on
man as a mere reflection of contemporary social and economic
conditions, it is the fashion to emphasize his 'humanism', citing
in defence particularly his earlier writings. From what has
been said above it can be seen that Marx himself openly
claims to be regarded as a humanist, a claim which will be
vigorously resisted by the critics of Marxism, who point out
the element of ruthlessness in the Marxian ethic,[13] to say
nothing of the cruelties and horrors of the degenerate regime
of Stalin. We shall later have cause to come back to this
issue, but meantime a word must be said about the history

of the word 'humanism', and the much older outlook which it describes.

Like 'democracy', 'humanism' is a very ambiguous word, and is in fact a piece of verbal territory bitterly contested by a number of claimants, but particularly the opponents in the cold war between east and west. It appears to have been coined by the Bavarian educationalist Niethammer (1766-1848),[14] who saw the danger of education becoming a mere technical preparation for the pursuit of a trade or a profession, and argued that in view of their human nature, men had a higher aim than this, the true human goals being general knowledge, artistic creation, and religion. Niethammer appealed both to the thought and culture of the classical Greeks and Romans, to the Greek 'logos' conception, and also to the Johannine Christian one. Thus for him (and for the whole preceding and succeeding humanist tradition, since he invented only the word, and not the thing itself) the humanist movement has been an amalgam in which idealist and Christian elements were somewhat uneasily combined. Sometimes the idealist element has so preponderated as almost to stifle the Christian one, and this has caused temporary hostile reactions of Christian thinkers, which have given some pretext to the opponents of Christianity to label it as anti-humanist. Thus historically there have been types of humanism which claimed that justice could not be done to man's humanity so long as man's subordination to God was maintained, while other humanists, representing the Christian outlook, have claimed that if God be denied, man's humanity cannot in the long run but be endangered. These historical facts are however sufficient to hinder Christians from at once repudiating Marx's claim to represent a type of humanism, since he was neither the first, nor the latest atheist to lay claim to the title of 'humanist'.

4 Marx's Repudiation of Religion

Marx believed that religion was just another example of the phenomenon of alienation. 'In religion,' he wrote, 'men make their empirical world a mere thought-world, a world of ideas, which confronts them as a strange reality . . .'[15] The nature of religion is to be sought 'neither in the "nature of man" nor in the predicates of God, but in the material world which is presupposed at every stage of religious development'.[16] Thus religious ideas are not what they purport to be, but 'were produced by entirely empirical causes remote from all influ ence of the religious spirit. . . . The supernatural powers are mystifications of sociological dependences, masquerades of earthly conditions, but at the same time wear masks which correspond to the latter. The ways of thought and the con ditions of a cultural period can be read off from them.'[17]

And when men have overcome the social and economic alienation after the achievement of the classless society, they will also find that they have overcome the alienation which produces religion and religious ideas.

Meanwhile Marx concedes that religion has a comforting power, especially for those who suffer from economic bondage It transfers to another and future world the consolations of which men despair in this world. It is 'pie in the sky when you die'. And since even those who profit from the situation are also sufferers from it they also have need of the consola tions of religion. So religion is the universal ground of consolation and of justification of the world as it is.[18] Thus not only the proletariat but also the capitalists are 'taken in': religion is more than merely a matter of cynical exploitation Marx's position in relation to religion can now intelligibly be summed up in the first paragraph of one of his early writings.[19] 'For Germany, the *criticism of religion* has been largely completed; and the criticism of religion is the premise of all criticism. . . .

'Man, who has found in the fantastic reality of heaven where he sought a supernatural being, only his own reflec tion, will no longer be tempted to find only the *semblance* of himself – a non-human being – where he seeks and must seek his true reality.

'The basis of irreligious criticism is this: *man makes reli gion*; religion does not make man. Religion is indeed man's self-consciousness and self-awareness so long as he has not found himself or has lost himself again. But *man* is not an abstract being, squatting outside the world. Man is *the human world*, the state, society. . . . Religion . . . is *the fantastic realization* of the human being inasmuch as the *human being* possesses no true reality. The struggle against religion is

herefore, indirectly a struggle against *that world* whose spiri-
ual *aroma* is religion.

'Religion is . . . the *opium* of the people.

'The abolition of religion as the *illusory* happiness of men,
s a demand for their *real* happiness. The call to abandon their
llusions about their condition is a *call to abandon a condition
which requires illusions. . . .*

'The criticism of religion disillusions man so that he will
think, act and fashion his reality as a man who has lost his
llusions and regained his reason; so that he will revolve
about himself as his own true sun. Religion is only the illusory
sun about which man revolves so long as he does not revolve
about himself.'

5 Marx's Relation to Feuerbach

As Marx must be understood in his relation to Hegel, so also
we must understand his relation to Feuerbach. In both cases
it is a relationship, on the one hand, of dependence, and on
the other hand, of reaction. The famous first sentence of *The
German Ideology,* quoted above, 'For Germany, *the criticism
of religion* has been largely completed', is in fact a reference
to Feuerbach's work which, for all his differences from it,
Marx greatly admired. Marx here takes it for granted that, in
the main, Feuerbach has established his case. How unjustified
this assumption was has later to be indicated. In his books,
Feuerbach assumes that 'all religion – the God of Christian
faith is unhesitatingly reckoned as one of the gods of the
religions – is a product of human need, and, what is more,
of unsatisfied human need. . . . Thus in religion man relates
to himself, he is the producer, he is also the disguised object
of these ideas.'[20] Man thinks, however, that he is speaking
about God, regarding God as substance, and himself as
predicate. 'If man makes himself a predicate of his predicate,
then in the self-abasement of this abstraction he is untrue
both to his dignity and to his bodily nature; he regards and
treats himself, together with nature, to which he belongs, as
something inferior, in order to gain a supposedly more valuable spirituality.'

Here we see two motifs that Marx adopted. First, the
assumption that God has no independent reality, and that those

who believe in him are deluding themselves. Secondly, the claim is made that in so doing they are guilty of projection, of alienation, and therefore are condemning themselves to a loss of the substance of reality. Similar claims will appear in a different form in the thought of Sigmund Freud, and it may be pointed out that Marx's economic and sociological version of the projection theory is not wholly compatible with Freud's.

But while Marx admits his dependence on Feuerbach, he has considerable reservations to make. First, that Feuerbach was too individualist in his outlook, and did not realize that man is involved in the very texture of society, and, secondly, – and this is not unconnected with the first point – that it is not enough theoretically to set forth the truth about religion, hoping that it may prove convincing, but that it will be necessary to remove through action the contradictions in society which produce religious alienation, before these illusions will wither away. These two points are made in Marx's theses on Feuerbach, the first in the sixth thesis, and the second in the fourth.[21]

6 *The Epistemological Basis of Feuerbach's and Marx's Atheism*

This excursus about Feuerbach has been necessary because of his influence upon Marx, and not least because of Marx's unquestioning acceptance of Feuerbach's main thesis about the illusory character of belief in God. For in Feuerbach it is the result of a very crude type of epistemology. In reaction against the over-rarefied thought of the German idealists, Feuerbach and his generation were 'gripped by the passion for the tangible, concrete, individual, perceptible, as the truly real . . .'[22] There is much to be said for such a desire for the concrete, for a realism to be set over against what F. H. Bradley called 'the unearthly ballet of bloodless categories'. But when it finds expression in such terms as Feuerbach's 'Only the senses give me . . . being', Gollwitzer is right in pointing out that 'Confronted by this "criterion of palpability" it is clear that the whole field of religion cannot stand the test.' Christian thought, he continues, has always known that the assertions of faith are not derived from sense-perception, 'consequently they cannot be empirically checked and verified by an "objective" observation.' Were it otherwise there would be some point in the Russian cosmonauts' triumphant declaration that there could be no God since they had not encountered him in their travels through outer space.

The statement 'only the senses give me being' is a mere assertion, it proves nothing but a resolution on the part of the man who makes it to define reality so narrowly that only what the senses can perceive is declared to be real. The epistemological foundation of Feuerbachian and Marxian atheism is as inadequate as this. Our critical remarks here confine themselves to the atheism which the Marxists have adopted, and do not apply to the political and economic analyses of Marxian theory, which have to be judged on their own merits.

7 The Marxian Ethic, Its Inner Dynamic and Its Ambiguity

One of the central problems, and indeed, one of the still unclarified ambiguities of Marx's thought is his view of our relation to our neighbour in his humanity. Does our neighbour in himself, in some way by his very existence, impose a limit upon our action of a kind different to that imposed upon us by material obstacles?

There has been a certain amount of discussion as to whether Marx believed that there was something common to all men which marked them out from animals and inanimate nature. It has become customary to refer to this 'something' as the 'humanum'. It is clear that Marx, who was a hater of abstractions, found this kind of thinking very uncongenial. His historical approach made him much more inclined to look on man in the context of his continually changing concrete situations, interacting with his environment, altering it, and being altered by it. In a famous passage criticizing German idealism, and emphasizing their concrete empirical approach, Marx and Engels say, 'In direct contrast to German philosophy which descends from heaven to earth, here we ascend from earth to heaven. That is to say, we do not set out from what men say, imagine, conceive, nor from men as narrated, thought of, imagined, conceived, in order to arrive at men in the flesh. We set out from real, active men, and on the basis

of their real life-process we demonstrate the development of
the ideological reflexes and echoes of this life-process.'²³

Thus nearly the whole weight of Marx's interest lay on what
men have been in the course of their history, creating themselves by their productive interaction with nature and with
each other. His suspicion of philosophizing about man's
nature in general terms was thus understandable, if we see it
as a reaction from the idealistic philosophy of his day. There
was the further fear in his mind that such doctrines could
only too easily be misused as an ideology, in defence of
entrenched class-prejudice, to paralyse revolutionary activity. It
is often only too easy to be unjust to a writer, particularly
if one does not attend carefully to the context of what he is
saying. When in the sixth thesis on Feuerbach, Marx says
that 'the human essence is no abstraction inherent in each
separate individual; in its reality it is the ensemble of the
social relations', he is probably not reducing man to nothing
but a function of social relations, as some exponents of modern
sociology are inclined to do, he is asserting, rather, that the
men we have to do with in the world are concrete, historical
human beings. Thus far then, we may say that it is not
necessary to fault Marx because he has this intensely empirical
approach.

However, as a matter of fact, the problem of the 'humanum'
cannot be permanently evaded, however sharp a distaste any
particular writer may feel for generalities. And, as a matter
of fact, as Vernon Venable remarks, 'at one point or another,
Marx and Engels mention most of the commonly remarked
human differentia. Man is a fire-using animal. He tames other
animals, and puts them in his service. He clothes himself
artificially, and creates his own shelter. He communicates with
his fellows, and has a highly-developed brain. In *The German
Ideology* Marx and Engels say "Men can be distinguished
from animals by consciousness, by religion, or by anything else
you like. They themselves begin to distinguish themselves
from animals so soon as they begin to produce their means of
subsistence" – and man produces, not like some animals, by
instinct, for "The labour process ends in the creation of something which, when the process began, already existed in the
worker's imagination, already existed in an ideal form".'²⁴

This characteristic of planned production offered by Marx as a criterion of the 'humanum', the specific characteristic of man, must be of great interest to the Christian, for this planned production (in the wide sense of the term, as indicating the conscious productive interaction of man with nature in order to provide himself with a human subsistence) is clearly closely akin to the biblical concept of man's dominion, which is an important component of the image of God in man.

Thus it is clear that in spite of his impatience with generalities, Marx has his own conception of man's specific nature, the 'humanum', and it is also clear that his use of the term the 'truly', the 'genuinely' and the 'really' human, would be meaningless without a normative conception of humanity, and the very notion of alienation involves the same concept, for it denotes a declension from the authentic humanity whose consummation is the goal of the communist philosophy.

But, strangely enough, while this ideal goal provides the dynamic of the Marxian ethic, it also turns out to be its most dangerous component. Venable expresses Marx's line of thought about the attainment of this goal in a few clear sentences, thus: – 'When he (man) fully understands and accepts the fact that history can become truly human history only when classes cease to struggle; when he realizes that classes, by their very nature, can cease to struggle only when classes cease to be; when he concludes, therefore, to the basic principle of thought and action that there can be but one ethical course to follow – that which will eventuate most directly and with the greatest dispatch in the total elimination of class division from society – then, they believe, he is fully free.'[25]

This is the one overriding ethical goal – the shortest way to the elimination of the class-war, by the expropriation of capitalism. It would appear that all personal consideration of loyalty to friends, undertakings solemnly given, respect for the sacredness of personality, must, if need be, be sacrificed to this end. This totalitarian aspect of communist ethics is the thing which has, more than anything else, shocked the conscience of the human race, and created an impression of cynical ruthlessness, which has largely overshadowed the fine humanist element of which we spoke earlier. And it would seem impossible to claim that it is entirely due to misunder-standings, by Lenin and others, of Marx's own teaching. Like the other elements, it has its place in the teaching of the two famous founders of modern communism themselves.

Near the end of his book, Venable says, 'It remains now only to ask what place this ethics of action, pugnacity, and partisanship can occupy theoretically in the tradition of which it forms, historically at least, a part – classical equalitarianism. . . . This doctrine has been variously formulated in such com-mandments to the individual as that he treat all men as ends, none as means, all as subjects, none as objects; others, when-ever and wherever, as though they were himself – the theory being that whether other individuals be friends or foes, whether they be aids or obstructions to the conditions of an ultimately genuine equalitarian humanism, the principle of rational justice states axiomatically that each nonetheless bears as he stands the inalienable right which follows from the numerical unique-ness of his own personhood – namely, the right to the good will of others.

'Our obvious problem here is to discover whether Marx's and Engels' view of human responsibility, which centers obli-gation on the conduct of the class struggle, on militancy and practical hostility toward large numbers of human beings – though still a distinct minority – can be seen as in any way compatible with this injunction to the indiscriminate exer-cise of good will.'[26]

At this point we must make a distinction. Two positions were possible for Marx to adopt. We must see whether he adopted the one or the other, or whether he spoke at this point in muffled and indecisive tones. The first position was that of a modified, and not absolute, cynicism. The enemies of communism misuse such ideas as justice, good will, the sacred-ness of the personality, and therefore he treats their assertions with suspicion and cynicism, as mere ideology. But the ideas in themselves are not ideology and nothing more. If this be Marx's position, then he has the right himself to speak of justice of true humanity, and of progress in ethical standards.

The second position is one of absolute cynicism. There is nothing in these ideas and standards but ideology. They are nothing more than weapons in the war of the classes. In that case Marx will have no right to speak of justice and the like. There is nothing at stake but the pure will to power. The war of expropriation and the ideal of the classless society are themselves pure ideology. The result of such complete cynicism would be ethical nihilism.

But it is to be observed that the danger of making the prosecution of the class war to a successful conclusion the one criterion of ethical action, to which all other scruples and considerations must be sacrificed, is not in itself a nihilist, but a fanatical view of ethics, though when it is carried out to the letter its results are about as repellent as the results of pure nihilism. The end in this case which is regarded as unconditional, and overriding all other considerations is the pursuit of a vision which may be called Utopian, but it has an ideal character of a sort, and is distinguished by its elevation from the mere struggle for power.

We have now to ask ourselves whether Marx did finally commit himself to the purely cynical position. Venable points out that though he frequently stated that 'Right . . . whether it be equal right or any other kind, "can never be higher than the economic structure of society and the cultural development thereby determined" '[72] and Engels expressed himself still more strongly to the same effect, yet Marx himself 'contributed to ethical thought that famous ideal of distributive justice – "From each according to his abilities, to each according to his needs".' This, says Venable, 'represents, from anyone's standpoint, the flowering, completion, and synthesis of all the most able saws of the classical equalitarians'.[28]

Yet we must reflect that this principle, which seems to embody a high respect for justice and for persons, does not, according to Marx, apply until the classless society has been achieved, and thus can never come into competition with the absolute obligation to achieve that society. Our general conclusion must be that Marx on occasion, or even frequently, speaks as if he were a pure cynic of relativist in the matter of moral values, but that he is not in fact cynical, since he not only talks about real humanity, advances in ethical standards, and so on, but makes an absolute ethical demand for the achievement of the classless society.

It is a pity that Venable slightly confuses the issue by

equating the Kantian demand that men should never be treated merely as means, but also always as ends, as persons, with equalitarianism, which is a much more questionable concept. The main motive power behind the doctrine which urges us to treat persons as ends, is the Christian teaching of the Fatherhood of God and the image of God in man.

The question then remains as to what place in Marx's ethic the individual human being and respect for him can hold. Is there any constraint upon our action laid by the fact that this particular being is a human being? This is a point at which Marxism speaks with a most uncertain voice, and it must be claimed that in Marx there is a fundamental incoherence, if not a sheer contradiction, at this point.[29]

The most important question which we have to put to Marx is whether having repudiated belief in God, he has not cut away the one secure foundation on which my fellow man can stand, and be protected from the invasion of my lust for power, or my fanatical attempts to play the part of providence in history, forgetting that my views may be mistaken, and that the results of my action may be very different from what I intend. Helmut Gollwitzer recalls in his book *The Christian Faith and the Marxist Criticism of Religion*[30] the famous statement of Marx, 'Man is the highest being for man.' He says, 'Anyone who for years has read daily that Marxist sentence inscribed on a transparency over the gates of prisoner-of-war camps in the Soviet Union, has had time enough to reflect upon it, and also to perceive the contradiction between the meaning of the sentence and the reality which he could see around him.' Gollwitzer goes on to point out the ambiguity of this saying. He says that the question 'was left open whether the highest being for me was to be my concrete fellow-man or an idea of man in the future. Were the first his meaning, that would lead him in the direction of the Christian love of our neighbour. . . . But if he meant the idea of man . . . as Marx hoped to find it realized in the society of the future, then . . . the fellow-man who but now was so exalted, becomes without significance, and can be manipulated without redress by appealing to the idea. . . . When humanism deposed God in the name of humanity, it cut away the ground from under its own feet.'[31]

Karl Marx's Conception of Man

This is the final ambiguity of the Marxian ethic for man. Is its result humanism or terror?

When we attack, and with justice, the ruthless element in Marxian ethics, we must remember also that the Christian doctrine of the sacredness of man has had far too little political and social application in the past, and that far too often the Church itself has been a gross offender against it, though at other times it has stood forth nobly in its defence.

8 Conclusions

Looking at Marx's doctrine of man in its main profile and characteristics, we must first reject his atheism as insufficiently grounded, though seen against its historical background it is not inexcusable. We must point out how his unquestionable humanitarian enthusiasm is endangered by it. 'Man is now alone in a world where it is very easy to replace him, in which he has only a fleeting and soon-forgotten place, a world as little capable of giving him enduring value as it is of receiving it from him.'[32]

Man then becomes only too easily the victim and fodder of the fanatical and unscrupulous planner, who sacrifices him to the idol of a future imagined for him.

On the other hand, for all its ambiguous characteristics, there is much in the Marxian view of man that may be accepted. It roots man firmly in his natural environment, and pleads that justice should be done to the under-privileged, arguing that human dignity is a phantom with little substance so long as it does not find expression in a fair share of freedom, opportunity, and planned control of the forces of production; that the notion of universal humanity is a mockery so long as men, classes, and nations are divided into the haves and the have-nots, a situation which is debilitating and estranging for all alike. If man's dominion is an authentic component of human nature and a mark of the image of God, it is largely frustrated so long as it is the monopoly of a few, and exercised in their interest. Social and planned production seem therefore to call for social ownership of the means of production. Until this is achieved, human nature will be to a considerable extent thwarted.

Marx's claim that communism is the true elimination of the

conflict of man with nature and with other men, the solution of the riddle of history, is a piece of rhetorical exaggeration, which Marx's own later writings do not echo. Gollwitzer admits that 'The concept remains optimistic enough if we understand it in a more relative manner, as the idea of a socialistic revolution within what is humanly possible, i.e. within the limits, and with the retention of the essential tensions which naturally belong to man as we have known him hitherto.'[33] Such a condition of man seems remote enough from us today, and we cannot depict in advance the ways in which it may find fulfilment, but it can be taken up into a Christian understanding of the authentic nature of man, and the enjoyment of the dominion which has been promised to him.

CHAPTER XVI

Sigmund Freud's
Conception of Man

The second thinker whose conception of man we have chosen
for comparison and contrast with the Christian one is Sigmund
Freud. There are few studies which in our day have made so
large a contribution to thought about human nature as dynamic
psychology. And there are no contributions to mental health
which can be compared with that made by the accompanying
discipline of psycho-therapy. Both dynamic psychology and
psycho-therapy owe far more to Freud than to any other
person. For all these reasons an attempt will be made here
to give, however perfunctorily, some sketch of those aspects
of his thought which are most relevant to the doctrine of man
in the world.

1 Freud's Intellectual Background and Interests
Freud grew up in the latter half of the nineteenth century. As
Guntrip points out,[1] he 'belonged to the era of Helmholtzian
physics and physiology. Behind the work of Helmholtz lies
that of Newton one hundred and fifty years earlier. . . .
Helmholtz died in 1894. By 1905 Einstein propounded his
theory of Relativity, initiating a radical revision of all basic
physical concepts. Freud's scientific orientation belonged to
the pre-Einstein era. . . . It reflects a scientific ideology which
had held sway some two hundred years when Freud began
to explore the psyche. The Newtonian scheme was a dualism
of matter, time and space on the one hand and force on
the other.'

This mental background naturally inclined Freud, whose own
early studies had been in the field of physiology, to interpret
psychological material as far as possible in biological and
physiological terms. In fact it may be said without exaggeration that Freud's conception of the self as an entity propelled
by the dynamic of the instincts is conceived on the analogy
of the Newtonian dualism.

In his great biography of Freud, Ernest Jones writes, 'The language of physics and cerebral physiology . . . was Freud's natural one, to which he in great part adhered later even when he was dealing with purely psychological problems. . . . In the realm of the visual, of definite neural activities that could be seen under the microscope, he had for many years felt entirely at home; he was as safe there as at the family hearth. To wander away from it and embark on the perilous seas of the world of emotions, where all was unknown and where what was invisible was of far greater consequence than the little that was visible, must have cost him dear.'[2]

It will be a central thesis of this chapter that Freud did indeed move away to some considerable extent from this early biologism, though he never explicitly broke with it, and that this change took place under the pressure of a flood of data coming from his psycho-therapeutic practice, which forced him to use concepts of a different order, which related to the development of personality in the early life of the child in its dealing with other people, particularly its parents. The fact that he did make this change at such a time and in such an intellectual environment, is a mark less of his inconsistency than of his greatness.

2 *Some of Freud's Central Concepts*

It is not easy to give a general sketch of Freud's theory, since its shape was continually developing, as new suggestions were made to account for phenomena observed in the treatment of patients, and new areas of the self were in turn brought under closer examination. Looking at the whole picture, it is however possible to pick out some of the most important concepts which were characteristic of Freud's work almost from the outset of his long career. Here we must distinguish between two kinds of concept. The first class are so near to the phenomenon itself that anyone who carefully examines the latter must agree with Freud as to their requirement for the interpretation of it.[3]

The first of these concepts is that of repression, of which Freud himself wrote 'The doctrine of repression is the foundation-stone on which the whole structure of psychoanalysis rests.'[4] In this context he also mentions resistance

and the existence of the unconscious.[5] All these he declares
to be, not assumptions, but theoretic inferences drawn legitimately from innumerable observations made in the course of
the analysis of patients.

To explain and correlate these and other concepts of the
first class, Freud evolved certain other important but more
speculative theories, chief among which were the doctrine of
the Oedipus complex, and his own particular type of instinct
theory. These more speculative theories belong to the second
of the two kinds of concept mentioned above.

In his *Introductory Lectures on Psycho-Analysis*, Freud
lists a number of everyday phenomena, slips of speech, forgetting, day-dreaming, and dreams. These things led him
early to the conclusion that in the mental and emotional life
of normal people as well as in that of neurotics, there were
conflicts of which they themselves were unaware. This uncon-
sciousness of underlying conflict was due to the phenomenon
of 'repression', which was different from the act of consciously suppressing a memory, feeling, or thought. In repression some thought or feeling which is unacceptable to the
conscious self is, as it were, thrust down into the unconscious,
but remains latent there. Repression is not a conscious act,
certainly not in the later stages. The act of suppression is not
necessarily injurious to health, but the result of repression is
often the rise of neurotic conflicts within the self, which waste
much energy, and are apt to find expression in anxiety,
compulsive actions, ideas, or phobias, which dominate the
person concerned, though he is unable to explain them.

Resistance was another of the concepts of the first type to
which Freud drew attention. It is a phenomenon universally
to be observed during the course of psychiatric treatment. In
spite of their sufferings, and their desire to be rid of them,
patients come up against feelings of blankness or blockage
in minds which they cannot overcome. The treatment makes
only slow and painful progress, and the patient will often
bring forward excuses for discontinuing it, or will forget to
keep appointments. The reason for this, at least in part, is
that he has already achieved some kind of balance in his
mental and emotional life, although an unsatisfactory one,
and fears what may happen if it is upset.

Among the more speculative concepts introduced by Freud to explain the facts encountered in psycho-therapy we have mentioned the Oedipus complex, and Freud's own particular type of instinct theory. The Oedipus complex received its name from the old Greek story of Oedipus, who killed King Laius, who turned out to have been his own father, and then married Laius' wife, Queen Jocasta, his own mother.

In this complex, Freud claimed to find one of the most important origins of repression. The young child has a sexual desire for the mother. The father comes to be regarded as a powerful rival for the mother's love, so that, with the affection and admiration which the boy feels for him, there is also an element of fear and hatred. But this hatred is repressed, and with it the incestuous desire for the mother. The same kind of thing will happen in the relationship of the small girl to her father, though this time the mother is the chief rival, and here again there is repression.[6] The Oedipus complex is one of Freud's concepts which has a continuing importance.

Freud's special form of instinct theory is another speculative concept of the second class. This theory passed through several stages in Freud's hands, but finally he decided that there were two main instincts as the sources of energy in the human psyche – the instinct of sex, or the libido, which he equated with the life instinct, and the instinct of aggression, which he equated with the death instinct. 'These libidinal and destructive drives were both innate, operated prior to experience, and were at perpetual warfare in the organism.'[7] In the work of Freud this form of instinct theory was linked with the notion of psychical energy, canalized in the instinctual channels, or in modifications ('sublimations') of them. Freud did not derive this theory of psychical energy from the practice of psycho-analysis, he brought it to analysis. It represents 'an attempt to conceptualize the data of psychology in terms analogous to those of the physics and chemistry' current in the second half of the nineteenth century.[8] Newtonian physics dealt with matter and force. Freud wished to introduce into dynamic psychology the concept of a psychical energy, quantitatively measurable, and seeking for discharge. No one today questions the fact that in psychical phenomena physical energy is involved, but the notion of a specific, quantitatively measurable, psychical, energy has been largely dropped, particularly because, unlike physical energy, it appears to be untestable in practice, a crippling defect in any scientific theory.[9] We shall later enter into a more detailed criticism of Freud's instinct theory.

3 *Freud's Interpretation of Human Action and Growth in the Terms of His Theory*

At first Freud thought that the conflicts whose existence he had inferred from his clinical experience, were conflicts between the conscious and the unconscious. The latter had instinctual wishes which were either of an aggressive or a sexual character. These were repugnant to the conscious self, and so were unable to emerge into consciousness. The unconscious was primitive, self-assertive, and animal, moved by the pleasure-principle. Increase of tension was accompanied by pain, discharge or decrease by pleasure.

Freud's dominant view was that the ego was a superficial structure in the psyche. It was its misfortune to be subject to pressure both from the external world and from the instincts within. In order to avoid retribution from without, it accepted the standards of society, even when these conflicted with the urges from the unconscious. These unlawful urges were thrust down by the process of repression, and emotions associated with the repressed material were also thrust down, and so lost to consciousness. It was the existence of resistance which led Freud to make one important modification in his theory. Previously he had been working with a duality of the conscious and the unconscious. Now the ego itself was discovered to have various levels, some of them primitive and unconscious.

Freud tried various ways of planning the map of the human self, about which more must be said at a later point, but a permanent new feature in his thinking was the concept of the super-ego. And since in his thought this concept was extremely important in the context of his attitude to religion, a word or two must be said about it here.

As we saw, he taught that through introjection many of the parents' injunctions and standards of behaviour are accepted

by the growing child, and become a kind of inner mentor.
Thus a part of the self was built up through the early years
of childhood into what was at first called the ego-ideal, and
later, the super-ego, which was held to be, in part, unconscious,
that is, its contents were not directly open to introspection.
As the parents had both loved the child and disciplined it,
so the super-ego had a double function of cherishing and
disciplining, and was also regarded in an ambivalent way by
the self, it was the object of mingled love and resentment.
Where the relation to the parents had been unsatisfactory in
early childhood, the oppressive and harsh side of the super-
ego predominated. It is generally accepted that Freud here
disclosed a profoundly significant element in the structure of
the self, and in his writings on religion, particularly in his
book *The Future of an Illusion* (1928), he makes great use
of it. However, it is by no means necessary to go the further
step with him that belief in God is nothing more than a
cosmic projection of the super-ego.

4 *Later Stages of Freud's Thought, and Some Developments From It*

At first Freud's attention, as we have seen, was concentrated
mainly on the unconscious, which he interpreted in terms of
instinctive libido. But there came a point in the early 1920's,
when his attention was drawn to the growth of the self and
its structures, and here he was dealing with the relations of
the growing child and its environment, and at once began to
use another type of interpretative category. Guntrip says
here 'Freud's theory of psychic structure was an attempt to
create a true *psycho*-dynamic theory, a psychology of man as
a person, after the false start of instinct and process theory.
In analysing ego-structure Freud was dealing with man as a
person whose psyche became internally differentiated and
organized as a result of his experience in personal object-
relations.'[10]

Guntrip argues that the evidence for this partial breakaway
of Freud from his organic and biological categories occurs in
his two books *Beyond the Pleasure Principle* (1920), and
Group Psychology and the Analysis of the Ego (1921). Like
most of Freud's books, these are difficult, and may be inter-

preted differently according to our judgment of the comparative importance of the various strands of thought contained in the work. Hitherto Freud had regarded the conscious self as merely the repressing agent censoring and keeping away from consciousness contents which would cause disturbance if they were admitted to it. Now he seemed to be working with a new group of concepts. It is true that in *Beyond the Pleasure Principle* he makes much use of the conflict between libido or positive instinct and the aggressive death instinct, both of which he regards as innate components of human nature. But libidinal elements are now admitted to be active, not only in that primary process which later came to be called the id, but also in the ego. In fact, instead of being regarded as a secondary repressing agent on the surface, as it were, of the unconscious, the ego is here looked on as the basic unitary self, which is subsequently split into opposing systems as a result of difficulties encountered in external object relations.[11]

In Freud's next book, *Group Psychology and the Analysis of the Ego*, the life and death instincts seem to be more or less, for the time, forgotten. The starting point is not the instincts regarded as innate in the organism, but 'distinctions which arise in the ego after birth as a result of experiences in object-relationships'.[12] Guntrip comments that at this point it would have been possible for Freud to have made a revision of his entire theory . . . and worked out a theory of neurosis and personality structure as explained by post-natal developmental changes and differentiations within the psyche as primary unitary ego. This was in fact the line of development followed to some extent by Melanie Klein, and more systematically by W. R. D. Fairbairn, which Guntrip also himself expounds. This opportunity was, however, lost, for in his next book *The Ego and the Id* (1923), Freud recurred to his earlier instinct theory, taking once more a narrower view of the ego as simply that part of the primary self which is exposed to the solicitations of instinct from within and the pressures of the world from without. But if this point of view is taken, then the id can hardly have self-character at all, since 'ego quality' is divorced from the sources of psychic energy.[13] Here we see once more the evil effect of Freud's biological and physiological concepts, which in the later work *The Future of an Illusion*, were to produce so depressing a view of human nature and its relation to society.

According to the object relations school there is from the beginning of life a rudimentary self, which is object-centred and personal in character. When this psychical unity begins to break down (as always happens to some extent in early childhood), it splits into various structures, each possessing its own libidinal component, each of self-character, each attached to objects, whether exterior or interior. A part of the object relations theory is the division of objects into external and internal or endo-psychic. The latter are claimed to have been introjected, and repressed, and with them the libidinal attachment of the self to them has been repressed also. These internal objects are therefore in a sense illusory or unreal, but since they form part of the internal world which helps to constitute the psyche, they are real and powerful in their influence upon the actions of the self. It is not necessary or possible here to give an account of the extremely elaborate manner in which the structures of the self are split and attached to these endo-psychic objects, as Klein, Fairbairn and Guntrip[14] have suggested, though these details may be extremely important in the diagnosis, treatment, and cure of various types of neurotic and psychotic illness. For our purpose it is enough to say that on this view human nature, whether its objects be external or internal, is not built up of components both impersonal and unfitted for any community or fellowship of men, so that human life in society is not inevitably an unhappy compromise between imperious instincts seeking discharge of tension and a hostile society. And society itself is not of necessity condemned to a precarious unstable balance of contending forces.

According to the object relations school, there is no original death instinct; the aggression which admittedly plays so large a part in the growth of the psyche, only becomes excessive when libido or love has failed to find adequate satisfaction in childhood, and is therefore a secondary and pathological thing. This view regards man's nature as not merely reactive to innate instinctual pressures, but as being from the start essentially outward-directed towards objects and goals. Here the components of human nature are clearly compatible with a theistic, and indeed, a Christian faith. These writers claim that they are themselves following pointers offered by the work of Freud himself, so that they can be regarded as standing in the true Freudian tradition.[15] It is also clear that Fairbairn and Guntrip do not share Freud's contemptuous rejection of religion, although they naturally admit that there is a good deal of neurotic religion and neurotic Christianity.

5 Freud's Repudiation of Weltanschauungen and his own Weltanschauung

Like many other people who have expressed their hostility to philosophy, Freud paid for his neglect. Guntrip tells us that he 'frequently expressed a hostile attitude to philosophy and religion, both of which he regarded as "nothing but" purely speculative attempts to evolve a set of beliefs primarily designed to serve as a basis for personal security, and representing nothing but wishful thinking. Philosophy and theology were to him intellectualized forms of the phantasy life, aiming at the creation of a *Weltanschauung,* a comprehensive view of the universe by the aid of which the thinker can feel defended against uncertainty and insecurity.'[16]

In 1926 Freud wrote[17] about the reaction of some readers to this book, *The Ego and the Id.* He said 'In that book I drew a picture of its (the ego's) dependence upon the id and upon the super-ego which revealed how powerful and apprehensive it was in regard to both and with what an effort it maintained its superiority over them. This view has been widely echoed in psycho-analytic literature. A great deal of stress has been laid on the weakness of the ego in relation to the id and of our rational elements in the face of the daemonic forces within us; and there is a strong tendency to make what I have said into a foundation-stone of a psycho-analytic *Weltanschauung.* Yet surely the psycho-analyst, with his knowledge of the way in which repression works, should, of all people, be restrained from adopting such extreme and one-sided views. I must confess that I am not at all partial to the fabrication of *Weltanschauungen.* Such activities may be left to philosophers, who avowedly find it impossible to make their journey

through life without a Baedeker of that kind to tell them all
about everything. Let us humbly accept the contempt with
which they look down on us from the vantage-point of their
superior needs.'

As Guntrip points out, philosophy cannot be so easily dismissed as this, and one of the penalties that Freud paid for his
contempt was that he was not able to criticize the philosophical
assumptions that underlay his own theorizing.[18] As we shall
see, the inferences drawn by many of his readers about the
Freudian view of the ego, the libido, and the nature of man
and his place in society, were not unwarranted, and an
'imaginative world-view' (as we might translate the word
Weltanschauung) even more clearly underlies works like *The
Future of an Illusion*. This world-view has various sub-species,
one of which has been inaccurately described as scientific
materialism, and is akin to certain types of positivism, one of
the central articles of faith in all these views being that the
physical sciences are the only authentic path to reality, and
that knowledge is only respectable in so far as it approximates
to the standards of scientific experiment and verification used
in these sciences. 'Scientific' materialism is not in fact scientific,
since it makes use of assertions of a general character about
man and the universe which are well beyond the range of
scientific verification or falsification. This does not entirely
explode the claim of such a philosophy to rationality, but
disallows its claim to be 'scientific'.

Freud himself later apparently modified his claim that no
Weltanschauung was implied by or expressed in his psycho-
analytic views, though to some extent he protected himself
by a qualifying clause. In his *New Introductory Lectures*
(1933) he stated his opinion that the young science of psycho-
analysis was in no state to formulate a *Weltanschauung,* but
must share the common *Weltanschauung* of science, which he
thought hardly merited such a high-sounding name.[19]

There can, however, be little doubt that Freud himself
subscribed to a full-blown *Weltanschauung* whose incom-
patibility with the Christian faith it should not be hard to
demonstrate. This was one of the varieties of naturalism.

6 Freud's Attack on Religion

Freud dealt explicitly with the theme of religion in his book *The Future of an Illusion*. This book starts with the familiar material about the anti-social instinctive drives in the individual, which are held in check by external sanctions and internal psychological structures within the individual. But the amount of frustration that can be tolerated in a society is limited, and in any community where the advantages of culture, wealth and instinctual satisfaction are too unevenly distributed, there will come a moment of fission, and all the cultural gains stored up by the society will be scattered to the winds, and society would be at an end. It is to society's interest to see that there is some kind of balance between desire and satisfaction, and that there are sanctions of force to hold at bay the elements leading towards revolt and disintegration. But there are certain evils which society cannot hold at bay; it can never defend man wholly from death and the elements.[20] Therefore men undertook the task of humanizing nature; they created the gods. The gods are personal, we can come to terms with them, we can try to exorcize them, bribe them, appease them.

The gods have three functions: they defend us from the terrors of nature, they reconcile us with the cruelty of fate and of death, and, as guardians of morality, they make amends to us for the sufferings that communal life has inflicted upon us.[21] This situation had its prototype in our infancy, when our parents, especially our fathers, were our protectors. They were loved, but also feared, as the upholders of justice. With their conception of Jahveh the father, the Israelites unconsciously revealed what had lain all the time behind the notion of the gods, the fear and love of the human father. These religious ideas, Freud continues, are prized as the most treasured possession of culture, men suppose that life would be intolerable without them.

Freud goes on to ask: 'what is the psychological significance of religious beliefs?' Scientific statements, he says, may be confirmed by perception, but religious beliefs can offer no such self-justification. It is maintained by theologians, when questioned, that our ancestors held them. If that is not enough to silence criticism, proofs of little value from antiquity are adduced, and finally we are forbidden to raise the question of their authenticity.[22] If we ask for present-day confirmation, the only answer is the kind of response given by Vaihinger, the creator of the As-If Philosophy, which is really equivalent to an admission that religious beliefs are fictions which have an unequalled importance for the maintenance of human society.[23] In short, Freud concludes, religious ideas are illusions, which cannot be disproved, but certainly cannot be proved by science, and some of them are so very unlike the evidence which we have laboriously discovered about the nature of the world, that one may well call them delusions.

Then comes a revealing sentence: '. . . to many questions science can as yet give no answer; but scientific work is our only way to the knowledge of external reality.' What we have then, behind this book of Freud's, is nothing more than the old positivist prejudice, using, it is true, a new and more subtle technique. For the old positivism held that knowledge which could not be verified by scientific experiment or sense-perception, was not true knowledge. All such statements as appeared to make cognitive claims and could not fulfil these conditions were mere expressions of emotion, or the like, 'hurrah noises' as one modern positivist put it.

Freud goes on to make one or two more reflections. 'Are not other assumptions,' he asks, 'such as those that regulate our political institutions, illusions also? There are certainly erotic illusions in our relations between the sexes. Is the conviction that science itself discovers anything about reality itself an illusion? . . . I have not,' he continues, 'time to follow these inquiries, though I think they would partly result in an affirmation of this doubt.'[24] However, we hear no more of the doubt, it appears to sink back into Freud's unconscious with a suspicious celerity. But at the end of the book he returns to the subject for a moment. '. . . Science,' he now declares, 'is no illusion. But it would be an illusion to suppose that we could get anywhere else what it cannot give us.'[25] This however, is not rational argument, it is mere assertion. It reminds us of what the late Harry Lauder used to say in one of his stage impersonations: 'Ah'm tellin' ye!'

Possibly the thought that was in Freud's mind when for a

moment he permitted himself to doubt the truth of science was this, that the assertion of uniformity in nature which underlies its other assertions is one which itself cannot be confirmed by experiment, but must always precede every experiment. And so science itself may not be able to come up to the standard set for knowledge by this school of thought, and so may have to be reckoned by it as no more than a beneficial illusion.

To continue our summary of *The Future of an Illusion*, Freud imagines a dialogue between a critic and himself. The critic says 'Granted that religion is an illusion, you must conclude that it is a beneficial one, and if its promises and safeguards were removed, most men would become nihilists.' 'No,' answers Freud. 'In effect, this would not happen.' In the long run culture would benefit by cutting its link with religion. Religion was a necessary stage in man's history. As a child cannot become mature without passing through a pathological conflict of soul called a neurosis, so mankind must pass through a pathological stage called religion, on its way towards maturity.[26] But through that stage mankind has already in large measure passed. It will be a grim world where there is no opiate of religion to hand, but by withdrawing his expectations from the other world, and by concentrating all his energies upon this world, man will probably attain to a condition where life will be tolerable for all, and no one will suffer oppression any more.[27]

7 The Incompatibility of Classical Freudianism with Christianity

Here again it will be impossible to do justice to the richness and variety of the subject-matter, and the various stages through which Freud's thought passed. But it would be fair to say that all along the two concepts of libido and aggression, the life instinct and the death instinct, were central to his thought. At the beginning libido was for Freud closely associated with sexuality. But in the end it became for him a kind of maid-of-all-work, it could be attracted towards the self, and when sublimated it could be transformed into a selfless devotion which would appear to have little connection with sex, as Freud pictured the latter. Equally original in the human constitution, according to Freud, was the death instinct, the source of our aggressive and destructive tendencies, both those directed towards ourselves, and those directed towards others. As Guntrip says, Freud never really departed from the view that libido (sex), and aggression are dangerous innate forces operating without regard to social necessities and moral values, and the ego must defend itself from them at all costs. Thus 'Freud is landed in the dilemma that the denial of instinct is necessary for culture and civilization, whilst the gratification of instinct and the relaxation of culture is necessary for health. This pessimistic conclusion should arouse our suspicions. Social life, on this view, can never be any other than unending warfare between instinct and morality, the needs of the individual and the demands of the group. . . . Civilization, culture and social life would have no real roots in the inner nature of the individual – who, apparently, is not formed for society in spite of the fact that on other grounds he needs it.'[28]

In fact, what we have in Freud is a doctrine of man in society very like that of Thomas Hobbes, who regarded man's nature as basically alien and hostile to society, and regarded his instincts as being held in check only by the threat of external sanctions adopted by society for its own protection against him. Freud has added the subtle thought, unknown to Hobbes, of the introjection of sanctions of society which are thus felt internally as the admonitions of the super-ego. Such a view of man, quite apart from Freud's rejection of God and religion in general, is surely incompatible with Christian faith, according to which man is basically created for his neighbour, society, and God, and can find true satisfaction only in these relationships. This pessimistic dualism is impossible material from which to build a theistic or Christian universe; this is a construction which could at the best achieve only a miserable and precarious balance among its contending atoms. And Guntrip's comment is very much to the point: 'We have here a full scale social psychology, or rather a psycho-biological theory of culture and civilization. It can be controverted only if the fundamental premise of instinct-theory is wrong.'[29]

It must not be assumed that Freud's critics belonging to the object relations school deny the powerful pressures of libidinal forces in the individual, or the tensions which exist between the desires of individuals and the needs of society. They have discovered other, and as they believe, more satisfactory categories of interpretation, which do not lead to Freud's dismal conclusions about the stuff of human nature. Freud, they hold, went wrong because his instinct concepts, built up on the model of the concepts used in the physics of his day, were inadequate to deal with the social and personal realities which were asking for interpretation and amelioration. In short, so strange are the raw materials of human society in Freud's theory, that Ian Suttie, in his brilliant study *The Origins of Love and Hate,* had little difficulty in showing that society could never have come into being at all, had man's instinctual and natural endowment been what Freud maintained it to be. Freud's doctrine of man does not even seem to fit some of the facts that are easily accessible to common sense. In his picture of the pleasure-seeking libido and the death instinct he seems to have no place for other-regarding love, or even for anything which might develop into it, no place for a rudimentary desire to give as well as to receive, to be related to an object for that object's sake. All other-regarding elements in man seem to be entirely the result of sublimation, when the primary instinct of libidinal desire is deprived of its direct goal. It is, however, never convincingly explained how these other-regarding qualities, so different, and by all agreement so desirable and fine, are produced by the mere existence of a barrier to direct libidinal satisfaction. Surely the natural thing for such a barrier to do would be merely to produce exasperation, or the pursuit of some other libidinal object, unless there were elements of tenderness and disinterested affection there from the start.

7 *Rejection of Freud's Contention that God is Merely the Projection of the Human Father-Idea*
The first Christian line of argument against a doctrine of religion like Freud's is to say that he has no a priori right to question the possibility of a contingent historical revelation of God. He never troubles to think of this possibility, prob-

ably because he treats of religion in general, and does not take seriously the Christian claim to revelation as a unique event. Historical event is not in the same dimension as wish-fulfilment.

Freud's account of belief in God attempts to discredit it by means of a psychological account of its origin in the life of the child. He maintains that when the child discovers that its parents are not morally perfect or all-powerful, it instinctively feels that there must be some great Power to protect the self, and prevent the disintegration of the personality. The ego, even with the help of the super-ego, is unequal to this task. So an act of projection takes place, and the figure of an Almighty Parent is projected on to the heavens. He has both the protective and the punitive functions of the human father. God is, or the gods are, thus created in our own image, or rather, in the image of our parents.

By this theory Freud is able to account for certain phenomena which the ordinary sociological sceptical theories of religion are unable to account for. It has been objected by Christians that God cannot be a wish-fulfilment, since he not only loves us, but judges us. Freud has here his answer ready. For one of his discoveries is that the super-ego has the same double function of protecting and punishing that the human father had. Again, when the sociological interpretation of moral obligation is suggested, that obligation is simply the pressure of the community upon me (Durkheim), and the Christian refutes it by saying that men feel bound by a law higher and sterner than that of the human community, Freud can answer, 'Yes, of course, the super-ego.' Thus, we may imagine, he would have interpreted the act of Antigone, who buried her brother Polyneices against the commands of King Creon, because she felt herself bound by an eternal and higher law.

This reduction by Freud of our belief in God and moral obligation is worthy of a fuller and more detailed treatment than I have yet seen it receive. It will not do merely to say that Freud shows *how* an idea of God arises, and that origins have nothing to do with validity. As Flügel says, the conviction of a peasant girl that a prince will come to marry her cannot be proved to be fallacious, for such things *have* happened. But that conviction is so very much in line with what we might expect to be her wishes, that we would do well to suspect her to have no rational grounds for it. As usual, the Freudians seem to have loaded the dice in their own favour. It is a case of 'Heads I win, tails, you lose.' If God's existence be regarded as a source of gladness, the answer will be 'wish-fulfilment', if it is regarded with anxiety, the rejoinder will be 'the super-ego'.

But it must be repeated that the edge of the Freudian attack cannot be turned by a simple declaration that origins have nothing to do with validity. We would be right in saying that the question of validity is a different one from that of origins. But there are cases where the origin of a belief only needs to be explained for the gravest doubts to be cast on its validity. For example, if it is explained to me that I have just had a car crash, and that my head has gone through the windscreen, then there is every reason to believe that the stars which I am seeing are not astronomical, but merely projections!

How then in particular can Christian apologetics refute such a claim as Freud's to have explained away our belief in God, as a mere projection of our relation to our human parents? Emil Brunner has given a fruitful hint as to one line of argument. 'Behind the crude formula, "Men make a god out of their wish" there lies the problem, as to how a wish can be made into God. Animals also have wishes, but they have no gods.'[30]

To put it differently, even idolatry, which is the making of something relative into an absolute, suggests that somehow God must have revealed himself. This is not a proof that would be fully cogent to unbelievers, but the Christian can see that there must have been an absolute confrontation, and that this could never have been engendered out of the conflict between instinctual drives and the prohibitions of the super-ego, with the ego as umpire, which are all that Freud characteristically allows to go to the make-up of human nature.

Here then, we have the same problem which has confronted us already in another context. Now we see the inner reason for Freud's inability to account for a truly *human* society. He does indeed admit the necessity of the confrontation of

The Image of God in Man

the human self by other selves, hinting that without this the super-ego and even consciousness itself might not exist. But he has no explanation why this society should be a characteristically *human* society. He does state that men had to combine in society, and so subjected themselves to the denials of instinct without which society would disintegrate. But why, one may ask, has man to combine in a *human* society? Do the animals not have very satisfactory societies of their own, built up on the pure basis of instinct, as it would appear? Our answer will be that man had to combine in a *human* society because he is created in the image of God. The essential thing here about man's humanity is that every man is confronted by the Absolute Thou, and only because our confrontation with each other is interwoven with this absolute confrontation, is it different from the confrontation of beasts with each other. It looks therefore as if the absolute confrontation were not a projection of the super-ego, but as if, in some sense, the reverse were the truth; without the absolute confrontation the super-ego would never have come into existence. There is in all of us, despite all sin, a relationship, not only to each other but also to justice and righteousness which goes to make up our relationship to the human thou. And this in our opinion suggests an immediate confrontation with God. We may concede that it would be illegitimate to demand of the Freudian psychology an acknowledgment of the validity of the belief in God. To do this would be to ask it to transgress its legitimate boundaries just as much on the side of faith as in fact Freud transgressed them on the side of unbelief. Yet it is fair to point out how inadequate the Freudian construction is in its account of the formation of characteristically human traits which we as Christians associate with man's sacredness, his standing as one created in God's image, as one directly confronted with God and responsible to him.

Thus we cannot accept Freud's suggestion that our conception of God is merely a projection of our own early idea of our human parents. But we must admit that the *content* of our conception of God is distorted if we have been unable to attain to a mature relationship with our human fathers, and

250

with authority in general. Those whose super-ego is hard and tyrannical, will have a hard and tyrannical conception of God. Freud's attack is a valid criticism of a bogus Christianity. In an exactly parallel way, Marx's criticism of our religion is a valid criticism of pathological elements in our faith. He claims that religion is – among other things – a weapon of the economically dominant classes for maintaining their domination. We must confess that to far too great an extent our religion has been perverted in this way. It has often been done unconsciously. But true Christianity is uninjured by the shafts of Marx and Freud.

Why are we unable to accept Freud's suggestion that our conception of God is a projection upon the clouds of heaven of our own infantile father-idea? Were the charge true, then there would be no more content in the concept of God than there was in the original father-idea of which it was a projection. And there would be no reality to correspond to it.

There is nothing on the cinema screen which is not on the film whose picture is projected upon it. That is the reality, the origin of the picture which is 'blown up' on the screen. Were the projection theory true, it would indeed be pathological for a grown man to feel dependent upon God, for at that age he ought not to feel dependent on his human father. And for Freud belief in God is a mark of immaturity in the individual and in the race.

Yet Christian faith maintains that while the human term 'father' is used of God, the predication is analogical. That is, the Fatherhood of God is not the same as the fatherhood of man. It is because in relation to God we are in touch with a reality which has its own independence, that there is this difference in the content of the concept. In fact, our relation to God is more intimate than the relation to our human father, for of them we could never say 'In whom we live and move and have our being', nor yet could we say of any one of them that 'in his service is perfect freedom'.

So from the standpoint of faith we must maintain that even where the relationship to God perhaps seems at the beginning a unity undifferentiated from the relationship to the human father, this is merely an appearance.[31] For the I-

251

thou relationship to God is one of the original constituents of our human nature. As Christians we can see that it is the absolute confrontation with God which is the foundation of our awareness of sacredness in other human beings. And I would suggest that there is a very general though often obscure awareness of this fact among men.

CHAPTER XVII

The Contribution of
Teilhard de Chardin

When this book first appeared, nearly twenty years ago, the name of Teilhard de Chardin was little known among Protestant theologians. In the works of Barth, Brunner, and Tillich there is, apparently, no single reference to him. This silence, in the light of his present fame, might have appeared inexplicable, until we recollect that owing to the veto of his Order and the Holy Office, he was prevented from publishing in his lifetime what he believed to be his most important works.

The theological atmosphere has changed considerably in the interval, and while many influences have contributed to the change, there is perhaps no single writer who has had more influence than Teilhard, so that there is some reason for including a chapter on his contribution rather than that of any other recent thinker, in a new edition of this book.

1 The Nature of Teilhard's Central Theological Work

Teilhard is a writer about whom the most various estimates have been made, both on the part of scientists, and on that of theologians and philosophers. The cause for this divergence has in no small part been due to uncertainty as to the genre of his most controversial works. His writings fall into four main categories. First, there is his correspondence; secondly, there are certain publications which are universally acknowledged to be of a scientific kind; thirdly, there are his devotional Christian writings; and fourthly, the books clustered around what is undoubtedly his main work, *The Phenomenon of Man*. It is on the strength of this last class of works that his reputation in coming years as a theological thinker is bound to stand or fall. Since his inclusion in this book can only be justified if he is agreed to be a seminal thinker, some attempt to say what he succeeded in doing in these works is required at this point. It will be our argument that the sharpest attacks

253

made on him are to some extent due to a misunderstanding of what he was doing, a misunderstanding for which he was unfortunately partly to blame himself. It is a risky thing to incur the charge of claiming to understand a great writer in some respects better than he understood himself, but the reader will understand that the epistemological analysis which follows is felt to be essential to the vindication of Teilhard in the hope that it may help to make some of the critic realize that he has been too easily dismissed by them.

There is an important passage in the Preface to *The Phenomenon of Man,* where Teilhard sets forth what he believes himself to be doing in the rest of the book. There is no other passage in Teilhard's writings where he writes anything contradictory to this, so it will be worth-while dealing with it at some length.

In this Preface he presents us with man as a phenomenon, as the object of purely scientific reflection. This reflection he contrasts with the 'farther-reaching speculations of the philosopher and the theologian', and tells us that 'Of set purpose I have at all times carefully avoided entering into that field of the essence of being.'[1] Elsewhere[2] he describes metaphysics as that discipline which employs the concept of the absolute best, or of causation, or of finality. This would seem to delimit metaphysics as the discipline which uses the Five Ways of Aquinas, his fivefold proofs of God's existence from the contingent as a starting point. However this may be, science for Teilhard has to do with empirical phenomena and their sequences. So we would appear to have a division of reality into two fields, on the one hand phenomena, which are in principle accessible to all men. This is the field, not only of daily experience and perception, but also of natural science. On the other hand we have the unseen realities with which philosophy and theology concern themselves. At several stages in the book he points out that what he is trying to do is to describe the phenomena and is leaving open the metaphysical issue of what deeper significance may underlie it. To give one of these instances to illustrate what he means; the fact of evolution is stated to be a phenomenon, while the question of whether God may have been at work in it is a theological or metaphysical question.[3]

254

But now Teilhard goes on to introduce a third area lying between these two. His book, he claims, deals with man the phenomenon, but with the whole phenomenon. And this is the field, not of philosophy or metaphysics, but of hyper-physics, or, as he elsewhere terms it, of ultraphysics. And he adds, 'Without contradicting what I have just said . . . it is this aspect which might possibly make my suggestions *look* like a philosophy. During the last fifty years or so, the investigations of science have proved beyond all doubt that there is no fact which exists in pure isolation, but that every experience, however objective it may seem, inevitably be-comes enveloped in a complex of assumptions as soon as the scientist attempts to express it in a formula. But while this aura of subjective interpretation may remain imperceptible where the field of observation is limited, it is bound to become practically dominant as soon as the field of vision extends to the whole. . . . science, philosophy and religion are bound to converge as they draw nearer to the whole . . . without ceasing, to the very end, to assail the real from different angles and on different planes. Take any book about the universe written by one of the great modern scientists, such as Poincaré, Einstein or Jeans, and you will see that it is impossible to attempt a general scientific interpretation of the universe without *giving the impression* of trying to explain it through and through. But look a little more closely and you will see that this "hyperphysics" is still not a metaphysic.'[4]

Now surely it is just this discipline of hyperphysics whose epistemological status is ill-defined by Teilhard. He is right in saying that every experience is involved in a network of assumptions, and that so long as the disputants are required to submit to the test of verification or falsification, the differ-ence between their varying assumptions is kept within bounds. But in proportion as the field extends to what Teilhard rather naïvely calls 'the whole phenomenon', this kind of checking becomes more and more difficult.

Teilhard himself is aware that two very important presup-positions govern the whole of his own thinking. First, there is the primacy accorded to the psychic and to thought in the stuff of the universe', which a sentence later he re-defines as 'the pre-eminent significance of man in nature', and, second.

'the "biological" value attributed to the social fact around us',
which also is re-defined by him, in the next sentence, as 'the
organic nature of mankind'.[5]

From the rest of his writings it is clear that the first principle refers to the notion that there is an advancing wave of
evolution in the universe, and that, in spite of his physical
smallness and the brevity of his life, man rides on the crest
of that wave, and is thus justified,[6] to change the metaphor, in
thinking that his perspective is not merely subjective, but that
the cross-roads of the universe are really where he stands.

The second principle, if I understand him rightly, is that
the social development of man, which points to a coming
unity in which man will be bound together in love with man,
is a continuation of biological evolution, carrying on the same
development which it began.[7]

These are not irrational presuppositions, but are they necessary? Clearly not, at least in the sense that it is quite possible
for highly intelligent people to repudiate them, as Sir Peter
Medawar does, maintaining that there is no sense in which one
product of evolution can be regarded as 'higher' than another,[8]
and later castigates 'the . . . superficial and ill thought out
view that the so-called "psycho-social evolution" of mankind
and the genetical evolution of living organisms are two episodes of a continuous integral process (though separated by a
"critical point", whatever that may mean).'

Therefore we are forced to ask whether Teilhard does not
first define 'phenomenon' as a reality which is knowable
independent of special presuppositions not necessarily shared
by every thinker, and then, by introducing talk about the
whole phenomenon', move into a field where verification, if
not impossible, will have such a different shape, that we are
no longer talking about science, but apologetics.

Emil Brunner once said that the nearer you come to the
centre of man's being, the more difficult it is to avoid the
influence of determining presuppositions of one kind or another.[9] Surely, this is a case in point.

Teilhard justifies the choice of his two presuppositions by
saying that they alone can give 'a full and coherent account of
the phenomenon of man'.[10] He implies consequently that in
pointing to this coherence, he is not merely testifying to his

faith, but appealing to the rationality of his partners in the debate. On both sides, each of the contestants claims that he is arguing rationally. Medawar's claim is that 'higher' and 'lower' are inappropriate terms to use in speaking of evolution, and, further, that 'evolution' is a concept which cannot be legitimately extrapolated beyond the biological sphere. Teilhard, I suggest, is speaking from the standpoint of an imaginative world-picture (*Weltanschaung*). Medawar claims that it is an ill-based world-picture. Whether he is himself building upon an alternative world picture, that of naturalism, does not appear.

In relation to discussions about man, I can therefore hardly believe that strictly speaking the word 'phenomenon' is altogether apt, since the very way that we see man depends in part upon the divergent presuppositions which we bring to our seeing. To some extent this can be said about other realities which we investigate, but man is so near to us, as it were, that our very seeing and our different valuations are more closely interwoven here than elsewhere. This leads to a complicated situation; it might lead us to abandon any attempt at rational discussion about man with people whose positions are widely divergent from our own. But in fact, man is so important a subject for us all, that this does not happen, nor can it be allowed to happen. In the last resort we are compelled to ask our interlocutors, 'Try to look at this reality, which confronts us both, through my eye-piece. Do you not get a clearer, less distorted, and more coherent image than your own eye-piece has been giving you?' And this kind of understanding or insight is what, in my opinion, Teilhard's project in *The Phenomenon of Man* endeavours to give to us. Thus we would place his work in this field, not within the boundaries of strict science, but within those of apologetics.

Now it must be admitted that Teilhard claims that he is speaking as a scientist in *The Phenomenon of Man,* and working within the field of science. Clearly his definition of science is very different from that of Medawar, who in the critical review cited above, remarked caustically, 'Teilhard practised an intellectually unexacting kind of science in which he achieved a moderate proficiency. He has no grasp of what makes a logical argument, or of what makes for proof.'[11]

Medawar, further, is not the only scientist who is unwilling
to regard Teilhard's claim to be writing scientifically as unjustified. Yet this does not mean that the work is to be regarded
as valueless, even if the criticism be just. In a recent book
Teilhard Reassessed, written by a number of authors, there is
both negative and positive confirmation of the view I have put
forward here.

The negative confirmation comes from F. A. Turk, a
scientist, who writes, 'But if it is not a philosophy; if neither
the method nor the conclusions may, in any strict sense, be
accounted scientific, what, in fact, is it? Has it value? If so,
how best may we use it?' Turk goes on to conclude that
Teilhard was a thinker who 'played his hunches', and that,
indeed, scientists often do this – but that the main value of
such hunch-playing is the production of hypotheses which
themselves may indirectly produce verifiable or falsifiable
consequences, and he goes on to indicate one or two such
fruitful conjectures of Teilhard's. Turk further suggests that in
'Teilhard's account of evolution . . . his facts are "coloured"
by his theory, both as to selection, interpretation and presentation', and Turk himself brings forward some other theories
which 'have been founded upon, roughly, the same range of
data'. He does this in order that his readers may be able 'to
obtain an "objective", if only very partial, "apparatus criticus"
of Teilhard's whole system'.[12] It seems that here we have an
awareness that we are moving in a field where we are not
simply concerned with phenomena, but also with differing
fundamental principles of interpretation and valuation, which
make different people see and estimate these phenomena in
divergent ways.

If Turk to some extent gives negative support to our viewpoint, Professor Anthony Hanson, the editor of the book,
gives some positive confirmation of it. In his essay, he describes Teilhard as being, if a philosopher at all, a process
philosopher akin to Whitehead and Alexander. Hanson writes:
'But the Christian philosopher was rightly described by Anselm
as *fides quaerens intellectum*, and his first duty is to keep that
faith intact; to see to it that the deliverances of science or of
autonomous reason do not end by denying Christian experience. His faith in God, and therefore in the universe, con-

vinces him of course that faith and reason cannot ultimately
conflict. I would regard Teilhard de Chardin's work as a
noble effort to vindicate this faith.'[13] While this statement
might be misunderstood as subscribing to the old view of
theology as Queen of the Sciences, dictating to them the
results to which they must come in their own legitimate
spheres, it is clear that Hanson regards Teilhard's main work
as lying within the apologetic field.

The Christian thinker must be convinced that the God in
whom he believes is the ultimate reality, and therefore he is
bound to try to work out the consequences of this faith as a
man of his time, living in his intellectual environment which
he shares with his contemporaries, using their concepts in so
far as they serve him, and attempting to preserve the coherence
of his own mental world while so doing. Yet his starting point
is the Christian faith, and the main current of his thinking
flows from the revelation of God, towards the world, and
not in the opposite direction. This cannot, of course, mean
that the apologist's Christian faith entitles him to deny the
findings of science in any sphere where science exercises its
legitimate authority. This, in general, is a description of the
work of the Christian apologist, and this is what in these
central works under consideration, I take Teilhard de Chardin
to have been.

2 An Account of Teilhard's Imaginative World-View

Our next task will be to give an account of Teilhard's imaginative world-view, without troubling to specify what elements
in it are the result of actual scientific observations, and
what are drawn from his Christian beliefs. Clearly, both
elements are here closely interwoven, and there will be a
chance later to suggest that at points where he thought that
certain conclusions could be drawn on scientific or general
grounds, he owed more to his faith than he often realized.
At the moment, however, our task is to set forth what he says.

His is a wide-ranging theology which includes a doctrine of
man, a doctrine of the world, and a doctrine of God. One of
the most striking characteristics of his doctrine of man is its
dynamic character; man is here understood as part of a moving
and changing universe, a universe still in the process of

creation, and advancing towards a consummation where man, and not only the individual, but the race, will find fulfilment in God. This eschatological trait is to be seen most clearly in the New Testament, but it was to some extent lost sight of in the course of the history of the Church. It is, curiously enough, Teilhard's doctrine of evolution which enabled him to recover an understanding of this dynamic forward thrust, for it helped him to regard creation not as something over and done with by an original divine fiat, but as a process which is going on – this is still an incomplete world, which will not find its perfection until 'God is all in all'.

Teilhard tells us that though the universe in general gives an impression of immobility, in the sense that it seems to have been always as it is, and will continue to be so, yet this is an illusion.[14] It is in movement everywhere, and this is not merely physical movement, but 'complexification' – evolution of the more complex out of the more simple. At first this change was so immensely slow that it would not have been observable had there been anybody there to look for it. But as it progresses, it gradually attains momentum, and not only does it do so, but the rate of change itself accelerates. The universe was at first an environment in which the elements were enormous in their number, and almost entirely unorganized, each being very much the same as the rest, the totality approximating to an aggregate rather than a structured whole. (The term 'elements' is here of course not used of the chemical elements, but in the sense of particles or primitive entities.) Teilhard continues: 'We will define the "complexity" of a thing, if you will allow, as the quality the thing possesses of being composed – (a) of a larger number of elements which are, (b) more tightly organized among themselves.

'In this sense an atom is more complex than an electron, a molecule more complex than an atom, and a living cell more complex than the highest chemical nuclei of which it is composed, the difference depending . . . not only on the number and diversity of the elements included in each case, but at least as much on the number and correlative variety of the links formed between these elements. It is not, therefore, a matter of *simple* multiplicity but of organized multiplicity; not simple complication, but *centrated* complication.'[15]

260

Thus Teilhard traces this movement in the universe towards centred unity, until at last he comes to the vastly complicated molecules which we associate with the phenomenon of life. He here takes a step which has horrified some scientists, he speaks of a 'within' of things which corresponds to the 'without' of things,[16] which latter alone can be examined by the microscope and the electron microscope. Life is not a magical or supernatural substance infused into matter at one stage, everything below that level being dead. Life is simply the 'within' of matter, which at a certain level of complexity becomes sentient, and is clearly seen by us to be so. But he feels that there is every reason to believe that this 'within' is present at a level far below that at which it is apparent to us; there being no matter from which it is entirely absent. Thus life evolves out of that which seemed inanimate, and mind evolves from what was merely psychic, to take two apparently cardinal moments in evolution. The universe is in motion towards life and mind.

Teilhard agrees that if we look at the universe in terms of mere extension in space and time we shall naturally be intimidated by the brevity and apparent insignificance of the phenomena of life and of mind. But if we think in terms of this movement towards complexity and higher consciousness, we shall arrive at a complete reversal of values and perspectives. 'Despite their vastness and splendour the stars cannot carry the evolution of matter very much beyond the atomic series; it is only on the very humble planets, on them alone, that the mysterious ascent of the world into the sphere of high complexity has a chance to take place.'[17] The planets, few though they may be according to modern scientific estimates, are 'finally nothing less than the key-points of the Universe. It is through them that the axis of Life now passes', through the vegetable and animal kingdoms, until at one point thought was born, and, still more important, reflection. It is true that, structurally speaking, man is extremely close to the existing animal species, from whom, or from collaterals of whose ancestors, man is descended. It would, however, be false modesty to soft-pedal the difference constituted by the act of reflection, through which we have achieved access to a whole dominion of reality which is closed to the other animals, and in which we can move freely.[18]

Now, having reached the present day in his lightning journey through the ages, Teilhard looks into the future. He has pointed out that in the growth and development and survival of life, the different branches of the tree have, as it were, spread out and diverged from each other, each one of them differentiating itself from the rest so as to fit in with its particular environment. There has indeed been also a subsidiary phenomenon of convergence, where the same environmental influences have forced species of different origin to become extraordinarily alike. Still, up-to-date, the main trend of evolution has been one of divergence.

But now, with the coming of man, who has subdued the earth and will subdue it further, covering it with a network of his culture, civilization, and communications, this divergence gives place to, and becomes subordinate to, a movement of convergence, in which races, people, and nations consolidate one another, and complete one another by natural fecundation. And this is bound to happen, not only in the physical mixture of races, but at all levels, not in the production of a mediocre uniformity, but in the discovery of our common humanity. What we are faced with is the inevitable collectivization of mankind.

At once, on hearing this, our minds are filled with apprehensions like those awakened by reading Aldous Huxley's *Brave New World* or George Orwell's *1984*. But Teilhard's mind is not filled with such dismal prognostications, though he does see the dangers facing the human race. In an essay on 'The Planetization of Mankind', he writes: 'Whether we like it or not, from the beginning of our history and through all the interconnected forces of Matter and Spirit, the process of our collectivization has ceaselessly continued, slowly or in jerks, gaining ground each day. . . . It is as impossible for Mankind not to unite upon itself as it is for the human intelligence not to go on indefinitely deepening its thought! . . . Instead of seeking, against all the evidence, to deny or disparage the reality of this grand phenomenon, we do better to accept it frankly. Let us look it in the face and see whether . . . we cannot erect upon it a hopeful edifice of joy and liberation.'[19]

262

The Contribution of Teilhard de Chardin

One may ask whether two world wars in close succession have not made such an outlook implausible, but Teilhard rejoins, 'No; during these six years, despite the unleashing of so much hatred, the human block has not disintegrated. On the contrary, in its most rigid original depths it has further increased its vice-like grip upon us all. First 1914-1918, then 1939-1945 – two successive turns of the screw. Every new war, embarked upon by the nations for the purpose of detaching themselves from one another, merely results in their being bound and mingled together in a more inextricable knot. The more we seek to thrust one another away, the more do we interpenetrate.'[20] And he thought he saw signs, not least in the world of science, of such a growing realization of man's common humanity, and the awareness of the mutual inter-dependence of men everywhere, independent of what religion, if any, they possessed.

There was, he believed, something providential in the very structure of our planet, which was forcing upon mankind this convergence. The narrow layer of soil, water, and atmosphere, which surrounds our earth, and within which life is possible, was itself by its very shape compelling the human race to live in harmony if it was to survive at all, and he believed that the wise exercise of man's dominion over nature would enable him to overcome the nightmare threats of overcrowding and contamination which have so dominated recent thought. While realizing the darker possibilities, he regarded the challenges of the present and the future much more as an opportunity than as a threat.

As a Christian believer his faith at this point assured him that God would not allow the whole vast enterprise of cosmic and human history to founder. The planetization of man was inevitably upon us, and the only way in which its possibilities of good could be realized, was that men everywhere should realize that they belonged together, and should freely choose to love one another.

At this point the most difficult place in Teilhard's thought is approached. He appears to believe that if we accept his reasoning, without for the moment leaving the field of the science of man for the domain of Christian faith and revelation, we can predict that mankind is bound for the destiny of socialization, of union with man, a condition in which new forces of love will create cohesion, thus leading to a great increase in man's dominion over nature and his control over his own evolution. Ahead of us there looms a point in time; Teilhard called it Omega Point. Of it we cannot say very much, but apparently beyond it, and still claiming to speak as a scientist, he foresaw a kind of breakthrough, in which even death would be overcome.[21]

What are Teilhard's reasons as a scientist for this apparently fantastic statement? Apparently that the cosmic drive of evolution must succeed, and it could not do so unless men had a hope that neither the individual nor the race and its achievements are due for final extinction. Therefore some kind of consummation must be reached which is beyond the destructive powers of time and the second law of thermodynamics.[22] This appears to be his line of thought, though he admits that much in the future is obscure, and on at least one occasion he leaves room for the possibility of a final choice in which men will be able to accept or reject finally the divinely-chosen destiny, some accepting life, and others choosing death.[23]

At this point, if not before it, the Christian faith and revelation come in to reinforce for Teilhard the conclusions of what he calls 'hyperphysics' or 'ultraphysics'. What science can say about Omega Point is deepened and given added content and assurance by Christian revelation and theology for those who are able to accept the Christian faith. The human race will in no way be able by its efforts to raise itself to Omega Point, which is the gift of divine grace, yet just as there was such a thing as 'the fullness of time' in which, through providence, the world became ready for the coming of Christ, so the divine providence is preparing a condition of the world which will be ripe for the ineffable consummation which is yet to come.

Here then we have, in the very briefest possible compass, Teilhard's picture of the past history of the universe, and of the past, present, and future of man. He was, of course, a transformist, believing that Darwin's general picture of evolution had once and for all made any other view impossible for men of integrity and intelligence. He did not deny the importance of the struggle for survival, and the role in evolution of biological mutation, though he did not think that these factors alone, even on the level of scientific explanation, could account for the appearance of life and mind. He believed in continuity of development, but also in that form of discontinuity which can coexist with continuity, when very gradual changes can suddenly produce what from certain points of view is an entirely new thing.

3 *Teilhard's Doctrine of Creation*

Thus far we have been talking of evolution, and the reader may have been tempted to ask whether Teilhard did not make a god out of the evolutionary process. The answer to this would be 'Definitely, no!' It is interesting to note that in conscious differentiation of his thought from Bergson's, he used to speak of 'Evolutive Creation', while Bergson had spoken of 'Creative Evolution'. This view of Teilhard's, or something very like it, is surely necessary for those Christians who, as their faith requires, look on God as the creator, and who are at the same time convinced by Darwinism that evolution, rather than the distinct creation at one blow of each of the different kinds of plants and animals, is the way in which life has come to possess its present shape. That there are difficulties for faith connected with such a view cannot be denied; for example, it may be asked whether the groping, wasteful processes of evolution are consistent with the Christian conception of God – but the wastefulness of nature is a problem for all believers, not only for those who are convinced that Darwin has made his general case good. This, however, is not the place to grapple with these difficulties.

This brings us to Teilhard's doctrine of creation, which is to be found in his earlier writings. To use his terminology, this is very clearly a metaphysical or theological doctrine, and therefore lies outside the realm of science, and also outside the realm of hyperphysics, to which in his later writings he tried to confine himself. In these later writings he described the process of evolution as advancing from disorganization to organization, from mere aggregates towards centred complication. These terms describe what is in principle observable,

When Teilhard goes on to speak of Creation, he is clearly moving into another field. In the writings where he does this, he states that God creates by uniting, to be created is to be united.

If the objection be made, that uniting presupposes the existence already of something to unite, Teilhard rejoins that if we are to conceive, as he does, of God's act of creation as an act of union, 'we must reject the time-honoured evidence of common sense concerning the real distinction between the mobile [the movable element] and the movement.'[24] This is tantamount to describing God's transcendent act of creation as being above the antithesis of matter and form. Our own acts of creation assume an existent material to which we give new form. We do not need to go into further detail on this question; it is, however, clear that Teilhard did not assume that God's creative act presupposes the existence of some eternal entity which is of equal standing with him. It is quite clear that he takes the position that God did not need to create, he could dispense with the created universe, and his act of creation is a free act of grace. The general effect of Teilhard's reasoning on this subject, which is not altogether clear, is to emphasize the synthetic element in God's creative act.

What emerges is the picture of the creation of a structured reality in which there are finite centres, each possessing its systematic unity and its corresponding element of inwardness and freedom. The plan of the universe finds ever more explicit fulfilment as the tide of evolution rises through the material, vegetable and animal kingdoms. A universe is being very slowly created which is a real entity over against its creator, with its own ever evolving centres of inwardness and freedom. Finally comes the stage where the human race appears, and biological evolution is supplemented and enormously reinforced and accelerated by social evolution. And at last divine providence and grace are leading men to realize that what is in process of creation is a great human family, destined to live together in harmony and love. Thus the element of structure, inwardness and centredness is seen not to have been a mere random characteristic of parts of the world, but a promise of the future, pointing forward to a great body of humanity which in the end of the day is to become identical with the community of Christ, the body of Christ, which is to reach its consummation through union with him, a union in which the whole created universe will play its part.

So through Teilhard's view of evolution and its theological interpretation, as God's method of creation, we begin to get his picture of God as a loving creator, calling into being a universe whose finite centres, each in their own degree mirror his own being, and where man, the latest of nature's products, is being shaped and given the power to respond to the creative love of God.

There are certain passages in Teilhard's writings where he seems to be saying that man is not the culmination of the evolutionary movement, but merely a means to the existence of a superman, or super-organism made of all human individuals, just as the biological individual is made up of cells. There can be no doubt that he did not believe that with the creation of man, evolution had come to a standstill. His vigorous advocate and fellow-Jesuit, Henri de Lubac, admits that at this point there is a certain vagueness in his thought, and sees the risk that such a development might be, not the consummation, but the destruction of personality. Yet he defends Teilhard on the ground that this development of the ultra-human does not in fact mean the swallowing up of individual persons, but their union 'centre to centre' (through love, not mystical absorption) in the one new humanity, in Christ.[25]

When he endeavoured to construct the human future as a project in ultraphysics or natural theology, hoping to carry his readers by arguments that would be convincing to all reasonable thinkers, and by extrapolating into the future tendencies already at work in the world, Teilhard's arguments seem often weak and visionary, his logic is unconvincing and muddled.[26] It is obvious that he is more dependent than he often realizes on the support of Christian revelation. If this be so, he spoke no more than the truth when in a moment of insight he wrote, 'The universe fulfilling itself in a synthesis of centres in perfect conformity with the laws of union. God, the Centre of centres. In that final vision the Christian dogma culminates. And so exactly, so perfectly does this coincide with the Omega Point that doubtless I should never have ventured to envisage the latter or formulate the hypothesis rationally if, in my consciousness as a believer, I had found not only its speculative model but also its living reality.'[27]

4 *Teilhard's Conception of the Image of God in Man*

Although the doctrine which has given its title to our study is seldom, if ever, explicitly mentioned by Teilhard, his picture of man is one which now can be seen to harmonize rather closely with much of the material dealt with in our earlier chapters. And this kinship is made clearer in a very interesting study in *Teilhard Reassessed* by R. B. Smith, on 'God and Evolutive Creation', who points out that according to Teilhard, the pattern of man's nature is similar to that of the divine nature, and how, indeed, even in what appear to be inanimate structures in nature there are the first faint traces of this same pattern. Smith writes,[28] 'Self-giving is the pattern, not only of human action but of the whole of creation from the beginning, for it is necessary to any true union. As we have seen, the revelation of God's Triune nature shows us the same pattern even in him, Father, Son, and Holy Ghost each giving himself completely to the others in a union which does not diminish distinction or confuse the Persons, but increases it so that they are both totally identified and totally differentiated. Then, as has been suggested, the beginning of creation must be understood as another act of self-giving, God as Trinity giving up his lack of limitations and posing over against himself a "nothingness" from which he might create.

'Now we must recognize that for creation to be complete God must elicit from it a response similar to his own action, a response which in the end must be a free response. . . . Throughout evolution, from matter to life to man, the pattern remains the same. At each new stage a response of self-giving is called for from the elements which are to enter into the new union. So also human evolution brings about further advance, as a result of union, until the point is reached at which the final stage of creation can begin and creation give back to God a response similar to his own self-giving.'

We do not need to, and cannot, lay very much weight on the lower rungs of this ladder, which perhaps rest upon somewhat dubious poetical, or even fanciful, analogies. But the vision of human nature as created for grateful self-giving to the God who both within the Holy Trinity and in his relations to the created universe is such free self-giving love, and who in his relations to created beings repeats the pattern of what he is within the mystery of his inner being, has numerous echoes with the thought of writers like Karl Barth and Emil Brunner. In Teilhard, as in these other two theologians, the image of God in man is conceived of, not so much as a sharing in being, as an existence in responsive grateful action, and with his emphasis on the relationship of men one to one, and one to all in the body of Christ, makes, like the other writers, the image of God as much a matter of relation to our human neighbour as to the divine thou.

5 *Does Teilhard's Thought rest on a too naïve Optimism?*

The question may be asked whether Teilhard's whole way of thinking does not lean too heavily on evolution and take too little account of the crucial importance of man's need for repentance, and the cost of man's salvation.

It is true that there are passages in which he appears to regard the divine consummation of history almost as if it were a natural process, whose successful conclusion was not only a matter of faith, but something that could be rationally predicted. Yet there are a number of things to remember in this context. The main emphasis in this theology is on the unfolding and the forward thrust of the divine purpose, and even a writer like Paul, who cannot be accused of underestimating the cross, when he is looking at things from the standpoint of God's purposes, emphasizes the majestic sweep and the unfolding of these purposes, which are to culminate in God's final victory. Teilhard's project in theology was an attempt to set the plan of salvation against the vast cosmic back-cloth for all human events which modern science has disclosed to us, and therefore it is natural that his main emphasis should be laid on the doctrine of creation as an original and continuing activity of the divine will which he believed to underlie the history of man and the world.

This is not the place to develop his whole teaching of man's perfecting through both activity and passivity or suffering, through domination of the natural world, and through pain and diminution when God sends it. This is one of the central themes of his devotional book *Le Milieu Divin*. It is clear that here he spoke from his own experience, and the story of his life is certainly not one which would naturally give rise to a too easily optimistic theology. In fact one of the most admirable and lovable things about him was the quiet patience with which he bore the exasperating and unending delays of authority, and the final veto on publication of what he knew to be his life's main work. There is no doubt that he personally knew what the cross meant, through the trials which he had to suffer, and which he patiently endured.

6 *Teilhard's Main Contribution*

What was Teilhard's main contribution to the doctrine of man? It was not so much the enunciation of original propositions; it consisted rather in the changing of emphases, the altering of perspectives, the opening of windows to the light and the wind. He was deeply influenced by the thought of St Paul, and there is no better key to his thoughts and hopes about the universe and human history than the great chapters in the second half of the Letter to the Romans, especially the second half of the eighth chapter, so much of which was not only obscure, but actually opaque to much of the Christian thinking of last century. This opacity was due to a temporary and partial loss of the Christian cosmic and historic hope, and a tendency to limit hope to the future of the individual believer. Fifty years ago many heads were being shaken over the visionary and prophetic words of St Paul in this passage. It is true that even today we feel that human language and thought are here being strained to the uttermost. But it would not be wrong to say that by his imaginative view of history and the universe, Teilhard has made this language again luminous for many of our contemporaries.

It must be clear to the Christian that his faith is committed to a view which in some way regards man as of very great, I might almost say of central, importance in the world. The doctrine of the incarnation, the doctrine of the love of God and his grace to man, the doctrine of the image of God in man, and the Christian doctrine of the world all imply that for Christianity God and man are very closely linked, that man

has a God-given dignity, and that in the divine purpose the
destiny of man plays an important, even a decisive part.

There are certainly naïve and childish formulations of this
belief, the cosmology of the ancient world favoured one of
them, with its picture of the invisible heavenly spheres rotat-
ing around the earth. Man was geographically at the centre
of things.

Modern astronomy has once and for all destroyed this
picture. As Teilhard says, the impression we get on a winter's
night of 'a serene and tranquil firmament twinkling with a
profusion of small, friendly lights, all apparently at the same
distance' is an illusion. The reality is one of 'immensities of
distance and size, huge extremes of temperature, torrents
of energy'.[29]

But is it only the naïve formulations of faith which appear
to be discredited by the findings of modern science? In the
old days, when the size and age of the universe were not
realized to be so vast as we today know them to be, the
story of the divine plan in history was conceived of as the
working-out of a great drama. A drama is thought of as being
enacted upon a stage, and a stage is regarded as well served
if its wings are so many yards long. But suppose that suddenly
it is discovered that the wings are not so many yards long,
but millions of miles long, then the question inevitably arises,
was this 'theatre', this 'stage' created for this, or indeed, for
any drama? And yet is not this notion of the divine-human
drama of history not an essential concept of the faith, with
which Christianity stands or falls? Surely it is much more
than an expendable piece of mythology.

The results of such reflections are almost bound to be
depressing and unsettling. The facts seem powerfully to suggest the truth of the speculative world-view of naturalism,[30]
which has been expressed in emotive language by Sir James
Jeans.

'Is this, then, all that life amounts to? To stumble, almost by
mistake, into a universe which was clearly not designed for
life, and which, to all appearances, is either totally indifferent
or definitely hostile to it, to stay clinging on to a fragment
of a grain of sand until we are frozen off, to strut our tiny
hour on our tiny stage with the knowledge that our aspirations

are all doomed to final frustration, and that our achievements must perish with our race, leaving the universe as though we had never been?'[31]

Teilhard has himself written, 'the "malady of space-time" manifests itself as a rule by a feeling of futility, of being crushed by the enormities of the cosmos. The enormity of space is the most tangible and thus the most frightening aspect.'[32] What he says here has been put with equal vehemence by Pascal,[33] by Bertrand Russell in *A Free Man's Worship*,[34] by Lord Balfour in *The Foundations of Belief*,[35] by William James in his *Pragmatism*,[36] by W. T. Stace in his *Religion and the Modern Mind*,[37] and with not less imaginative power by Tennyson,[38] Matthew Arnold, and others in their poetry.

Famous among the attempts made to ease the pressure of this problem was Pascal's. 'Terrified by the immensities of space and time' he consoled himself by reflecting that even if man were destroyed by the senseless forces of the universe, even if he were only a reed, yet he was a 'reed that thinks' and thus was superior to the thoughtless universe that in the end destroys him.[39]

This was not Pascal's final word on this issue, but when we look at it, we see that it does not give us much help, for the reason that a fundamental philosophical dualism seems to underlie it. It is not much consolation to man to know that he is superior to the forces of the universe, if at the end of the day, the universe annihilates him. A similar dualism seems to underlie the often-quoted passage in Russell's *A Free Man's Worship*.

Now it would appear that Teilhard really offers a contribution to an answer to this problem; more than that is probably not within the power of the human mind in our conditions of limited knowledge. Teilhard is not the only theologian to give this insight,[40] but he gives much more body and detail in its working-out than any other writer up-to-date. The universe is not wholly alien and indifferent, it is 'in motion towards life and mind'.[41] The perspectives in which man sees reality are not a mere illusion caused by his point of view; the place where he stands is really a crossroads of the universe. Teilhard, with his knowledge of science, has pictured in some detail a universe which is not incompatible with the Christian doctrine of God, of man, and of the world. Indeed, it draws its inspiration from the Christian faith, yet it is not in contradiction with the disclosures of modern science. It therefore constitutes a legitimate alternative to the extremely depressing world-view of naturalism, as outlined by Jeans and others. Clearly, neither of these world-views can refute the other on strictly scientific terms – there are no laboratory experiments which could verify the one and falsify the other. But Teilhard's imaginative world-view, which we do not need to accept in every detail to benefit by it, does ease the pressure on the human imagination which naturalism has exerted for well over a century, and it may be that this is his greatest achievement as an apologist, if not his greatest contribution as a thinker. The result is a feeling of liberation and hope which are very much needed and welcome in the world today.

Teilhard should therefore be described as a 'theologian of hope', and he himself summed up his vocation and perhaps his achievement in a letter written on board ship, 'within sight of St Helena' about eighteen months before his death: 'Without for once being concerned to respect any orthodoxy (whether scientific or religious) in the way I express myself – though at the same time in the consciousness that I am simply acting out of loyalty carried to its extreme limit, to my two-fold vocation as a man and as a Christian: this is the astounding panorama that, simply by adjusting our vision to what we can all see, I would like to bring out for you with unmistakable clarity.

'This is not a thesis, but a presentation – or, if you like, a summons. The summons of the traveller who has left the road and so by chance has arrived at a viewpoint from which everything is bathed in light, and calls out to his companions, "Come and look!" '⁴²

CHAPTER XVIII

The Dignity of Man

1 Introduction

This subject has been misunderstood and mishandled, both by non-Christian humanists and orthodox Christians. Our general thesis in this chapter will be that both sides have adopted the same false presuppositions, and have come to opposite conclusions.

The humanists have affirmed man's dignity, equating it with his moral goodness, or claiming at least that he is able in his own strength to attain such goodness. They resent as· an intolerable affront to man the suggestion that he is dependent on God for pardon or salvation.

And some orthodox theologians have accepted the presupposition that dignity implies moral goodness, and felt compelled to deny the dignity of man while affirming the Christian faith, just as the others have affirmed human dignity and denied the faith. So penetrating a writer as C. S. Lewis felt compelled to say: 'The infinite value of each human soul is not a Christian doctrine. God did not die for man because of some value he perceived in him. The value of each human soul considered simply in itself, out of relation to God, is zero.'[1] It may be that Lewis was misled by this false presupposition, that value of personality implies moral goodness; but he was only able to maintain his case by making a false abstraction. Our quarrel with this statement of Lewis is to be put in one sentence from the Gospel: 'What therefore God hath joined together, let not man put asunder.'[2] It is illegitimate for Christians to think of man 'considered simply in himself, out of relation to God'. As we have seen, man is essentially to be thought of as doubly dependent on God; in continual confrontation with God, and as created for salvation by union with Christ. Thus the text we quoted of the marriage bond has a singular fitness when used of the relation of man to Christ, for man is a member of that humanity which God plans to unite as the Church, the bride; with the bridegroom his own son.

C. S. Lewis' statement has its value as an attack on those who think of man's value as something existent in its own right over against God but, seeing that he does not draw attention to the invalidity of the abstraction, he runs the danger of being classed with the orthodox who have accepted the fallacious rationalist presupposition that dignity implies moral goodness.

It will be worth-while to examine in greater detail the work of two writers who hold, respectively, the humanist and the orthodox positions, and both rest their case on the same false presuppositions. This will make our case clearer.

2 *A Rationalist Example*
The writer whom we shall criticize is Herschel Baker, whose book, *The Dignity of Man,* is written from a non-Christian humanist position. A general criticism of the book is not possible or necessary, but one fairly long quotation will make the author's views on the dignity of man clear to us.[3]

In a concluding paragraph of the first part of his book, called 'Retrospect', Baker considers the Greek view of man at the time when it had produced the two systems of Stoicism and Epicureanism. These he regards as both showing signs of degeneration, each in its own way, from the nobler humanism of Plato and Aristotle.

He says: 'None the less, the memory of the great tradition is yet green. By maintaining the primacy of reason, the Greeks were able to formulate the ethics of humanism. Virtue is knowledge: the pronouncement of Socrates not only implied the supremacy of reason; it also made it possible for man, by using the reason which is one of his natural faculties, to attain the good life. Morality, thus, is not a superimposed canon to which men blindly and dutifully conform. The Greeks would not have understood that the fear of Jehovah is the beginning of wisdom. They held virtue to be knowledge, which was every man's innate birthright. Their ethics were immanent. . . . They respected man too much to subordinate him . . . to a remote Setebos of a god who decreed right and wrong, and who parceled out pain and pleasure arbitrarily, or in return for services rendered. In their judgment, man was himself his own best master simply by exercising his prerogative of reason. His goal was not "salvation" – the concept of being saved from innate sin was foreign to the Greeks, save the Orphics – and for sin they had no word. Man could live brutishly, enslaved by animal passion and bound to matter; or he could live divinely, satisfying the natural demands of his sensitive soul under the guidance of reason. The chariot of his soul was drawn by all the forces of his intricate nature, but reason, proudly triumphant, was the driver who held in check the plunging beasts.'[4] I have quoted this passage at length since it makes very clear the standpoint of the author. God is first held at arm's length and regarded as alien to man's nature, and then his rights are denied. The attitude to revealed Christianity is that of the rationalists of the eighteenth century.

It is not, however, Baker's obvious preference for his conception of the Greek view of man to the Christian one, which concerns us here, for to this view he has his right. It is rather to the underlying presuppositions that attention must be drawn. He regards man as in reality a being who can be fully understood apart from God. And if this point be granted, it is inevitable that God should be regarded as 'a remote Setebos, a God who decrees right and wrong, who parcels out pleasure and pain arbitrarily, or in return for services rendered'.

3 An Orthodox Christian Example

The second writer whose views on human dignity we shall have to criticize is Professor Werner Kümmel. In his excellent book, *Man in the New Testament*, he writes as a New Testament scholar, and with his general conclusions the present writer would not wish to disagree. But in the chapter where our special interest lies, Kümmel is on more debatable ground at more than one point.

In his chapter on 'Jesus in the Synoptic Kerygma', his first point is that Jesus called all men to repentance, and claims that this means all men are sinners. Discussing two objections to this claim that sin is universal among men, he says of the second: 'A. von Harnack has, as is well known,

maintained in his lectures on *The Essence of Christianity* that
in the text "For what shall it profit a man, if he shall gain
the whole world and lose his own soul?" Jesus puts the highest
possible value on man's natural worth. "He who can say
'Father' to the Being who rules Heaven and Earth, is raised
above Heaven and Earth and has himself a value that is
higher than all the structure of the world." If that were right,
one would have to conclude that Jesus could scarcely have
maintained the common sinfulness and need for salvation of
all mankind; for if man has an infinite value in God's eyes,
he cannot face God as being completely reliant on his forgiveness and succour.'[5] Our answer to this statement is that
there is no such inference at all.

Kümmel goes on to examine the two sayings (Mark 8:35
and 36) which are the basis of Harnack's statement. These
are 'For whoever would save his life will lose it; and whoever loses his life for my sake and the gospel's will save
it.' (Mark 8:35) and 'For what does it profit a man, to gain
the whole world and forfeit his life? For what can a man
give in return for his life?' (Mark 8:37) He suggests that
it is likely that the real meaning of verse 35 is that it is better
to give up one's life on earth in order to win an eternal life
in heaven than the reverse, and that verse 36 means that the
loss of eternal life cannot be made good by the winning of the
whole world. (The word in both verses is *psyche,* which means
here, not 'soul', but 'life'.) He concludes that 'these two texts
just do not take for granted the special value of the human
soul: on the contrary, they are intended to warn man about
the danger of losing eternal life.'[6]

One might ask, however, whether there is not a certain
dignity in that being before whom there hangs, by God's
grace, even the *possibility* of an eternal life?

In the next paragraph Kümmel goes on to argue that Jesus
sees man only in relation to God, and that he chose for his
eschatological preaching the concept of God's coming king-
ship, which was not a common one in the eschatological Jewish
hope. Man is confronted in Jesus' preaching with God as
his ruler and judge, his position is one of complete dependence, without the possession of any security against his
creator. The animals are also God's creation, but men are of

higher value than them (Matthew 6:26-30, 10:31). 'For Jesus, man is certainly the crown of creation, but he does not conclude from that a special value for man in God's eyes but rather man's great obligation. God created man with a special task: man must bring forth fruit.'[7] Man is compared to a slave who comes home tired from the field, and must go on working for his master.

The unspoken presupposition in all this argument is that man has only a value if he has certain rights over against God or has a status independent of God. The gospel in these passages quite clearly tells us that man has a particularly high value for God, but Kümmel thinks that he has neutralized this statement by saying that Jesus means here to teach not the specially high value of man for God but man's obligation to God. As a matter of fact, this thought of man's obligation to God is not found in either context (Matthew 6:30 and Matthew 10:31). And in any case the fact of man's absolute obligation to God, which is admittedly a central concept of Jesus' teaching, in no way conflicts with the concept of man's high value to God. It can only be thought so to conflict with the thought of man's value if man's value implies that man has certain rights and independence over against God, so that he does not require to give him an absolute obedience. But this is again the rationalist fallacy, that man may be adequately thought of as a quite independent unity over against God. And, we must ask, is not the same false presupposition which we saw lying behind the quotation from Herschel Baker evident here in the writings of Werner Kümmel?

There is one passage further on in the same chapter which is relevant to our purpose.[8]

It deals with a question which we have already discussed in our exposition of the New Testament teaching on the image. Kümmel asks: 'Does not Jesus' view of man as the *child of God* imply that he is especially valuable to God?' He points out that German Christian expositors in recent years have wished to suggest that Jesus thought of God only as the Father. If this view of God be right, must not the conclusion follow that Jesus thought of all men as God's children? There can be no doubt, Kümmel says, that Jesus laid great emphasis in his preaching on the fact of God's fatherhood of men,

But it is equally true that there are only a very few passages which speak of men as God's children, and, further, these passages all refer to those who believe, who only become God's children by their repentance and faith.

It will be remembered that this is not our own conclusion, and here, venturing into the realm of New Testament exposition against a New Testament scholar, we venture to say we are convinced that a universal sonship of a kind is implied in the parable of the Prodigal Son, and elsewhere in New Testament teaching. But it is more to the point to draw attention to the fact that the value of man to God does not essentially rest on anything that man has achieved, or on his response to God. Every gift comes from God, and God can value the gifts that he has put into humanity, which sin has not been able to destroy, just as he looked on his creation at the first, and saw that it was good.

4 *Human Dignity no Ground for Claim against God, but a Reason why we should have Reverence for Other Men*

In his discussion of the vexed question of Jesus' beliefs about man's value for God, Kümmel says that this depends on the role that man's position before God plays in our Lord's thought. It is emphasized that this position is one of utter dependence. As God's creature, man is a being who owes full service to his creator, and can have no value in his sight, and no rights over against him.

We have already rejected the notion that the universal sinfulness of man implies man's worthlessness in God's sight. Now, on the other hand, we must deny that the notion of man's dignity implies any human rights against God.

Even in the relationship between a loving human father and son the question as to the son's rights can become nearly meaningless, although the possibility remains that the father may do harm to the son through ignorance or folly or ill will. But apart from such aberrations, we may say that among the members of a loving family the question of rights does not arise. It may be said: 'It does not arise, but the rights are there.' This is true, but in the relationship to God the situation is different. In the relation of a son to a human father, the son's rights are there, just because it is possible and conceivable that the father might act foolishly or sinfully towards his son. To suggest that man might have rights over against God is to harbour the thought that God might act out of ill will or folly towards one of his creatures, or be in some way less than wholly loving and just. To ask this question about human rights over against God is thus already to doubt God; and that means that we do not see him as the God and Father of Jesus Christ. Whatever harm may come to man in his relations with God is not the result of God's action to him, but of his own rebellion against God or failure to trust him.[9]

But, it may be objected, does not the Bible picture God, not only as exempt from all duties to man, but also as treating man like a mere thing? This point must be examined, for if it were true, then would there not be some truth in Herschel Baker's description of him as 'a remote Setebos'?

We do not, of course, deny God's supreme power, but claim that this power is in the hands of perfect wisdom and love and justice. We can in fact see that God treats men with a very great deal of respect and delicacy, usually refusing to batter his way into their lives. And yet we know that we are absolutely in his hands and that he has a thousand ways of approaching us, and a power over us and all his creatures that would be absolutely terrifying if he were not absolutely good and loving. Are there, then, any passages in the Bible where he is pictured as mere power dealing with men as with mere things? There are two passages where this comparison of man with a thing in the hands of God is made, and it is worth looking at them in some more detail.

The first passage is in the forty-fifth chapter of Isaiah, and the most important verses are the ninth and the tenth. Those read: ' "Woe to him that strives with his Maker, an earthen vessel with the potter. Does the clay say to him who fashions it, 'What are you making?' or 'your work has no handles'? Woe to him who says to a father, 'What are you begetting?' or to a woman, 'With what are you in travail?' " '

If we look at the context, we shall see that the rebuke is addressed 'To religious people, who professedly accept God's sovereignty, but wish to make an exception in the one case against which they have a prejudice – that a Gentile (Cyrus) should be the deliverer of the holy people. Such narrow and imperfect believers are reminded that they must not substitute for faith in God their own ideas of how God ought to work . . . that God does not always work even by his own precedents; and that many other forces than conventional and religious ones – yea, even forces as destitute of moral and religious character as Cyrus himself seemed to be – are also in God's hands, and may be used by him as means of grace.'[10]

Here, then, men are not actually treated as things but are reasoned with, and are told that they must not dictate to God the details of his providence. They must trust in him, that whatever comes from him to them, he is wise and good. They are not merely battered down into submission, or treated as irrational beings but are urged to understanding and the most personal of all acts, a faith and reliance on the God who has in the past revealed himself as the God of truth, who will never desert his people. And this they must continue to believe even though he may use strange ways of delivering them from Babylon.

Even more, they are not to be simply overawed by the knowledge of divine omnipotence, but are encouraged to ask God for the meaning of the dark and strange events of history, and he will reveal them to faith. So verse 11 continues the argument: 'Thus says the Lord, the Holy One of Israel, and his Maker: "Will you question me about my children, or command me concerning the work of my hands?[11] I made the earth, and created man upon it; it was my hands that stretched out the heavens, and I commanded all their host. I have aroused him (Cyrus) in righteousness, and I will make straight all his ways; he shall build my city and set my exiles free, not for price or reward," says the Lord of hosts.'

The conclusion of our discussion of this passage is that while Israel is reminded that God is in heaven, while Israel is on earth, as dependent on him, as a potsherd on the potter, yet God does not treat his people as mere things, but calls them from a questioning doubt to an unquestioning faith, and uses an appeal to their reason to help him in his task, and even encourages them to ask him questions, provided that they be questions asked in faith and not in querulous doubt.

This passage was quoted in an even more famous passage

in the New Testament, by St Paul in the ninth chapter of the Letter to the Romans.

Here, one must confess, at the first the impression is much stronger that man is battered into an inert acceptance of God's will by the use of the divine omnipotence. The whole passage is relevant, but we may quote from verses 17-24:

'For the scripture says to Pharoah, "I have raised you up for the very purpose of showing my power in you, so that my name may be proclaimed in all the earth." So then he has mercy upon whomever he wills, and he hardens the heart of whomever he wills. You will say to me then, "Why does he still find fault? For who can resist his will?" But who are you, a man, to answer back to God? Will what is moulded say to its moulder, "Why have you made me thus?" Has the potter no right over the clay, to make out of the same lump one vessel for beauty and another for menial use? What if God, desiring to show his wrath and to make known his power, has endured with much patience the vessels of wrath made for destruction, in order to make known the riches of his glory for the vessels of mercy, which he has prepared beforehand for glory, even us whom he has called, not from the Jews only but also from the Gentiles?'

One must confess that the impression given by this passage is of a questioner browbeaten into silence, reduced to the status of a thing, and not roused to a faith that, whatever the events of history may seem to declare, God rules in justice and love.

We must indeed remember that the suggestion that God could be anything but just, is twice rejected as unthinkable by St Paul in the Epistle to the Romans.[12] But the trouble is, that in the passage quoted above, God's righteousness is defined in such a manner that Christ's revelation of the Father is denied, and faith, far from being encouraged, is stifled. Who could trust in such a God as this? This passage is surely the origin of some of the most unattractive things in Calvin's *Institutes,* where the same type of argument is used: 'But who are you, a man to answer back to God?' In both cases the thing would have been better put if this statement had run: 'But who are you, a man, to answer back to *me*?'[13]

We must remember that if in the heat of argument St Paul

does at this point suggest unworthy things of God, this suggestion is only made, as it were, in parenthesis, and his view about the rejection of Israel is later made clear. This rejection is not final, but only temporary until the Gentiles shall have come into the kingdom. 'For God has consigned all men to disobedience, that he may have mercy upon all',[14] and the vision of the end of history is such as to call forth from Paul a song of praise: 'O the depth of the riches and wisdom and knowledge of God! How unsearchable are his judgments and how inscrutable his ways!'[15] Does our admission that man is right 'to reply against' Paul's picture of God as given in these verses mean that man has a right over against God? Surely not. It is because Paul's verses indicate a view of God untrue to the revelation given by our Lord that we object to them. This god, then, is not the true God, or let us rather say that for the moment St Paul's understanding of God is imperfect. If God were like this, then there would be some justification for the views of Herschel Baker. But against the God and Father of Jesus Christ, the real God, we have no rights except the right to love and trust him unconditionally.[16]

We must, however, affirm that human dignity, while it gives man no rights over against God, yet makes every man an object of reverence to other men, and gives him right over against them. These rights must not be considered as absolute claims, in the sense that, whatever the situation, he has, as it were, a right to his pound of flesh. But in every situation he must be treated as in an essential sense equal with all other members of the human race. It is not our purpose here to go into detail on this matter, but rather to trace the source of this universal sacredness and worth of man, as seen by Christian faith.

This dignity depends firstly on the self-giving love of God, who created every man for communion with himself, and who sent Christ for the salvation of men. This love is the origin of our being. It created us out of nothing. It is not the love which, as Nygren sometimes claims, is given only to the worthless and undeserving. It is, indeed, given to them, but it is also the love which the Father has for the Son and the Son for the Father. It expresses itself towards man in grace

and in forgiveness of sins. But it is a love which forgets itself
and is given without regard to the worth or worthlessness of
the object. This is its essence, and not the fact that it is given
to the worthless.

It is this love which gives man his being in confrontation
with God; it is this love which gives man his destiny of
union with Christ. It is this love which expressed itself in the
life and death and resurrection of Christ, and in the gift of
the Holy Spirit. If we love God, then we must also love,
irrespective of their worth, all the men whom he has so
loved and given us to love.

Secondly, every man thus created, whether he is a sinner,
greater or less, or in human eyes a saint, has a dignity in our
eyes because of the personal being that God has given to him.
Having given this dignity of personal being to man, God
also values it, though it is all the gift of his grace. And
this dignity of man, universal, whether man be sinner or saint,
is also something that we must call good, and which we
must value.

And, thirdly, and less essential, there is a comparative
sense in which man may have value and dignity. Some may
have much of this kind of worth, and others little or none.
There is surely no reason why God should not value some
human beings more than others for their goodness and love to
him and to men. We must remember that in this sphere, as in
the last one, all goodness in any man comes from God. And
we must not so define value in man as to leave the impression
that God is in need of it, imperfect without it. It is of his
grace that we are there at all, and the persons of the Holy
Trinity have all blessedness in their mutual love. But surely
there is a sense in which God can find more value in one
man or woman than in another. There is a deep truth in the
words of the Fourth Gospel: 'the Father himself loves you,
because you have loved me and have believed that I came
from the Father.'[17]

To put a very insignificant illustration beside a great saying,
a friend of mine once said to me: 'God must love So-and-so
very much; she is such a fine woman.' Surely there is a truth
in such a saying, made in conversation without theological
reflection. If we know what we are saying, when we say a

thing like that, we are doing no violence to the great principle
of salvation by faith alone and the fundamentally gracious
nature of God's love to us.

This part of our discussion cannot be better concluded than
by a quotation from Calvin's commentary on Genesis 9:6.
Calvin writes: '. . . God declares that he is not thus solicitous
respecting human life rashly and for no purpose. Men are
indeed unworthy of God's care, if respect be had only to
themselves; but since they bear the image of God engraven
on them, he deems himself violated in their person. Thus,
although they have nothing of their own by which they obtain
the favour of God, he looks on his own gifts in them, and is
thereby excited to love and to care for them. This doctrine,
however, is to be carefully observed, that no one can be
injurious to his brother without wounding God himself. . . .
Should anyone object that this divine image has been obliterated, the solution is easy; first, there yet exists some remnant
of it, so that man is possessed of no small dignity, and,
secondly, the celestial creator himself, however corrupted man
may be, still keeps in view the end of his original creation, and
according to his example we ought to consider for what end
he created men, and what excellence he has bestowed upon
them above the rest of living beings.'

5 Prospect for the Future

Barth has a very striking passage in *Dogmatics*, Vol. III, 2,[18]
where he says that the last war, and what preceded it, and
what might yet follow from it, has brought before us afresh
the problem of humanity. What are we to make of the
rights, the dignity, the sacredness of our fellow men? Man
today stands at the cross-roads. Will mankind, in its future
development, declare itself for or against man? This decision,
Barth says, will be taken here with one result, there with
another, according to the doctrine of man and the corresponding ethic practised. And the question will arise with all its
urgency whether there is any ethic and doctrine of man,
other than the Christian one, which is able to resist the surge
and weight of an inhuman doctrine of man which despises persons as having neither sacredness nor worth.

It can be seen, if we accept Barth's views here, that this

argument which we have been conducting with some of the orthodox Christians as to the dignity of man is not a mere matter of words. It is a matter for great concern if Christians should feel themselves by an error in logic bound to deny that the doctrine of the dignity of man is compatible with an evangelical faith. And while Christianity is not to be commended simply on the grounds that 'only if there is an element of the sacred in human personality can society get oxygen enough to breathe',[19] but because it is true, yet if its truth has in it the oxygen that can save society from the poisonous gases of totalitarianism, why should we not clearly say so? Since God has declared himself so unequivocally to be on man's side in Jesus Christ, it would be strange if our Christian faith were to declare itself against him.

And those who are apt, often without much knowledge, to sling abuse at the dialectical theologians should notice that not only Calvin, but also the two great neo-Calvinists of yesterday, Barth and Brunner, both declared that the dignity of man, rightly understood, is a part of the faith. Calvin and Barth on the subject we have already quoted. Brunner says that the divine eternal election is the ground, and indeed the sole and sufficient ground, of the unconditional value of the self. There is no such thing as personal value in abstraction, but the value of the person as person is based upon the fact that man has been created in the personal word of God.[20] This I understand to mean that Brunner refuses to think of man apart from his relation to God in the word, just as we ourselves, in asserting man's dignity, refused to sever what God had joined together, God himself and man.

In the future we may be faced by a Marxism whose inhumanity has been intensified and made more fanatical by the opposition it has met in the world, a Marxism where the nihilistic element has obtained a sweeping victory over the remaining elements of longing for justice and social good. Or we may be threatened by the power of the totalitarian social engineers, or the dominance of some new type of Fascism.

What of the powers of resistance of idealism? In the notion of a spark of the divine in each soul, or in the faculty of reason, there may be some such power, but since in many that spark is so weak, is there not the temptation for the idealist to value men, not because they are human, but because they are gifted, and to despise those who are not? Thus Plato's *Republic* expresses contempt for the common man, and describes as the ideal community a city in which there is a government which might be fairly described as a totalitarian rule by the intellectuals.

There is another type of philosophy, the renaissance cult of the creative genius, which works out at pretty much the same thing. Sir Osbert Sitwell is a good exponent of this view of man. He charms and disarms his readers by his real affection for interesting and independent character in men and women. He is free, or fairly free, from the snobbery of social class, but in the end he cannot hide his disgust for the commonplace man. *Noble Essences,* the last volume of his memoirs, shows his most attractive side, his earlier volumes show his lack of sympathy for ordinary, humdrum people.

And what hope is there for the world from the mystical humanitarianism of Aldous Huxley, with his call for detachment and religious union in God, as advocated in *Ends and Means*? As Desmond MacCarthy has pointed out in a review of Huxley's novel, *Ape and Essence*, there is in this book, as also in Huxley's earlier novels, an underlying cynicism and disgust with man. MacCarthy says: 'Though this novel is called by the publisher "a cautionary tale, a prophetic nightmare", written to warn men what must happen if they persist in their totalitarian follies, it fails in its ambitious beneficent purpose. For Mr Huxley is the last man qualified to write it. He does not care enough for his fellow men, although with his intellect, aesthetic sensibility, and wide knowledge, he has often fed their minds. For he despises them too much, and disgust with human nature has ever been his strongest imaginative stimulant as a creative writer, from his first novel to this, his latest.'

Is not this a true diagnosis? If I do not know that man is the one for whom Christ died, and with whom God wills, with all the force of his grace, to be joined in incarnation, death and eternal destiny, then is not disgust with humanity almost an inevitable result of a prolonged survey of the human scene, particularly if I am a man of Huxley's temperament?

And, if this disgust were to be our own last verdict, would there not be some temptation to think that the cynical brutalities of the totalitarians were understandable, and that, even if they were not, they did not matter so very much after all?

T. R. Glover records a story about the scholar Muretus who in the year 1554 was ill, and the doctors proposed to try an operation upon him. It was of the nature of an operation, but so slight were the chances of success, and so little was their interest in healing him, compared with their desire to see what the symptoms would be before death intervened, that it would be fairer to call it an experiment in vivisection. Not knowing who the patient was, or that he spoke Latin, one doctor said to the other, '*Fiat experimentum in corpore vili*'. (Let the experiment be tried on this worthless body.) '*Vilem animam appellas*,' came a voice from the bed, '*pro qua Christus non dedignatus est mori?*' (Dost thou call that soul worthless for which Christ was content to die?)[21]

What other view of man can compare with this for splendour, for power to awaken compassion and resist injustice? It was a sudden insight into its grandeur that made Manley Hopkins write of his own future, and, in God's intention, of every man's, thus:[22]

> '. . . Enough! the Resurrection,
> A heart's-clarion! Away grief's gasping, joyless days, dejection.
>   Across my foundering deck shone
> A beacon, an eternal beam. Flesh fade, and mortal trash
> Fall to the residuary worm; world's wildfire, leave but ash:
>   In a flash, at a trumpet crash,
> I am all at once what Christ is, since he was what I am, and
> This Jack, joke, poor potsherd, patch, matchwood, immortal
>   diamond,
>   Is immortal diamond.'

Notes

I THE OLD TESTAMENT TEACHING

1. Quotations from the Bible here as everywhere in this book, are from the Revised Standard Version.

2. A. Nygren, *Agape and Eros* (S.P.C.K., London, 1933) Vol. I, p. 181, approving a statement of E. Lehmann.

3. von Rad in Kittel, *Theological Dictionary of the New Testament* (Eerdmans Publishing Co., Grand Rapids, 1968) Vol. II, p. 390.

4. W. Eichrodt, *Theology of the Old Testament* (S.C.M. Press, Ltd, London, 1967) Vol. II, XVI, 1.I.

5. von Rad, op. cit., p. 390.

6. It will later be maintained that there is a close link between the image and man's dominion.

7. It is possible that in the story of the mark set on Cain (Genesis 4:15) there is some suggestion of a similar truth to that contained in the story of the creation of man in God's image.

8. von Rad, op. cit., p. 391.

9. Eichrodt, op. cit., XVI, 1, IIc.

10. C. R. Smith, op. cit., (Epworth Press, London, 1951), pp. 29-30.

11. Eichrodt, op. cit., XVI, 1, IIc.

12. von Rad, op. cit., p. 391.

13. *Church Dogmatics* (T. & T. Clark, Edinburgh) Vol. III, 1, pp. 193 seq.

14. Ibid.

15. Ibid., p. 196.

16. Here Barth is adopting the view of Justin Martyr, Theophilus of Antioch and other Fathers.

17. von Rad, op. cit., p. 242.

18. Exodus 34:29.

19. von Rad, op. cit., p. 242.

20. 2 Esdras 7:97.

21. C. R. Smith, op. cit., pp. 94-5.

22. Eichrodt, op. cit., XVI, 2, VI.

23. Except in the case of Moses, which we cite later.

24. Genesis 12:3, 18:18, 22:18.

25. The passage 1 Corinthians 11:7 does not refer to a universal

image, but to the man in distinction from the woman. This sense of the term is only once found in the Bible.

26. *The Man Born to be King* (Victor Gollancz Ltd, London, 1947) p. 225. See Tertullian, *De Idololatria*, 15, I, 47, 25. The interpretation given here has recently been taken up by G. Bornkamm with approval in *Jesus of Nazareth* (Hodder & Stoughton Ltd, London, 1960) p. 207.

27. It is supported by the articles by von Rad, and Kittel in Kittel's *Theological Dictionary of the New Testament* (articles *eikon* Vol. II).

II THE NEW TESTAMENT TEACHING

1. Cited by A. S. Peake in *Expositor's Greek Testament*, ed. Nichol (Hodder & Stoughton Ltd, London, 1903) Vol. III, p. 503.

2. The reference may rather be to The Wisdom of Solomon 7, where wisdom is spoken of in terms like those which Philo uses of the Logos. Here, in verse 26, wisdom is called the image of God's goodness.

3. Luke 20:24. The passage 1 Corinthians 11:7 considered by Emil Brunner in *Man in Revolt* (Lutterworth Press, London, 1939) p. 500 and others as a reference to the universal image, surely refers to the man alone being in the image, while the woman is not. It is thus irrelevant in this context.

4. Acts 4:12.

5. See Strachan in *Expositor's Greek Testament* on 2 Peter 1:4; also Hauck in Kittel *Theological Dictionary of the New Testament*, Vol. III, article on Koinonos, p. 804.

6. See also Colossians 1:27, where St Paul writes: 'Christ in you, the hope of glory.' The gift of the Spirit is in many passages the pledge or hope of glory. To assert that the one experience is being alluded to is not the same thing as to identify the Spirit with the Son. In all Christian experience all three Persons of the Holy Trinity are present.

7. *Paul and Rabbinic Judaism* (S.P.C.K., London, 1948) p. 86.

8. As Davies points out.

9. Romans 7:24-5.

10. *The Doctrine of the Trinity* (James Nisbet & Co. Ltd, London, 1943) p. 32.

11. J. Scott Lidgett, *The Fatherhood of God* (Epworth Press, London, 1902). See also books, both entitled *The Fatherhood of God*, written last century by Professor R. S. Candlish and Professor Thomas J. Crawford. Candlish denied the universal Fatherhood; Crawford, in controversy with him, maintained it.

III THE IMAGE OF GOD IN THE
MYSTERY RELIGIONS

1. Reitzenstein, *Hellenische Mysterienreligionen* (Leipzig, 1927) p. 7.

2. Ibid, p. 25.

3. A. D. Nock, *Conversion* (Oxford University Press, 1933) pp. 144ff; quoted by Davies, op. cit., p. 92.

4. Reitzenstein, op. cit., p. 29.

5. Ibid., p. 30.

6. J. G. Frazer, *The Golden Bough*, abridged edition, (Macmillan & Co. Ltd, London, 1929) p. 358.

7. H. A. A. Kennedy, *St Paul and the Mystery-Religions* (Hodder & Stoughton Ltd, London, 1913) p. 216, quoting Cumont, *Les Religions Orientales*, p. xxii.

8. See Kittel, Vol. II, pp. 255-6, where this suggestion is made to explain the singular and non-classical sense of the word *doxa* in the mystery religions, a sense very like that of the Septuagint and the New Testament.

9. Kennedy, op. cit., p. 50.

10. Reitzenstein, op. cit., p. 30.

11. Ibid., p. 31.

12. Galatians 2:20.

13. Quoted by Kennedy, op. cit., p. 292.

14. I have used the clumsy term 'divinization' to express the teaching of the Fathers named, to express something less than deification, which is the teaching of the mystery religions.

IV HUMAN REASON AS A SPARK OF THE
DIVINE FIRE

1. It should be noted that this is quite a different thought from that of the divinization of the believer.

2. In this chapter I am much indebted to James Drummond's excellent work, *Philo Judaeus; or, The Jewish-Alexandrian Philosophy* (Williams & Norgate, London, 1888).

3. Xenophon, *Memorabilia*, IV, iii, 14.

4. Ibid., I, iv, 8.

5. Sir Alexander Grant, *The Ethics of Aristotle* (Longmans, Green & Co., London, 1866) Vol. I, p. 307.

6. Aet. Plac., i, 6, I.

7. Plut. Sto. *Rep.*, 38, 3.

8. Acts 17:28.

9. Zeno, Stob. Ed., Ecl. I, 60.

10. Cornut, *Nat. Deor.*, c. XVI, p. 64.

11. Sen. Ep. lxvi, 12; for full references, see Drummond op. cit., Vol. I, pp. 107-8.

12. M. Aur., IX, 8.

13. Sen., *N.Q. Prol.*, 12.

14. Epictetus, *Disc.*, ii, 8, 12.

15. Drummond, op. cit., Vol. I, p. 110.

16. Ibid., Vol. II. p. 17.

17. Ibid., pp. 222-73.

18. Such passages would, of course, make it easier for the early Christian theologians to apply the Logos concept to Christ.

19. Drummond, Vol. I, p. 315, citing *Leg. All.*, II, 7 (I, 71).

20. Drummond's arguments against this point are unconvincing (op. cit., Vol. II, p. 230), and, if his interpretation of Philo be right, there is a weakness in Philo's teaching here.

21. Drummond, op. cit., Vol. I, p. 327, citing *Quod det. pot. ins.*, 22-3 (I, 206-7).

22. *Decem. Orac.*, 25 (II, p. 202).

23. Drummond, op. cit., Vol. I, p. 329.

V THE TEACHING OF TWO THINKERS ON 'IMAGE' AND 'LIKENESS'

1. Ernst Klebba, *Die Anthropologie des Hl. Irenaeus* (Münster, 1894) p. 22. Quoted by John Lawson, *The Biblical Theology of St. Irenaeus* (Epworth Press, London, 1948) p. 200.

2. Arnold Struker, *Gottebenbildlichkeit des Menschen, ein Beitrag zur Geschichte der Exegese von Gen. 1:26* (Münster i. W., 1913) p. 92. This work is authoritative in the thoroughness of its study of the text.

3. A more detailed exposition, which would make the text unduly cumbrous, may be given in this note.

The second of the six passages mentioned above (III, 23, 1) and the third (III, 23, 2) both refer to Adam before the Fall. The fourth (IV, 38, 3) refers to man restored by salvation, and is thus eschatological. The same is true of the fifth (IV, 38, 4). And the reference of the sixth (V, 1, 3) is both to the unfallen Adam and to a regenerate humanity.

Thus, in these five passages, whatever his teaching about man's loss of the likeness through sin, Irenaeus would be justified in speaking of him as possessing it, for in no case is man spoken of as merely fallen and sinful.

There is, however, one of the six passages, the first (III, 18, 1), which refers to man as having possessed from the beginning both image and likeness, which are both restored to him in Christ, after their loss at the Fall.

Thus five of the six passages neither support nor contradict the view usually assigned to Irenaeus, that the likeness was lost at the Fall, while the image remains.

4. *Man in Revolt*, p. 93.

5. V, 16, 2.

6. This view has some difficulty in explaining certain passages in Irenaeus. But Struker points out that the Logos is also God's, and that therefore the term 'image of God' may be used where 'image of the Logos' is meant, while the terms 'flesh' and 'handiwork' may sometimes be used in a wide sense to include all human nature as well, including man's freedom and reason. So that at times man's flesh in this wider sense may be described as in God's image. *Expideixis*, II, which is very hard for Struker to explain, as it seems grossly anthropomorphic, he considers as an interpolation, since it is suspect on other grounds also. Struker, op. cit., pp. 92-100.

7. II, 7, 6-7; IV, 3, 1.

8. *Demonstr.* § 22.

9. Gross, *Divinisation du Chrétien dans les Pères Grecs*, p. 147.

10. The danger of this expression is that it goes beyond our knowledge, suggesting that there would have been an incarnation even had there been no Fall.

11. Brunner, *Man in Revolt*, p. 505. There is an uncertainty on this point. For an interesting and full discussion of it, see J. Lawson, *The Biblical Theology of St Irenaeus*, Ch. XII. Lawson gives the views of Klebba and Duncker, two main authorities, as well as his own conclusions.

12. Lawson, op. cit., p. 207; Gross, op. cit., pp. 156-7; Struker, op. cit., pp. 103-7.

13. *Adv. Haer.*, V, 8, 1.

14. Struker, op. cit., interprets these passages and others in the sense criticized in which the eschatological moment appears not to have justice done to it. Probably a case can be made out for both the conflicting interpretations of Irenaeus as the debate had not yet arisen when he wrote.

15. Op. cit., Ch. XI.

16. If Struker is right, we are not speaking of exactly the same thing.

17. Brunner, op. cit., p. 93, pp. 504-5.

18. Lawson, op. cit., p. 223.

19. Brunner, op. cit., p. 504.

20. Preface, 1, 3.

21. *Protreptikos* (Stählin's Edition), 120, 3.

22. Ibid., 120, 4.

23. *Paidagogos*, I, 11, 12.

24. *Stromateis*, VI, 136, 3. But see *Paidagogos*, III, 66, 2, where man's existence in the divine image and likeness is given as a

reason for avoiding cosmetics! This might indicate a view like that
of Irenaeus where the image has a bodily reference, if the passage
were to be taken seriously!

25. *Protreptikos*, 98, 4.

26. Dom Augustinus Mayer, *Das Bild Gottes im Menschen nach
Clemens von Alexandrien*, pp. 23-4. In this chapter I am much
dependent on Dom Mayer's study.

27. *Paidagogos*, III, 66, 2.

28. *Stromateis*, III, 42, 6.

29. It would be fairer to say that Karl Marx at least spoke with
an uncertain voice on this issue, as will appear in Chapter XV.

VI THE INWARD WAY TO GOD AND THE NEED OF HISTORICAL SALVATION

1. *Stromateis*, II, 102, 6.

2. *Harvard Theological Review*, 18 (1925), pp. 39-101.

3. Mayer, op. cit., p. 34.

4. Ibid., pp. 33-46.

5. *Stromateis*, V, 88, 2.

6. Lawson, op. cit., p. 161.

7. *Contra Gentes*, § 30.

8. Ibid., § 34.

9. Ibid., § 38.

10. Ibid., § 47.

11. A. Robertson, Introduction to translation of Athanasius,
Contra Gentes, p. 11 (Nicene and Post-Nicene Fathers).

12. *Contra Gentes*, § 2.

13. Ibid., § 34.

14. Ibid.

15. *De Incarnatione*, Ch. 14.

16. *De Trinitate*, IX, 2.

17. Ibid.

18. Ibid., X, 12.

19. Ibid., XIV, 8.

20. Italics mine.

21. *De Trinitate*, XIV, 5.

22. Ibid., XIV, 8.

23. St Thomas Aquinas, in his *Summa Theologica*, I, 93, 8, commenting on Augustine, quite explicitly commits himself to this
position.

24. *De Trinitate*, XIV, 16.

25. Ibid. XV, 8.

26. Gilson, *Introduction à l'Etude de St. Augustin* (Paris, 1943)
p. 140.

27. Op. cit., XIV, 8.

VII SANCTIFICATION AND SALVATION
1. Op. cit., p. 155.
2. Ibid., pp. 155-6.
3. Ibid., p. 165.
4. See also IV, 39, 2.
5. *Stromateis*, VII, 84, 7.
6. Ibid., VI, 71, 1.
7. Ibid., VI, 104, 1.
8. Ibid., VI, 103, 5.
9. 2 Corinthians 3:7, 18.
10. *Contra Arianos*, III, §§ 10-25.
11. Ibid., Discourse III, § 22.
12. Ibid., § 25.

VIII THE IMAGE AS RATIONALITY
1. *Adv. Haer.*, IV, 4, 3.
2. *Protreptikos*, 124, 3.
3. *De Incarnatione*, § 3.
4. Ibid., 6.
5. Ibid., § 14.
6. Brunner, *Man in Revolt*, p. 504.
7. Ibid., pp. 102 seq.

IX THE IMAGE OF GOD IN AQUINAS
1. *Summa Theologica*, I, 93, 2.
2. Ibid.
3. Ibid., I, 93, 4.
4. It is doubtful how seriously Aquinas himself takes this distinction, for he himself goes on to describe the *actual* love of the natural man for God (see below).
5. Op. cit., I, 93, 8.
6. Ibid., I, 12, 12; I, 56, 3.
7. Ibid., I, 60, 5.
8. The whole situation is complicated by the fact that Aquinas does not accept the Irenaean exegesis of Genesis 1:26, since he defines a likeness as something more general than an image (*Summa Theologica*, I, 93, 9).
9. Paul Althaus interprets Romans 7, with most modern scholars, as treating of the natural man, seen by the man of faith. And he takes verses 22-3 to mean that the natural man both loves and hates God. This is the desperate nature of the division in his soul (Althaus, *Paulus und Luther über den Menschen*, Gütersloh, 1938) p. 63.

10. *Revised Church Hymnary* (Oxford University Press, 1927). Hymn 319.

11. Op. cit., I, 12, 5.

12. 1 John 3:2.

X THE IMAGE OF GOD IN MARTIN LUTHER

1. Luther, *Werke: Weimarer Ausgabe*, 42, 51.

2. Ibid., 42, 248.

3. Augustine, *Confessions*, X, vi-xxvii.

4. Op. cit., 24, 49.

5. Ibid., 42, 41 seq.

6. *Summa Theologica*, I, 93, 4, Resp.

7. Ibid., I, 60, 5.

8. We shall ourselves develop a doctrine of the universal image, which we claim does not endanger the evangelical principle.

9. Op. cit., 42, 50.

XI THE IMAGE OF GOD IN JOHN CALVIN

1. *Institutes*, I, 1.

2. T. F. Torrance, *Calvin's Doctrine of Man* (Lutterworth Press, London, 1949) p. 36.

3. *Commentary on Psalms* 19:1.

4. 2 Corinthians 3:18.

5. *Commentary on Genesis* 3:1; *Institutes*, II, 1, 5.

6. *Institutes*, II, 2, 18; II, 2, 22; *Commentary on Psalms* 19:2, 104:2; *Commentary on Romans* 2:19.

7. II, 2, 17.

8. *Institutes*, II, 2, 12-15.

9. Ibid., II, 2, 18.

10. Ibid., II, 2, 22.

11. I am not aware that he ever uses this term for it.

12. *Commentary on Acts* 15.9.

13. *Commentary on John* 3.6.

14. *Sermon on Job* 2, 1 seq.

15. *Institutes*, III, 7, 6; cf. also *Commentary on Genesis* 9:5-7.

16. *Institutes*, II, 2, 18.

17. Ibid., III, 2, 14.

18. *Institutes*, II, 5, 15.

19. Ibid., II, 3, 6.

20. Ibid., II, 2, 12.

21. Ibid., I, 7, 4.

22. *Commentary on 2 Corinthians* 3:18.

23. *Institutes*, I, 15, 4.

24. Ibid., I, 15, 3.

XII THE IMAGE OF GOD IN EMIL BRUNNER

1. *Scottish Journal of Theology*, Vol. 4, No. 2, pp. 123-35, 'The New Barth'. There is little use made in this chapter of Brunner's pamphlet, *Natur und Gnade*, and Barth's answer to it, *Nein! Antwort an Emil Brunner*, since both Barth and Brunner later moved from the positions represented there, although no doubt both of them would still assent to much that they had said at that time. The pamphlets originally appeared in 1934, although they did not appear in an English translation until 1946, under the title *Natural Theology* (Geoffrey Bles, Ltd).

2. See p. 57ff.

3. Ibid., p. 62.

4. Ibid., p. 71.

5. *Urschöpfung*. What this means will be discussed later in this chapter.

6. Ibid., pp. 71-2.

7. Ibid., p. 67.

8. Ibid., pp. 78-9.

9. See especially pp. 96-9.

10. Ibid., p. 98.

11. Ibid.

12. Ibid., p. 106.

13. Ibid., where Brunner says: 'The human "thou" is not an accident of man's humanity, something which gives a new content and richness to his already existing humanity; it is rather the condition of his humanity.' This refers to the formal structure of man's humanity, his dependence on the human 'thou'. The next sentence runs: 'He cannot be man unless he loves.' This is clearly a reference to the true man.

4. 'The New Barth' in *Scottish Journal of Theology*, Vol. 4, No. 2, p. 127.

15. *Man in Revolt*, p. 387.

16. Calvin, *Commentary on Genesis* 1:26.

17. Op. cit., p. 89.

18. Ibid., p. 142.

19. Ibid., p. 117.

20. Ibid., p. 150. An unfortunate illustration, since administrators of the law of a state are only held morally responsible for their obedience to it on the grounds that there is a law above all positive laws, which they could have obeyed rather than the law of, let us say, Nazi Germany. Of this law above the laws Brunner has himself written movingly in his *Justice and the Social Order* (Lutterworth Press Ltd, London, 1945). Thus Nazi administrators were responsible and guilty just because they were not in their

actions wholly determined by Nazi law.

21. Ibid., p. 479.

22. Ibid., p. 490.

23. Both the biblical theology and the history of the doctrine are summarized by Brunner in the first appendix of *Man in Revolt* pp. 499-515.

24. Ibid., p. 513. Here Brunner says: 'Although in using this terminology I am making no innovation . . . I have now renounced the use of this expression "formal Image".' He claims that he has done this to avoid misunderstanding on the part of other theologians. The terms 'Old Testament image' and 'New Testament image', which I have used in this book, have been taken over from Brunner, and mean precisely the same thing as his earlier pair of terms 'formal image' and 'material image'.

25. Ibid., p. 500.

26. Ibid., p. 501.

27. Ibid.

28. Ibid., p. 93.

29. Brunner claims that Luther's interpretation had the result of destroying the false two-storey view of man's nature which the scholastics built up on Irenaeus' distinction between 'image' and 'likeness'. While agreeing that the two-storey view is an unfortunate one, I cannot but feel that Brunner is a little hasty in holding that this is the place where its origin is to be found. Firstly, Irenaeus did not hold the two-storey view explicitly himself, and was not an exponent of natural theology. And, secondly, Aquinas, who is the chief exponent of the two-storey view, does not use the Irenaean distinction between image and likeness; for him a likeness is something more general than an image (*Summa Theologica*, I, 93, 1).

30. Ibid., p. 96. This, I take it, is a reference in particular to Kant's final surrender in the *Opus Postumum* of the principle of radical evil in the noumenal self; cf. also ibid., pp. 126-7.

31. Karl Barth, *Natural Theology*, p. 88.

32. Perhaps this criticism would have to be modified in view of Barth's *Church Dogmatics*, Vol. III, 2, where it is repeatedly asserted that every man is by nature related to God through Jesus Christ. Barth still rejects Brunner's view that all men stand in confrontation with the Logos.

33. I have not tried to discuss the question of the point of contact thoroughly, feeling that I have no contribution to make to the subject.

34. *Natural Theology*, pp. 22-3. Brunner maintains that even in sin a 'formal' freedom remains. The sinner has still a power of

alternative choice. But he has lost 'material' freedom, the power
of doing perfectly what is God's will.

35. *Man in Revolt*, p. 105.
36. *Natural Theology*, p. 23.
37. Ibid., p. 10.
38. Ibid., p. 24. A discussion of this passage and criticisms of it
will be found in our fourteenth chapter.
39. See p. 193.
40. *Man in Revolt*, pp. 478-95.
41. *Natural Theology*, p. 31.
42. *Man in Revolt*, p. 536.

XIII THE IMAGE OF GOD IN KARL BARTH
1. First published in 1919.
2. *Commentary on Romans* (Oxford University Press, 1933) pp.
168-9.
3. *Church Dogmatics*, Vol. I, 1, Author's Foreword, p. vii.
4. Ibid.
5. *The Knowledge of God and the Service of God* (Hodder &
Stoughton Ltd, London, 1938).
6. Op. cit., Vol. I, 1, p. 273.
7. *The Knowledge of God and the Service of God*, pp. 40-51.
8. Op. cit., Vol. III, 1, p. 184.
9. Ibid., Vol. III, 2, 'Phenomena of the Human', § 44.2.
10. Ibid., p. 198.
11. Ibid., Vol. III, 1, p. 196.
12. Ibid.
13. Ibid., p. 184.
14. This subject, and Barth's views on it, will be discussed in
the next chapter.
15. Ibid., p. 188.
16. Ibid., Vol. III, 2, pp. 74-5.
17. This statement refers to an opinion of Barth expressed in
Vol. III, 2, p. 198, where it is said that because we are sinners, our
real human nature is concealed both from ourselves and others,
and known only to God.
18. Op. cit., Vol. III, 2, pp. 68-71.
19. Ibid., pp. 86-7.
20. Ibid., p. 142.
21. This question will be treated more fully in a later chapter.
22. Ibid., Vol. II, 1, p. 91.
23. Ibid., Vol. III, 2, p. 184.
24. Ibid., p. 196.
25. Ibid., pp. 132-202.

26. Ibid., Vol. III, 2, 'Real Man', § 44.3.

27. Ibid., p. 136.

28. Ibid., p. 198.

29. Brunner has drawn attention in an article in the *Scottish Journal of Theology* (Vol. 4, No. 2, p. 127) to many statements of Barth in Vol. III, 2, where the image is regarded as man's destiny rather than the definition of his being (cf. especially Vol. III, 2, pp. 319-20). This is equivalent to Barth's saying that the true man is the man of faith who loves God, Barth is able to slip over from the one sense to the other, perhaps because the word *Bestimmung* used by him can mean either 'definition' or 'destiny'. In a letter of 13 December 1950, Brunner sent me a copy of this article before its publication, and affirmed his complete agreement with the criticisms of Barth expressed in this chapter, which I had sent to him in draft form. The two criticisms of Barth, by Brunner and myself, had been written quite independently of each other.

30. Ibid., Vol. III, 2, pp. 207-16.

31. Ibid., p. 222.

32. Ibid., pp. 247-74.

33. Ibid., pp. 279-85.

34. Partly translated into English under the title *From Rousseau to Ritschl*, (S.C.M. Press, London, 1959) and about to appear in complete form in English.

35. Op. cit., Vol. III, 2, p. 277.

36. Ibid., Vol. III, 1, p. 186.

37. As Barth himself admits, Vol. III, 1, p. 196, 'The distinction between "I" and "Thou" in mankind has a sexual character, and this belongs to our nature as creatures, and not to the image.'

38. Ibid., p. 203.

39. We must, of course, remember that Barth decisively rejects the notion that the image is a power or capacity.

40. Op. cit., Vol. III, 2, p. 277.

41. Ibid., pp. 131-2.

XIV THEOLOGICAL CONCLUSIONS

1. Op. cit., Vol. III, 1, p. 184.

2. § 44.2.

3. Brunner, *Man in Revolt*, p. 102.

4. Barth's contention that responsibility thus defined is merely a last inner ring of possibilities and not the real man cannot be accepted. The responsibility is not the possibility; it remains, whatever possibility is chosen. It is the real man. The alternative, that the real man is necessarily the man who does God's will gladly, inevitably results in the conclusion that the sinful man is unreal.

5. Op. cit., Vol. III, 1, p. 184.

6. Ibid., p. 193.

7. Genesis 1:27.

8. Ibid., p. 184.

9. Ibid.

10. Ibid., p. 185.

11. Ibid., p. 196.

12. *Man in Revolt*, p. 96.

13. Calvin, *Sermon on Job*, 2, 1ff.

14. *Natural Theology*, p. 24.

15. *Our Knowledge of God* (Oxford University Press, 1939) p. 30.

16. See *Man in Revolt*, p. 229. 'What remains of man's original nature is the form of his existence as man, his personal existence, and the structure of his humanity, but this form is filled with a content contrary to its original content.'

17. *Natural Theology*, p. 88.

18. Ibid., p.. 79.

19. Ibid.

20. Ibid., p. 84.

21. It is only fair to say that Barth sometimes states a view on this point which is very like Brunner's own. He says: '(Man) did not disappear as man or change into another being when he became a sinner, but he confronts God, even as a sinner, as the being that he was when God created him, and consequently as the being whose nature consists in its freedom.' Then Barth goes on to deny that this existence as a human being is any contribution on man's part to his salvation. There is thus a parallel to Brunner, although man's actual humanity is not equated with the image in any sense, and freedom is probably differently conceived.

22. John 1:1-5.

23. Colossians 1:16-17.

24. *Man in Revolt*, p. 97.

25. *Man in Revolt*, p. 98. There are, however, a number of passages which seem to equate man's being (*Wesen*) with his relation to God, e.g., p. 483. On p. 541, Brunner denies that the concept of substance is applicable at all to man's being, but here he seems to be working with a much narrower concept of substance than I wish to apply to man.

26. Ibid., p. 104.

27. Romans 2:4.

28. Op. cit., Vol. III, 2, p. 274.

29. Ibid., p. 285.

30. Ibid., Vol. II, 1, p. 168.

31. Ibid., p. 167.

32. Ibid., p. 169.

33. For the whole passage, ibid., p. 162-72.

34. Ibid., p. 119.

35. Ibid., p. 120. Unfortunately the English translator has here missed out the crucial phrase 'they were always men who knew God.'

36. Ibid.

37. Ibid., p. 94. Here Barth's confusion of general revelation with natural theology leads him astray. The gods of natural theology are caricatures, but behind them is the real God in his general revelation.

38. Brunner, *Dogmatics* (Lutterworth Press, London, 1949) Vol. I, p. 132.

39. Ibid., p. 133.

40. Brunner, *Revelation and Reason* (S.C.M. Press, London, 1947) p. 33.

41. Ibid., p. 64.

XV KARL MARX'S CONCEPTION OF MAN

1. It is, of course, here conceded that there are wide areas of study where this relation makes little or no difference, and other matters concerning man where its influence is more or less peripheral.

2. Helmut Gollwitzer, *The Christian Faith and the Marxist Criticism of Religion* (St Andrew Press, Edinburgh, 1970) p. 9.

3. Bernard Delfgaauw, *The Young Marx* (Sheed & Ward, Ltd, London, 1967) p. 3.

4. Ibid., p. 3.

5. Ibid., p. 62.

6. Ibid., p. 30.

7. Karl Marx, *Capital*, Vol. I, pp. 680-1. Quoted by Erich Fromm, *Marx's Concept of Man* (Frederick Ungar Publishing Co., New York, 1961) p. 51.

8. As Fromm points out, not property as objects of use, but as capital which hires labour. Op. cit., p. 52.

9. Ibid., p. 127. *Economic and Philosophical Manuscripts*, 'Private Property and Communism'.

10. Ibid., pp. 58-9.

11. Cf. Clement of Alexandria and Athanasius.

12. In an unpublished lecture, referred to by Gollwitzer, op. cit., p. 75.

13. See below, pp. 225-31.

14. See a valuable essay by H. Gollwitzer on *Humanismus Ost und West*.

15. K. Marx and F. Engels, *The German Ideology* (Lawrence & Wishart, Ltd, London, 1965).

16. H. Gollwitzer, op. cit., p. 31.

17. Ibid., p. 32.

18. Ibid., p. 33.

19. *Early Writings* of Karl Marx, op. cit., pp. 43-4.

20. Gollwitzer, op. cit., pp. 53-5.

21. Ed. Burns, *A Handbook of Marxism,* (Victor Gollancz Ltd, London, 1935) p. 230. Theses on Feuerbach.

IV. Feuerbach starts out from the fact of religious self-alienation, the duplication of the world into a religious, imaginary world, and a real one. His work consists in the dissolution of the religious world into its secular basis. He overlooks the fact that after completing this work, the chief thing still remains to be done. For the fact that the secular foundation lifts itself above itself and establishes itself in the clouds as an independent realm is only to be explained by the self-cleavage and self-contradiction of this secular basis. The latter must itself, therefore, first be understood in its contradiction, and then, by the removal of the contradiction, revolutionized in practice. . . .

VI. Feuerbach resolves the religious essence into the human. But the human essence is no abstraction inherent in each individual. In its reality it is the *ensemble* of the social relations. . . .

22. Gollwitzer, op. cit., p. 48.

23. Fromm, op. cit., p. 198. Quoting *The German Ideology.*

24. *The German Ideology,* p. 20. Quoted by Vernon Venable, *Human Nature: The Marxian View* (Dennis Dobson, Ltd, London, 1946) p. 67.

25. Veneable, op. cit., p. 171.

26. Ibid., pp. 204-5.

27. *Critique of the Gotha Programme.* Cited by Venable, op. cit.

28. Venable, op. cit., p. 206.

29. We may note in passing that if we do not admit that the successful prosecution of the class war is the only standard by which we are to judge political or individual action, but must also keep in mind the fact that human beings as human beings, by their very existence impose a limitation of a moral character upon us, this does not give us any easy rule of thumb by which we can decide what to do in the particular case. Indeed, it will be far more difficult to decide than for a doctrinaire Marxian, who has only one supreme goal to aim at. The doctrine of the sacredness of personality does not absolve the Christian from agonizing moral problems, especially from problems involving coercion. Unless, that is, he can adopt the absolute ethic of non-violence. Anyone

who believes that coercion to overthrow an unjust government may never be used, but is permissible in the case of conflicts between nations, thereby reveals that his ethic is a mere ideology, such as Marx saw through and despised. The doctrine of the sacredness of personality does not allow the man who holds it to escape from the painful moral problem of what to do when it appears that the sacrifice of one life or a few lives could secure the safety of a great many.

30. Op. cit., p. 79.
31. Ibid., pp. 79-80.
32. Ibid., p. 113.
33. Ibid., p. 74.

XVI SIGMUND FREUD'S CONCEPTION OF MAN

1. Harry Guntrip, *Personality Structure and Human Interaction* (The Hogarth Press Ltd, London, 1961) p. 147. Guntrip is a writer to whom my indebtedness will be evident.

2. Ernest Jones, *Sigmund Freud: Life and Work* (The Hogarth Press Ltd, London, 1953, 1955, 1957) Vol. 1, pp. 420-1.

3. It is a measure of Freud's originality to have drawn attention to these phenomena and the interpretative concepts. It is only with hindsight that we can say that the use of the latter is inevitable if we are to understand the former.

4. Sigmund Freud, 'On the History of the Psycho-analytic Movement', *Collected Papers* (The Hogarth Press Ltd, London, 1924) Vol. 1, p. 297ff.

5. Yet another is the concept of transference, important in therapy, but not for a study of Freud's doctrine of man.

6. *Group Psychology and the Analysis of the Ego.* The Standard Edition of *The Complete Psychological Works of Sigmund Freud* (The Hogarth Press Ltd, London, 1951) Vol. XVIII, p. 105.

7. Guntrip, op. cit., p. 66.

8. John Bowlby, *Attachment and Loss* (The Hogarth Press Ltd, London, 1969) Vol. 1, p. 19.

9. Ibid., p. 41.

10. Guntrip, op. cit., p. 145.

11. Ibid., pp. 89-90.

12. Ibid., p. 91. See Freud, The Standard Edition, op. cit., Vol. XVIII, pp. 130-1.

13. Ibid., p. 93.

14. Ibid., p. 363.

15. A claim which is hotly contested by those who claim to be orthodox main-line Freudians.

16. Guntrip, op. cit., pp. 120-1.

17. Freud, *Inhibitions, Symptoms and Anxiety* (The Hogarth Press Ltd, London, 1936) pp. 28-9, cited by Guntrip, op. cit., pp. 99-100 and 121.
18. Guntrip, op. cit., p. 121.
19. *New Introductory Lectures* (The Hogarth Press Ltd, London, 1933) p. 232. Quoted by Guntrip, op. cit., p. 123.
20. *The Future of an Illusion* (The Hogarth Press Ltd, London, 1928) p. 24.
21. Ibid., p. 32.
22. Ibid., p. 45.
23. Ibid., p. 61.
24. Ibid., p. 59.
25. Ibid., p. 98.
26. Ibid., p. 76.
27. Ibid., p. 87.
28. Guntrip, op. cit., p. 69. A much superior theory of instinct has been propounded by John Bowlby in his important book *Attachment and Loss*. One of its advantages is that it does not use at all the ambiguous and untestable concept of psychical energy. In brief, Bowlby regards instincts as tendencies innate in animal species and in man, to perform certain types of action. These tendencies are there today as a result of their survival value in much earlier times – especially in the self-defence of groups of animals against predators. While this theory expressly rejects the notion of purpose in nature as not belonging to science, and explains instinctive behaviour, just as Darwin explained adaptation, as a product of successful survival, it is free from the pessimism of Freud's instinct theory. This modern form of instinct theory also leaves us free to say that beyond what the scientist can see in it, i.e. its effectiveness in aiding survival, such behaviour may have, or may contribute to, an intrinsic value.

A further advantage of Bowlby's theory is that, unlike Freud's instinct theory, it is not incompatible with the object relations theory of human behaviour, but actually supplements the latter. For this type of instinctive behaviour is not the only component in the attachment of the young animal or child to its mother or the group. There is here also an object relationship as well as an innate tendency to perform certain actions which will keep mother and child, or young animal and herd, together. It would thus appear that this type of instinct theory is by no means incompatible with a theistic or Christian faith. It does not picture the individual as fundamentally at loggerheads with his fellows.

29. Ibid., p. 69. But see note above on Bowlby's instinct theory.
30. E. Brunner, *Revelation and Reason*, p. 259.

31. If we may trust John Baillie's memories of his childhood, there are some who have been able from the earliest childhood to distinguish between these two relationships. (See *Invitation to Pilgrimage* (Oxford University Press, 1942) pp. 38-9. For all his admiration of Dostoevsky, Freud was never able to forgive him for not having lost his faith in God. This was apparently, like his submission to the Tzar, a mark of Dostoevsky's immaturity! See Freud, *Collected Papers* (The Hogarth Press Ltd, London, 1950) Vol. 5, p. 234.

XVII THE CONTRIBUTION OF
TEILHARD DE CHARDIN

1. *The Phenomenon of Man* (William Collins Sons & Co. Ltd, London, 1959) p. 29.
2. *Human Energy* (Collins, London, 1969) p. 90.
3. *The Phenomenon of Man,* footnote to p. 169.
4. Ibid., pp. 29-30.
5. Ibid., p. 30.
6. *The Future of Man* (Collins, London, 1964) p. 68;
   The Phenomenon of Man, p. 224, and passim.
7. *The Phenomenon of Man,* p. 30.
8. Medawar, *Mind,* LXX, (1961) Critical Article on Teilhard's *The Phenomenon of Man,* p. 103.
9. *Man in Revolt,* pp. 57-60.
10. Op. cit., p. 30.
11. Medawar, op. cit., p. 105.
12. *Teilhard Reassessed* (Darton, Longman & Todd, Ltd, London, 1970) pp. 4, 6 and 7.
13. Ibid., p. 175.
14. Cf., e.g. *The Future of Man,* p. 61.
15. *The Future of Man,* p. 105.
16. *The Phenomenon of Man,* pp. 53-6.
17. *The Future of Man,* p. 109.
18. *The Phenomenon of Man,* pp. 165-6.
19. *The Future of Man,* p. 128.
20. Ibid., p. 127.
21. In a famous passage, Henri Bergson hazarded a similar guess. 'As the smallest grain of dust is bound up with our entire solar system, drawn along with it in that undivided movement of descent which is materiality itself, so all organized beings, from the humblest to the highest, from the first origins of life to the time in which we are, and in all places as in all times, do but evidence a single impulsion, the inverse of the movement of matter, and in itself indivisible. All the living hold together, and all yield

to the same tremendous push. The animal takes its stand upon the plant, man bestrides animality, and the whole of humanity, in space and in time, is one immense army galloping beside and before and behind each of us in an overwhelming charge able to beat down every resistance and clear the most formidable obstacles, perhaps even death.' *Creative Evolution* (Macmillan & Co. Ltd, London, 1911) pp. 285-6.

22. *The Phenomenon of Man*, p. 289.

23. Ibid.

24. *Comment Je Vois*, note 29, and appendix. Cited by Henri de Lubac, *The Religion of Teilhard de Chardin* (Collins, London, 1967) pp. 199-200. For a discussion on this theme of Creation in Teilhard's thought, see this book, p. 196 seq.

25. H. de Lubac, op. cit., pp. 208-16.

26. In his criticism that Teilhard is always shouting at us, Medawar has really drawn blood.

27. *The Phenomenon of Man*, p. 294.

28. *Teilhard Reassessed*, p. 54.

29. *The Future of Man*, pp. 98 and 99.

30. The sense given to 'naturalism' in this chapter is quite different from that given to the term by Karl Marx who professed himself both a naturalist and a humanist. Karl Marx was in fact one type of philosophical realist, and what is here called 'naturalism' is very like the type of materialism (not historical materialism) which Marx repudiated.

31. Sir James Jeans, *The Mysterious Universe* (Cambridge University Press, 1930) p. 13. Quoted from memory by Teilhard in *The Future of Man*, p. 104.

32. *The Phenomenon of Man*, p. 227.

33. Pascal, *Pensées*, Articles IV, XIII, XVI, and XVII.

34. Bertrand Russell, *A Free Man's Worship* in *The Basic Writings of Bertrand Russell* (Allen & Unwin Ltd, London, 1961) p. 66.

35. Arthur Balfour, *The Foundations of Belief* (Longmans & Co., London, 1895) pp. 29-31.

36. William James, *Pragmatism* (Longmans & Co., London, 1907) pp. 104-5. (Quoting Balfour, loc. cit.)

37. W. T. Stace, *Religion and the Modern Mind* (Macmillan & Co. Ltd, London, 1953) pp. 144-8.

38. Tennyson, especially *In Memoriam* and passim.

39. Pascal, *Pensées*, Article XVIII, X.

40. E.g. William Temple hints at a similar view in *Nature, Man and God* (Macmillan & Co. Ltd, London, 1934) especially pp. 129-30.

41. *The Future of Man*, Chapter I, 'A Note on Progress'.

42. *Activation of Energy* (Collins, London, 1970) p. 376.

XVIII THE DIGNITY OF MAN

1. C. S. Lewis, *Transposition and other Addresses* (Geoffrey Bles Ltd, London, 1949) p. 41.

2. Mark 10:9.

3. Herschel Baker, *The Dignity of Man* (Oxford University Press, 1948). This book disarms the critic by a charmingly modest Preface. It is a pity that the author has such an inadequate understanding of Christianity. Attempting an impossibly wide review, he at least succeeds in being interesting.

4. Ibid., p. 105.

5. W. G. Kümmel, *Man in the New Testament* (Epworth Press Ltd, London, 1963) pp. 22-3.

6. Ibid., p. 24.

7. Ibid., p. 26.

8. Ibid., p. 34.

9. Here I do not suggest that all harm that comes to a man is the result of his *own* sin. Harm comes to him from other sources, and faith must hold that since God is supreme, he will be able to overrule even this for good.

10. George Adam Smith, *The Book of Isaiah* (Hodder & Stoughton Ltd, London, 1910) Vol. II, p. 174.

11. Moffatt's rendering: 'would you question me about the future?' if accepted, would weaken, though not destroy, our case. Adam Smith's translation confirms the Authorized Version.

12. Romans 3:4-6 and 9:14.

13. Romans 9:20.

14. Romans 11:32.

15. Romans 11:33.

16. For this reason, the account given by D. S. Cairns in his autobiography of an experience of his student days does not represent a rebellion against God. He says: 'I had been reading the ninth chapter of Romans, and when I came to the passage about the "vessels of wrath" and "Who art thou, O man, that repliest against God?" my mind gave a "mental spring" and said, in effect, "I do! This is an unjust and tyrannous endeavour to overcome conscience, and it *cannot* be God".' *David Cairns: An Autobiography* (S.C.M. Press, Ltd, London, 1950) p. 121. This was surely a perfectly right reaction of a conscience enlightened by Christ. To approve of it does not, however, mean that we conclude man to have any rights against God as revealed by Christ.

17. John 16:27. It is a sign of something far wrong with Nygren's

view of *Agape* that it forces him to cast some suspicion on this passage.

18. ??? P. 228.

19. Cairns, op. cit., p. 36.

20. See *Man in Revolt,* Chapter XVIII, 'Man in the Cosmos'.

21. T. R. Glover, *Jesus in the Experience of Men* (S.C.M. Press, Ltd, London, 1921) p. 226.

22. *That Nature is a Heraclitean Fire and of the comfort of the Resurrection.*

ng
he
ing
in
ey
o
e.
o
o
e
y
e
is

Index

Index

Index

Casey, R. P., 94, 294
Cleanthes, 72
Clement of Alexandria: on divin-
    ization, 50, 65, 78, 88-91,
    passim; is he Neo-Platonist?,
    93-5; how far influenced by
    Gnosticism?, 111-13
Confessio Scoticana, 171
Confrontation with God, uni-
    versal: taught by Calvin, 141-4;
    by Brunner, 153-5; denied by
    Barth, 155, 174, 185
Confucius, 181
Covenant, O. T., 36
Crawford, T. J., 290
Creation, 25, 27; relation of
    Christ to it, 41; image of God
    in creation, 135; not a fact in
    history for Brunner, 158-9;
    creation in Teilhard, 265-6

Darwin, Charles, 214
Davies, W. D., 52
Delfgaauw, Bernard, 216, 302
Demuth, 28, 173
Depravity, as taught by Calvin,
    137-40
Dialectic, contrast of Marxian
    with Hegelian, 215-16
Dignity of man, 26, 29, 35, 37,
    274-88, *passim*; Calvin's,
    Barth's, and Brunner's views
    on it, 285-8
Divinization of man, 50-1; in
    Irenaeus, 85, 108-11; in Clem-
    ent of Alexandria, 111-13; in
    Athanasius, 113-14
Dominion over nature: con-
    nected with the image, 28;
    interpreted by Marx, 218, 227;
    largely frustrated by economic
    inequality, 231
Dostoevsky, criticized by Freud,
    306
Drummond, James, 72-8, 291-2

Dubos, René, 15

Ebenbildlichkeit, 60
Eckhart, 65
Eichrodt, W., 27-9, *passim*
Einstein, Albert, his theory of
    Relativity makes Freud's early
    naturalism outdated, 233
Endowment and response, 198-
    202
Engels, Friedrich: cynical relati-
    vism in ethics, 229; on human
    differentia, 226
Eros, 180-1
Eschatology, 33, 35, 44, 45-50;
    missing from the mystery re-
    ligions, 63; in Irenaeus, 84-5;
    in Augustine, 105; in Aquinas,
    125; in Calvin, 150; in Teilhard,
    264, 266; in Manley Hopkins,
    288
Existentialism, Christian, 137,
    189-95

Fall: does not destroy dominion,
    28; likeness lost then, according
    to Irenaeus, 80; Adam and Eve
    children before it, 84; Aquinas
    underestimates it, 122-4; in
    Luther, 128; in Brunner, 160-1;
    Brunner does not believe in
    historical Fall, 191, 200; in
    Barth, 170
Farrer, Austin, 198
Fatherhood of God, 52-9
Feuerbach, 181; Marx's relation
    to him, 223-4; epistemological
    basis of his atheism, 224-5
Firstborn, 40-3
Flügel, 248
Formal image, in Brunner, 164-9
Frazer, James G., 291
Freud, Sigmund: his influence
    compared with Marx's and
    Darwin's, 214; his form of

314